SPORT, PLAY, AND

ETHICAL REFLECTION

RANDOLPH FEEZELL

Sport, Play, and Ethical Reflection

UNIVERSITY OF ILLINOIS PRESS

URBANA AND CHICAGO

Library of Congress Cataloging-in-Publication Data
Feezell, Randolph M., 1950–
Sport, play, and ethical reflection / Randolph Feezell.
cm.
Includes bibliographical references and index.
ISBN 0-252-02955-0 (cloth : alk. paper)
1. Sports—Moral and ethical aspects. 2. Sportsmanship.
I. Title.
GV706.3.F44   2004
175—dc22   2004002534

Contents

Acknowledgments   *vii*

Introduction   *ix*

PART ONE
SPORT: ATTRACTION AND PARADOX

1. Sport, Bodily Excellence, and Play *3*

2. The Freedom of Play *19*

3. Sport, the Aesthetic, and Narrative *32*

4. Play and the Absurd *46*

5. Sport and the View from Nowhere *58*

PART TWO
SPORT AND ETHICS

6. Sportsmanship *83*

7. On Cheating in Sports *97*

8. Sportsmanship and Blowouts *111*

9. Sport, Character, and Virtue *123*

10. Respect for the Game *143*

Notes *157*

Index *171*

Acknowledgments

It would impossible to mention everyone to whom I owe a debt of gratitude for helping me, either directly or indirectly, during the time I have worked on this project. Even if I could enumerate, although not exhaustively, the numerous intellectual and philosophical influences that have shaped and sustained my academic work, I would also have to mention significant influences from that other area of my life that may be of equal importance—after all, this is a book about sport. I want to thank all my friends and colleagues in two of the worlds I inhabit. The philosophy department at Creighton University has provided a congenial atmosphere within which to work, and some of them—Bill Stephens, Michael Brown, Dan Dombrowski in the old days—have not seemed to mind when I bugged them about some of the ideas that are discussed here. I have had hours and hours of valuable conversation with Craig Clifford about the topics in this book, and the final chapter on "respect for the game" has obviously been influenced by the discussion of that topic in a book we coauthored. I could go on and on about Craig, but one day he will read this and the last thing he needs is yet another boost to his self-esteem. Although we don't talk as much as we used to, my discussions with another fine philosopher, athlete, and human being, Curtis Hancock, deserve special mention. Many years of coaching and talking with Paul Davis have been valuable. That magic spring and summer with the Bluejays years ago taught me something about the joyous possibilities of sport. The experience reinforced my hope that the good things that can happen in sport sometimes do happen and my conviction that my favored metaphors for sport are not hopelessly unrealistic. Thanks Bluejays! Special thanks to my children, Travis, Evan, Tyler, and Allie, for putting up with me, as a father, intermittent coach, and gadfly, and for allowing the possibility of teaching each other about life and sport. Finally, what can I say, Barb? Thanks for the interest and encouragement over the years. I needed it.

I appreciate the financial support I received at various stages in the project from the Creighton College of Arts and Sciences and the Graduate School at Creighton University. Special thanks to Cheryl Woods for her superb help in the preparation and submission of my manuscript. Patrick Murray, chair of the philosophy department of Creighton University, was especially helpful at one point because of his flexibility in course scheduling. Patrick's support as a friend and colleague, as well as my department chair, is deeply appreciated.

I am grateful for permission to use parts of the following previously published articles. Permission to use parts of articles published in *Philosophy Today* was granted by DePaul University. Permission to use parts of articles published by the *Journal of the Philosophy of Sport* was granted by the Editor, acting for the International Association for the Philosophy of Sport. Permission to use parts of the article published by *The Modern Schoolman* was granted by Saint Louis University.

"Sport: Pursuit of Bodily Excellence or Play? An Examination of Paul Weiss's Account of Sport," *The Modern Schoolman* 58 (May 1981): 257–70.
"Play, Freedom, and Sport," *Philosophy Today* 25 (summer 1981): 166–75.
"Sport, the Aesthetic, and Narrative," *Philosophy Today* 39 (spring 1995): 93–104.
"Play and the Absurd," *Philosophy Today* 28 (winter 1984): 319–29.
"Sport and The View from Nowhere," *Journal of the Philosophy of Sport* 28 (2001) 1–17.
"Sportsmanship," *Journal of the Philosophy of Sport* 13 (1986): 1–13.
"On the Wrongness of Cheating and Why Cheaters Can't Play the Game," *Journal of the Philosophy of Sport* 15 (1988): 57–68.
"Sportsmanship and Blowouts: Baseball and Beyond," *Journal of the Philosophy of Sport* 26 (1999): 68–78.
"Sport, Character, and Virtue," *Philosophy Today* 33 (fall 1989): 204–20.

Introduction

This book is the product of two things: my lifelong interest and involvement in sports and a philosophical turn of mind. The combination may be relatively rare but hardly unique. At one point in my life I was convinced that the former, cultivated and developed in youth, had to give way to the latter, whose inchoate appearance blossomed as an undergraduate and seemed to trump my other interests as I entered graduate school. Like someone seeking to expunge bad habits, I sought to move on, to leave sports back there behind me where they belonged. I believed that significant involvement in sports and an earnest pursuit of an intellectual life were incompatible. I was faced with the burden of a Kierkegardian "either-or"—sports or philosophy? The choice was, in some sense, easy, because it was couched in a reflective atmosphere that produced a seemingly transparent but false dilemma. What did these practices represent to me? Youth versus maturity. Body versus mind. The material realm versus the realm of ideas. Ignorance versus wisdom. But most of all, what seemed to be crucial was the sense that the seriousness and importance of philosophy contrasted with the trivial and nonserious character of sport. Or, to put it differently, an engagement with philosophy necessitated an engagement with serious existential and social concerns, whereas involvement in sports seemed childish and superficial. As the reader will see, when I began to think seriously about nonseriousness, that is, about sport, several issues crystallized in my mind.

Having decided to study philosophy and forgo a life involved with sports, two further things contributed to the eventual production of this book. My recovery went poorly, and I found out that philosophy had become engaged in—surprise—thinking about such "bad habits."

Like most people who have studied philosophy seriously, after years of graduate work I had a decent sense of what had occurred in the history of philosophy and what was occurring in the contemporary philosophical scene. I had no sense that there was an area of thinking called "philosophy of sport." Ph.D. in hand, tenure track in tow, first paycheck in my pocket, I faced my academic future, knowing that my life as an athlete was an adolescent adornment to my professional existence, which would be spent thinking about the serious concerns of life, such as art, religion, and morality. To my university colleagues I sheepishly admitted that I spent hours playing in the gym and even more hours on the diamond coaching. But others have their vices, I thought. Some drink too much; other intellectuals actually watch television. At least my schizophrenia helped produce a relatively healthy body, and as long as I could be a good father and advance toward tenure, my involvement in sports could be seen as a harmless diversion. Philosophy and sports—vocation and avocation. But I began to wonder (which is important for a philosopher): Why can't I give up these games? What is the attraction? Why does this type of experience mean so much to me? I still recognized these activities as relatively trivial, but I experienced sport as splendid nonetheless. Christopher Lasch spoke of sport as "splendid futility"; I came to think of it as "splendid triviality."

At some point I stumbled across a book that awoke me from my dogmatic—or ignorant—slumber: *Sport: A Philosophic Inquiry,* by Paul Weiss, a well-known and highly respected American philosopher. At that time I had no idea that a Philosopher, that is, a real honest-to-God legitimate academic philosopher, could write a serious work on sport—and a whole *book* at that. It was a revelation. I approached the book with delicious anticipation and some pretense. After all, I had been a scholarship athlete at a major university known for its nationally reputed teams, and I played two other sports at a fairly high level. I had coaching experience, and I sat on the athletic board at a Division I university. I studied the sports pages like a difficult text on which I had to lecture. I had significant experience as a player, coach, and fan. I knew sport from the inside. On the other hand, I was a *real* philosopher, and how many philosophers could there be who had the experience in sports to go along with the academic intellectual training? It was going to be a serious responsibility to be the bearer of the truth about sports, but I could handle it. As the same time, I also realized that many would not be able to appreciate my contributions to philosophy of sport, since the academic prejudice against the lack of seriousness and rigor of such philosophizing is apparent, and the athletic world is populated by few who would appreciate my obscure reflections.

Years of thinking have left me much more humble. It didn't take long for me to realize that some first-rate minds were attending to some of these issues and that I had much to learn. Still, perhaps I could contribute. And if the professional philosophical community failed to recognize the importance or value of thinking about sport and play, that would not diminish the more personal value that these inquiries would have for me. I discovered that I was as compelled to understand my experience in sports as I was dragooned into other interminable reflections about the meaning of life, cosmic attitudes, and the foundation of our moral existence. In fact, I discovered that thinking about sport and play led ineluctably to some of these larger questions.

As I have said, Weiss's book was important. It gave me a point from which to start thinking, and it performed a legitimating function, for me as well as for many others. Two other texts were important for me early on: Johan Huizinga's classic study of play, *Homo Ludens,* and Michael Novak's passionate reflection, *The Joy of Sports.* Huizinga's work taught me to take seriously the category of play in relation to sport, while Novak's text reinforced the notion that one might unapologetically affirm the splendid qualities of sport and see in sports sources of meaning and represented qualities that bring to mind religious and aesthetic aspects of human existence. I also learned a great deal by thinking about numerous articles that appeared in the *Journal of the Philosophy of Sport,* first published in 1974 by a society of scholars interested in a vigorous and more sophisticated philosophical study of sport. After almost thirty years the scholarly material in this area has mushroomed, and I hope that this book is able to make at least a modest contribution to this relatively new tradition of inquiry.

The first part of the book attempts to engage Paul Weiss's initial curiosity about the attraction of sport. It is a truism to note the widespread interest in, or perhaps we should say obsession with, sports. To understand why sport attracts we must say something about what it is. Weiss's fundamental question "Why are so many people so involved in sports?" leads to reflections about the nature of sport and the kind of experiences it can offer to participants and fans. Yet the involvement, indeed the obsession, with sport is paradoxical, since in most cases sports involve activities arbitrarily and artificially constructed for no apparent external purpose. In an important sense, sports don't really matter, yet we often participate in and view sports as if nothing mattered more.

In the first chapter I critically respond to Weiss's insistence that the key to understanding the nature of sport is the young person's pursuit of physical excellence, best exemplified by the Olympic athlete. I argue that such a notion is a quite limited view of the nature of sports participation and that we should look for sport in the neighborhood of play. I discuss the famous accounts of play offered by Johan Huizinga and Roger Caillois, and I argue that a play theory of sport offers a more phenomenologically adequate account of the experience of the player in sports.

In the following chapter I reflect on some of the implications of viewing sport in relation to play, first by reflecting on the experience of freedom in sport and the way in which people often feel a sense of liberation when engaging in sports activities. I suggest that one of the reasons sport attracts so many relates to this experience of freedom, understood not as choice but as self-expression. The next chapter offers a different twist to the question of the attraction of sports. At least part of the undeniable appeal of sports, for fans as well as for participants, is related to the aesthetic possibilities of sports. Sports offer experiences that are rich in aesthetic value in the sense that such experiences have the temporal and developmental structures that are constitutive of what John Dewey called "an experience" and what others associate with narratives.

The following chapters explore the paradox of our serious attraction to nonseriousness when we are involved with sports. There is something absurd about the kind of play we associate with sports. We have reflectively available to us a perspective outside of our immediate participation in sports, and from this perspective we judge that our participation in sports activities is relatively insignificant. Yet when we cultivate this detached perspective and return to our immediate involvement it is not clear how to integrate the discrepant attitudes of detached observer and passionately involved participant. I consider how certain attitudinal responses, like humility and irony, are appropriate for participation in intensely absorbing yet trivial playful activities.

In the second part of the book I discuss some of the explicit ethical issues associated with sports, and I show the way in which conclusions about ethical behavior in sports are often closely related to the views of sport and play expressed in the first part of the book. I argue that sportsmanship is best understood by embracing the fact that sports are playful contests, activities that are both "serious" and "nonserious" at the same time. The good sport must combine in the unity of single attitude and in his behavior the generosity of the play spirit and the keen sense of fair play characteristic of a competitive athlete. The good sport is both player and athlete, and the virtue of sportsmanship should be seen in Aristotelian terms, as a judicious mean between excessive playfulness and excessive seriousness. Contrary to some recent interesting speculation about the issue of cheating in sports, I argue that the conventional view of cheating is correct. Cheating is wrong because it violates both the explicit and implicit agreements that are essential for the competitive equality of a game. I then attempt to defend, also in light of recent criticisms, the traditional view that it is unsportsmanlike to intend to "run up the score."

The next chapter attempts to show how sports might be important for character building and the development of important human excellences or virtues. Using Alasdair MacIntyre's notion of a "practice," I show both the strength and limitation of the view that sports are especially important because they are the locus of the growth of good character. Finally, I analyze "respect for the game" as a unifying principle and attitude of sportsmanship.

The view of sport that emerges in this book rejects any overly simple or reductive notion, especially any kind of purely instrumental view of sport. If sport is conceived as merely an occasion for winning, the locus of competition, or an instrument for amusement or entertainment, something of the complexity of this form of human activity will have been left behind. For me, to emphasize sport as play is not just another form of reductionism. Play is a concept that allows us to appreciate the multilayered, complex phenomenon we call "sport." To stress the notion that sport is found in the neighborhood of play is to hold that sport is an intrinsic good with its own internal purpose. In this sense, sport is analogous to Kant's conception of the work of art—"purposiveness without a purpose." To treat sport as an instrumental good is to fail to take it seriously *as* good in itself. To take sport seriously as an intrinsically valued form of human play is to view it as a fundamentally purposeless or aimless form of human activity in relation to other "serious" forms of human action. Thus I agree with Christopher Lasch's notion that the problem of sport in contemporary society is not that we take it too seriously from the point of view of the commercial and nationalistic ends for which sport is used. The problem is that we fail to take seriously the intrinsic value of such trivial activity. To insist that sport is fundamentally trivial is to resist a reductionist view of sport. That is the only way to take sport "seriously" qua sport and to see the other ends for which sport is used as secondary.

Two other important notions need to be stressed. Play is enjoyed for its own sake, but the enjoyment or pleasure that arises when participating in playful activities supervenes upon the activity. The end is not merely the pleasure or enjoyment or "fun," separate from the activity. A view of sport that stresses play is not reduced to hedonism. That would be yet another form of reductionism that reduces sport to something else that is good. Like Aristotle's notion that the good person will experience pleasure in the exercise of the virtues, the player who experiences the "joy of sports" aims at being fully engaged in the enjoyable *activity*, not the enjoyment itself. Furthermore, the activity at issue is a rule-governed, tradition-bound practice with standards of excellence, and thus goods, internal to the activity. To treat such an activity as good in itself and worthy of one's full commitment is to allow for the possibility of the display of good character in sport. The cheater who violates the constitutive rules of a sport isn't really engaged in the practice defined by these very rules. The point here is logical, not moral. The cheater also fails to take his sport seriously and reduces it to being an instrument for public glory and stolen pleasure. In contrast, the fairness, courage, and determination of the good sport are characteristic of one who respects the requirements of participating in an activity whose value is intrinsic to the practice itself, since he believes it is both enjoyable and important to attempt to become good at the sport in question.

I should also say a few words about the title of this book. Most readers will recognize the second part of the book as "ethical reflection." Discussions of sportsmanship, cheating, and good character seem obviously to be examples of thinking about ethical matters. But I also consider the first part of the book to be involved in ethical reflection in a broader sense. In the history of philosophy, ethical thinking has been concerned not simply with the rightness or wrongness of action, but with larger issues associated with the question "How should I live?" What kind of person should I be? What is a good life? What should I care about? These questions concern the goods that we seek and the basic attitudes that guide us in life. The first part of this book involves why sport matters to us, why some seem to care so much about it, and how to understand this in relation to other things in life that seem to matter more. Thinking about play, freedom, and the absurd is ethical reflection in this broader sense.

Although this book might be used as a text in certain kinds of courses, I did not write it as a text. My intent was not to canvass the contemporary ethical scene in sports; I have not attempted to examine every important ethical challenge in the sports world. For example, the book contains no extended discussion of performance-enhancing drugs and technologies, not because such issues are unimportant; they obviously are. However, my own interests have been somewhat different up to this point. I hope to write about other ethical issues in sports in the future.

As for making a contribution to serious reflection on sport and play, the reader will have to decide. Youthful pretense has given way to aging humility. The chapters are sometimes dialogical in character. My views emerge in dialogue with other thinkers and philosophers, some of whom explicitly discuss sport and play and some of whom have interesting notions that can be applied to clarifying sport and play although they have not explicitly made the connection. In some of these chapters I am a philosophical mosaicist, attempting to piece together concepts and ideas in a novel way in order to show something, that is, in order to allow the phenomena of sport and play to show themselves or be illuminated by philosophical thinking. In others, I respond to the interesting yet puzzling things I have heard others say about aspects of sport. G. E. Moore once famously remarked that it was neither the world nor science that occasioned his philosophizing; rather, the curious and puzzling things that other philosophers *said* about the world and about science caused him to start thinking. Some philosophers have been scandalized by his admission, as if such motivation were more appropriate for an undergraduate without a viewpoint of his own than for a mature thinker motivated by a sense of wonder and the idiosyncracies of his own autonomous reflection. I can't say that I'm scandalized by Moore's comments, although I would find this stimulus somewhat impoverished if one had no other motivation for philosophizing. As usual, our motives are mixed, but I find no problem in admitting that the attempt to respond to the views of others has motivated some of these chapters. In some cases my initial reaction was akin to Socratic aporia; in other cases my intuitive negative reactions carried convictions that led to arguments. In all cases I am thankful to others for evoking my own thinking and helping me to clarify some important issues.

Finally, there is nothing here that is so technical or jargon-ridden that it will be incomprehensible to readers unfamiliar with academic philosophy. There is nothing hopelessly obscure or technical about considering the notions of sport as play, as a rule-governed and tradition-bound activity, as a practice, or as "an experience." Such notions help us to understand and appreciate the existential and normative implications of participating in these activities that mean so much to some of us.

SPORT, PLAY, AND

ETHICAL REFLECTION

Sport:
Attraction and Paradox

1 Sport, Bodily Excellence, and Play

Where does one begin in philosophy of sport? What does it mean to take a philosophical interest in sport? Even for someone with a significant background in philosophy the answers to these questions are not obvious. Historically, philosophers have for the most part simply ignored sport as an appropriate topic of philosophical concern. Suppose for years you have unreflectively participated in and watched sports, and suppose you are also committed to the Socratic ideal of the examined life. A kind of vague existential imperative might naturally arise to seek a philosophical understanding of sport, but its method and its shape would be indeterminate. It's not that you want to keep a philosophical conversation going; on the contrary, you want to find a way *into* a philosophical conversation about sport.

In this context I believe it is appropriate to turn to the first systematic work on sport by an important contemporary philosopher. *Sport: A Philosophic Inquiry,*[1] by Paul Weiss, is important because it seemed to show, for some, that genuine philosophical reflection about sport might be possible. Much has been written about sport since that book was published. In it he offers an early, interesting account of sport. He is first interested in the Platonic search for the nature of sport. Philosophy of sport involves a variety of central concerns, and one might consult relatively recent publications to gain a sense of the subject matter and scope of such reflection.[2] The reader will find in these publications a wide range of topics examined, many of which are related, unsurprisingly, to the

3

central areas of philosophical inquiry: metaphysics, epistemology, ethics, aesthetics, and social and political philosophy. For example, one important part of philosophy of sport might be construed as applied ethics, in which such sport-related topics as sportsmanship, cheating, violence, competition, performance-enhancing drugs, and sexual equality are examined. Or one might reflect on the aesthetic aspects of sport and wonder whether there is a close relationship between sport and art. However, many would agree that an appropriate point of entry into philosophy of sport involves questions about the nature of sport and its relation to two other important concepts: play and game. This might be especially important if other considerations, including ethical ones, were essentially related to such grounding questions as What is sport? How is sport related to the nature of play and game?

In this chapter I primarily examine Paul Weiss's attempt to give an adequate account of the nature of sport. In doing this, I do not want to leave the impression that this is the only topic dealt with either in *Sport* or in his developmental meditation on sport, which mainly occurs in volume 5 of his philosophical diary, *Philosophy In Process*.[3] For example, Weiss attempts to give a relatively complete set of categories that describe athletic experience and enable us to classify sports and understand their differences.[4] He offers a phenomenologically nuanced examination of the nature of athletic acts. The categories of speed, endurance, strength, accuracy, and coordination are closely examined to capture descriptively the reality of "the athlete in action."[5]

Weiss's work also attempts to give the vocabulary of sports a precision and clarity it has not previously had by making distinctions among terms not ordinarily distinguished and by giving precise definitions of those terms. For example, he offers insightful discussions of such notions as "play," "sport," "game," and "contest."[6] Finally, there are discussions of topics such as women in athletics and amateurism versus professionalism. However, all of these topics are either directly or indirectly related to what I take to be his major concern in *Sport*, which is to offer and defend an account of the essential nature of sport. He states his view bluntly and straightforwardly in chapter 1: that sport involves the pursuit of excellence in and through the body. He further attempts to justify his theory by examining other "apparently more plausible views"[7] and by offering a description of athletic experience that would contribute to a more complete account of what it would mean to speak of "excellence" in athletics. I have little doubt that the pursuit of excellence is an important element in sports, but I have doubts about whether this is the element that defines the nature of sport. Weiss insists that he has written "a work in philosophy, and not in sport. It is a work in philosophy just as a philosophy of history or a philosophy of art is a work in philosophy and not in history or in art."[8] This means that Weiss offers arguments and invites a philosophic examination of his account of this historically neglected area of human activity. In the following I examine Weiss's view of sport and the arguments that support this view. Briefly, in the next section I attempt to sketch the account of sport offered by Weiss, emphasizing the important arguments offered early in *Sport*. This section is straightforwardly expository. In the following section I respond to Weiss's view of sport and tentatively offer a more plausible account based on the classic accounts of play offered by Huizinga and Caillois. Finally, I offer some speculative remarks on the experiential requirements for an adequate philosophy of sport and some brief comments concerning the importance of an inquiry into the nature of sport.

It is no wonder that philosophers are finally attempting to think seriously about sport. Sports have an almost ubiquitous presence in American culture and in other parts of the world as well. At a time when people find fewer and fewer things to care about, amateur sports are setting records for participation, and professional sports are setting records for spectator attendance. The sporting world offers to many people the context of their hopes, the locus of their momentary reprieve from a burdensome reality, or the repository for the only kind of heroism that they can appreciate at this moment in history. In the preface to his provocative book on sports, Michael Novak responds to the neglect of sport by serious thinkers:

> Considering the importance of sports to humankind—considering the eminence of stadia and gyms and playing fields on university campuses, comparing the size of the sports section to any other in the paper—our intellectual negligence is inexcusable. Only prejudice, or unbelief, can account for it.
> What "grabs" so many millions? What is the secret power of attraction? How can we care so much?[9]

In this same spirit, Paul Weiss begins his philosophic inquiry of sport by wondering why so many people are involved in sport.

> Sport does not only interest the young; it interests almost everyone. The fact compels a pause. Why are so many so deeply involved, so caught up emotionally in athletic events? Are they in the grip of some basic drive? Do they only express some accidentally acquired cultural habit of admi-

ration for successful violence? Are they really interested in perfection? Does it perhaps give them a special kind of pleasure?[10]

Weiss immediately adds that these questions have "philosophic import, dealing as they do—as we shall see—with what is close to the core of man, what he seeks, and what he does."[11] Yet there is some ambiguity in asking these questions that are said to have "philosophic import." Many people are "involved" or "interested" in sport. But what kind of interest or involvement is Weiss talking about? Are we talking about immediate participation in athletic activity? Or are we talking about spectator involvement? As we shall see, Weiss thinks that an answer to the first question—the one concerned with the athlete's participation in sports—also indicates why spectators are so fascinated by viewing athletic events. I am inclined to think that the fascination involved in these two orders of experience is somewhat different; perhaps something like the difference between the artist who creates an artwork and the spectator who completes the object by viewing it. But I will put off these considerations until later. For our purposes it should be noted that Weiss's account of sport primarily focuses on the athlete's immediate participation in athletic activity. So Weiss is initially asking the following question: Why does the active participant involve himself in sport?

Moreover, what is the sense in which this question has "philosophic import?" For Weiss, a philosophy of sport is embedded in a philosophy of human nature. A philosophic account of sport answers this guiding question by relating sport to the nature of the human person. As Weiss says, "If a study of sport is to be of philosophic interest, it should show its relation to men's basic concerns. It will then be able to make evident why sport is pursued almost everywhere."[12] A philosophy of sport, in Weiss's sense, would attempt to sift the complex elements involved in athletic experience and find the most basic factor or factors that would account for the fact that sport "interests almost everyone."

What is the "basic concern" of people that accounts for the widespread interest in sport? According to Weiss it is "concern for excellence." At first glance, it is not clear why Weiss thinks this is the most adequate account of why people engage in sport. Certainly the pursuit and appreciation of excellence is an important aspect of human existence, and this is the first premise in Weiss's argument. "Unlike other beings we men have the ability to appreciate the excellent. We desire to achieve it. We want to share in it."[13] If we accept this first premise, how are we led to the notion that sport is primarily understood in terms of people's concern for excellence? At this point Weiss makes a very curious—and I think misleading—move. The important clue that reveals the nature of sport is the fact that it is primarily "young men, though, who are most absorbed in sports. It is they who participate in it most passionately and most successfully."[14] Now the argument becomes clear. There are many ways in which people can become excellent, for example, intellectually, morally, or in terms of some skill or craft. All people supposedly desire excellence, but young people—Weiss unfortunately insists on speaking of young *men*—have neither the maturity nor the experience to become excellent in more important ways. Therefore, they turn to sport as a way to become excellent physically; sport must be understood as the arena in which the person can become physically excellent. "Sport is a traditionalized set of rules to be exemplified by men who try to become excellent in and through their bodies."[15] The young have the possibility of turning to sport in order to attain a unique aspect of self-completion, and they become physically excellent according to the unique demands made by the particular sport in which they participate.

> Those who are young cannot do much to maintain or to contribute to culture; they are not experienced or developed enough to see or do things in the round. Most of them find it quite difficult to attend to the important for more than an occasional, short period, or to be much occupied with what is not relevant to the satisfaction of personal desires and short-run concerns. Most young men are largely unformed and undirected. No longer boys, they are not yet full adults, able to function as prime factors in society, state, or civilization. The best that most of them can do is to be good at sport. And that is a goal well worth their devotion.[16]

Weiss sees sport as an arena in which people pursue the ideal of excellence by means of physical activity. Insofar as we are bodily beings, the pursuit of bodily excellence is a necessary element in a person's quest for self-perfection. It is, one might say, an often overlooked element necessary for what Aristotle called *eudaimonia,* or human flourishing, beyond the perfection of the intellectual and moral aspects of human nature. The young person channels her vitality toward satisfying the desire for excellence, a desire she supposedly shares with the rest of humanity. Weiss thinks this is important: "It makes good sense for a young man to want to be a fine athlete; it is not unreasonable for him to suppose that through his body he can attain a perfection otherwise not possible to him."[17] The "athlete" is the category that best describes the participant in sport who "strives to have a fine body and to use it well."[18] If this is an adequate account of why young people are attracted to athletics, we also have an explanation for why the spectator is fascinated by sports.

The spectator has the ability to recognize and appreciate excellence; therefore, the spectator's fascination with the game is also related to people's attraction to ideality.

> Few men work at becoming all they can be. Fewer still try to do this by achieving a disciplined mastery of their bodies. But all can, and occasionally some do, see the athlete as an expression of what man as such can be and do, in the special guise of this individual body and in these particular circumstances. In the athlete all can catch a glimpse of what one might be were one also to operate at the limit of bodily capacity.
>   . . . By representing us, the athlete makes all of us be vicariously completed men. We cannot but be pleased by what such a representation man achieves.[19]

These arguments offered in chapter 1 of *Sport* outline Weiss's view concerning the nature of sport. In the remaining parts of the book little or nothing is added to his definition of sport, although much more is added to describe more completely the way in which one might view athletic activity from this perspective. His explanation for the attraction of athletics is further defended in chapter 2. Here he critically discusses a number of other apparently plausible explanations for the attraction of athletics. Among the most important theories examined by Weiss are: that sports offer a way for the young to expel excess energy; versions of what Weiss calls the "social theory," suggesting that sport is an instrument for socialization or that sport "promotes the life" of participants by bringing about certain goods like honor and health; that sport is a character builder; and that sport is an accepted outlet for the natural aggressive tendencies of domination and subjugation.[20] I shall not look closely at all of these discussions, but in the next section, in which I critically examine Weiss's theory, I will look at the way he treats the play theory of sport.

At the end of his discussion in chapter 2 Weiss reiterates his view that sport enables one "to become excellent in and through his body," and that it is attractive to young people because "it is one of the most ready means . . . by which one can become self-complete."[21] The following eight chapters in *Sport* meticulously describe the

> stages the athlete goes through in his progress toward self-completion. There is first his *acceptance of* his body, carried out in training and practice. This is followed by his *identification* with the situation in which he is, particularly with the equipment to be used, thereby enabling him to enter into a contest, and these *define* what he is by what he does. Finally, there is his assumption of the position of a representative in a game,

where, without losing distinctiveness, he functions on behalf of, and so far exhibits the import of, others.[22]

After these extended discussions Weiss ends his reflection on sport by considering some other topics that are, for the most part, peripheral to our present concerns. Let us now critically examine Weiss's general account of sport and those parts of the more narrow descriptions of athletic activity that are critically relevant.

———————

I have little doubt that the athlete's pursuit of excellence is sometimes an important part of sport, but I think this account of sport is limited. At best, Weiss's theory can stand only as a partial truth. The reason why his view is plausible is that it seems to fit well with our conception of the dedicated athlete. As Keith Algozin has suggested, "For Weiss the model of the athletic display of bodily excellence is The Olympic Games. Men and women of all nations have trained their bodies to challenge the resistances of space and time with speed, endurance, strength, and accuracy and coordination prescribed by the various particular sports."[23] But can the emphasis on the idealized conception of an Olympic athlete capture the reality of the "universal interest" in sport cited by Weiss? I think the mistake here is rather like the mistake made by some philosophers of art who provide a plausible theory of one particular aspect of art but have insurmountable problems when the theory is extended to other types of art. For example, Suzanne Langer's notion that art is an iconic symbol of human feeling appears to be a plausible theory of music, but not a satisfactory theory of the novel or even of painting. I think Weiss is misled in his theory of sport by his initial suggestion that the crucial factor to be explained by and incorporated into a philosophy of sport is the fact that "young men" are most involved in sport. But why should this be taken as the most important clue to a philosophy of sport? It could very well be that even if Weiss's explanation for why young "men" engage in sport is true—and I don't think it is—this account would not explain why so many others are interested in sport. Weiss himself says, "Sport does not interest only the young; it interests almost everyone."[24]

The problem, moreover, is not just Weiss's misleading emphasis on the fact that it is young people who are most absorbed in sport. Weiss argues that the "athlete" is the category that best describes the participant in sports, and he wonders why young men want to become athletes, as if the athlete is the embodiment of bodily excellence. Thus "athlete" is a conception that represents the ideal of the physical being that the person ought to become. Once again, however, the category of the "athlete" seems to be limited. From Weiss's perspective one engages in sport in order to become an athlete, but if this is an ideal to be won—and for many an impossible ideal, given their bodily limitations—it simply cannot capture the larger reality of the participant or player who falls short of the ideal and its pursuit. This initial emphasis on the "young athlete" as the key to the nature of sport ignores all of the participants in sport who are neither young nor particularly athletic. Think of examples of sports participation that such a notion simply misses. It ignores high school or college intramural basketball players who are not excellent enough to make an organized team, players in adult city softball leagues, and middle-aged tennis players who are still addicted to their weekly matches. No one would ever call these persons "athletes." How about pick-up soccer games, weekly leagues for mediocre bowlers, Sunday flag football, adult hockey leagues, retired cross-country skiers, and golf for hackers? The list could go on and on.

Why do so many people, neither young nor athletic, engage in sport? Do they have anything in common with the "young athlete," considered by Weiss to be at the heart of sport? I am very hesitant to offer an answer in the guise of a definition, as Weiss seems to do. The post-Wittgensteinian attacks on essentialism are difficult barriers to overcome, and these arguments have appeared in the philosophy of sport, just as they have in the philosophy of art and elsewhere. For example, Frank McBride concludes an essay called "Toward a Non-Definition of Sport" by admonishing philosophers of sport. Because the intention and the extension of the concept "sport" are vague, "philosophers of sport ought not waste their time attempting to define 'sport.'"[25] Yet Weiss's question is important, and his answer is not irrelevant. At the least, his approach challenges us to come up with a better explanation. Definitions are hard to come by, but our concepts aren't empty, and our experiences aren't hopelessly diverse. Wittgenstein thought that such concepts need not be susceptible to the kind of definition Weiss attempts to offer. There may be no "essence" of sport, but there are surely overlapping properties of different sports activities, and such characteristics at least constitute what Wittgenstein called "family resemblances." On this model, a better answer to Weiss's question would be to highlight features of sport that are more inclusive, that are apparent across a wider spectrum of participants. The test of an explanation that would more satisfactorily answer the question "Why do so many people engage in sport?" would involve conceptual analysis and an appeal to the first-person lived experiences of the participants. Ideally, both the "athlete" and the nonathlete would find more common ground in another type of response. The aging athlete past her prime or the nonathletic participant would find it difficult to admit that her activity involved "the pursuit of bodily excellence," where the Olympic athlete is the best example of this conception. However, a least common denominator might still be possible such that the athlete might recognize in his own experience a root kinship with the nonathlete.

Since sport experience appears to be pluralistic and complex, I am hesitant to offer something like a "definition." People engage in sport because they find aspects of sport with which they deeply identify. Cultural factors are obviously important. Some people undoubtedly identify with the pursuit of excellence, the struggle of the contest, the development of good health, or the satisfaction of playing well. But none of these seem to me to be universal enough. I believe that the clue to sport experience is that it usually involves engaging in an immensely enjoyable physical activity. We choose to play our games or engage in such activities for no other reason, in many (or most) cases, than the intrinsic enjoyment involved. Some people who engage in sports may grow in virtue, some may enjoy the psychological domination of others, some may like the momentary pleasure of being the victor in a relatively trivial contest, or a few may even get paid to play their games. Yet without the initial possibilities associated with pleasure, satisfaction, or joy, who would play? Why do so many people engage in sport? Because it's fun! At the cost of offering an answer that seems trivial, banal, or too simplistic, this element of enjoyment or fun, which is an intrinsic part of participating in sports, leads me to consider play as an explanation for the attraction of sport. Sport might well be termed "enjoyment in play."[26] We find sport in the neighborhood of play, a particular kind of play.

Weiss is not unaware of the power of the play theory of sport, but the way in which he treats it is quite odd. In *Philosophy in Process* Weiss remarks:

> I have been struck recently by the number of men who have told me that they are primarily interested in sports as participants for the fun of the game, and they are interested in sports as spectators primarily for relaxation. The two contentions are related. They point up a dimension of sports which is related to play in that it involves a contrast with work, involves one in something which has value in itself, and which provides not revelation, or improvement, or the satisfaction of some deep drive, but simply pleasure of an uncomplicated sort.[27]

Given the nature of this statement, one might imagine that Weiss would consider the play theory of sport as one of the crucial theories to be critically examined. In chapter 2 of *Sport* Weiss discusses and critically responds to at least *seven* important alternative theories before strongly reemphasizing in the concluding parts of the chapter that athletics is attractive because it offers a way to become excellent in and through the body. When one considers this list of alternative theories, what is most surprising is the absence of any extended consideration of the play theory in its most significant form. Weiss briefly discusses the play of children in relation to a version of the social theory of sport—that the play of children develops them as social beings—but quickly discards the theory as it relates to sport, because "the sport of men and the play of children . . . are distinct from one another in structure. They have different results."[28] In addition, Weiss insists that this theory also fails to explain why people pursue more individual sports. But certainly Weiss does not deal adequately here with play and sport. It need not be offered in relation to a "social theory" of sport. Throughout the central chapters of his work he fails to treat the dimension of sport that relates to play. He finally discusses play in a later part of the book, only to dismiss play as a category that has little to do with the fundamental aspects of sport and the athlete.[29] The way Weiss treats the play theory of sport is all the more questionable given the significance of this theory, which is termed by Paul Kuntz, a sympathetic commentator on Weiss's philosophy of sport, "the best developed theory of sport since it has had two recent exponents, on whom Weiss depends, who have devoted two brilliant books to its exposition and modification."[30]

Kuntz is referring here to the works of Johan Huizinga and Roger Caillois, and Weiss considers the play theory of sport in relation to a discussion of their respective descriptions of play.[31] The comments by Kuntz are slightly misleading, because neither Huizinga nor Caillois have as a central goal to provide a philosophy of sport. But their discussions of play are enlightening when viewed as the foundation for a perspective that conceives of sport as play. If it is appropriate to examine Weiss's position in order to initiate our foundational reflections on the nature of sport, likewise, it is appropriate to examine the classic accounts of play offered by Huizinga and Caillois. Others have refined their analyses, but their initial reflections are pregnant with most of the key insights that are important for understanding the close relationship between sport and play.

Huizinga emphasizes the freedom of play and insists that "the *fun* of playing resists all analysis, all logical interpretation . . . It is precisely this fun-element that characterizes the essence of play."[32] Huizinga summarizes his notion of play in the following passages:

[play is] a free activity standing quite consciously outside "ordinary" life as being "not serious," but at the same time absorbing the player intensely and utterly. It is an activity connected with no material interest, and no profit can be gained by it. It proceeds within its own proper boundaries of time and space according to fixed rules and in an orderly manner.[33]

. . . play is a voluntary activity or occupation executed within certain fixed limits of time and place, according to rules freely accepted but absolutely binding, having its aim in itself and accompanied by a feeling of tension, joy and the consciousness that it is "different" from "ordinary" life.[34]

Caillois describes play as free, separate, uncertain, unproductive, and governed by both make-believe and rules.[35] Huizinga and Caillois offer these descriptions of play without explicit reference to sports. But when we reflect on these descriptions with sport experience in mind, they strikingly reveal the relevant phenomena in a more adequate manner than Weiss's account. I realize that it would not be difficult to generate counterexamples if we interpreted these statements as traditional real definitions. However, if we respond to them as guiding us to the most inclusive locus of sport (the "neighborhood" of sport, as I have said, metaphorically), as true "for the most part," we will be enlightened. We need not give an extended discussion of each of these terms and each part of Huizinga's account in order to point to the most important elements of play in relation to sport, but we do need to comment on some of them. Both Huizinga and Caillois emphasize that play is an activity with which one positively identifies, and in this sense it is free. Weiss explains it this way: "Play . . . is free in the sense that it is carried on by the player only while he desires to engage in it."[36] Huizinga stresses the freedom of play as its first central characteristic. Play is never necessitated; it is like an "ornament," he says. It is a gift, added to life, "superfluous" in the sense that it is not a product of biological, cultural or moral necessity. Closely related to the freedom of play is its separateness. Play is "separate" in the sense that when one plays there is a movement from the world of ordinary concerns to the immediate involvement in an activity that suspends the ordinary.[37] Huizinga also speaks here of the "disinterestedness" of play. When we play we momentarily transport ourselves from the world of work, moral duty, and human needs—the "serious" concerns of everyday life—to an alternative world that has an "as if" quality. Although play is not "serious" when contrasted to the world of work and human suffering, it is often wholly absorbing and engaging. It has its own internal "seriousness" that frees us from our usual everyday worries. Often, but not always, a play world is established, constituted by its own rules and bounded by unique orderings of space and time, internal to the play world. In this world of play, especially in the competitive playing of games, something is at issue. Meanings are clear here, actions have transparent significance in relation to the goals involved, and a peculiar order reigns. The order of the play-world is contrasted with the ambiguity of ordinary life. Finally, and perhaps most important, the activity is engaged in for its own sake. It is autotelic, intrinsically valued, not instrumentally desired. Play is engaged in for the sake of the intrinsic enjoyment of play itself. One might see the play of sport as a free and immensely enjoyable physical activity engaged in for its own sake. I think this conception of sport more nearly captures the sense in which it is of "universal interest." This is the element of sport that is absent neither from the dedicated athlete nor the pick-up basketball player, the weekend golfer, the tennis player, or the jogger.

Weiss comes close to endorsing this view.

> "Sport" comes from "disport," to divert or amuse . . . a good deal of sport, of course, is pursued for no other reason than the pleasure that it gives. There is delight in moving one's limbs with grace and skill: there is joy in testing oneself and one's opponent. Pleasure is rarely absent from any sport, even when one has pushed oneself almost to the limit of human endurance.[38]

Yet Weiss cannot accept this as more than a "subordinate phase" of sporting activity, because it ignores such elements as "self-sacrifice" and "self-denial." Yet this comment is seemingly topsy-turvy. Weiss admits that "pleasure in play" is rarely absent from any sport but suggests that such a view of sport ignores the element of "tension" involved in athletic competition, so we are prevented from "considering pleasure to be more than a subordinate phase."[39] But if such intrinsic enjoyment is rarely absent from sport, even if one is pursuing the ideal of physical excellence at all costs, then the more universal aspect of athletic experience is this pleasure in play, which would account for the experience of both the dedicated athlete and the part-time aging player who still loves the game. This is why Weiss's answer to "Why do people engage in sports?" is so limited. It is the "player who plays," not the "athlete," who is central to sport. The "player" may well be an athlete; he may not. But certainly the athlete is one who plays, and when the athlete can no longer play "at" or "in" his game, he will probably give it up. How many times have we heard even the professional athlete say that he was forced to give up the game because it was no longer "fun"? Engaging in sport is a self-contained activity bringing an immediate enjoyment; it is in this sense intrinsically valuable. I do not mean to suggest that this is the only important part of sport. The source of this immediate enjoyment involves a variety of factors, including the explicit affirmation of one's physical presence in the world—it feels good to run and jump—the bracketing of "ordinary" life, and the transparency of meaning attached to acts within the game. There are, of course, other elements. Paul Kuntz argues that we "cannot at the same time and in the same sense say that the value of sport is to educate men in responsibility and cooperation and that sports are for themselves, without utility or value other than immediate enjoyment."[40] I would not hold that the sole value of sport is either one of these alternatives, and I doubt if anyone who thought seriously about the matter would either. But the latter alternative is an essential element in sport in the way in which the first alternative is not. From the standpoint of the player the pure joy of sporting activity is often an irreducible element in his experience. I am forced very much to agree with Richard L. Schacht:

> At the risk of banality, I would suggest that athletic activity consists in engaging in some sport the rudiments of which one has mastered; and that the only "athletic goal" of which it makes any sense to speak, at least where all but the very finest athletes are concerned, is simply that intrinsic enjoyment which one may derive from engaging in the activity in question, through winning and/or playing to the best of one's ability and/or playing well.[41]

I would only add that the goal Schacht speaks of is also, I believe, a part of the experience of even the finest athletes, and that winning is not necessary for this enjoyment. It's neither winning nor even *how* you play that is most important; what is most important is simply *that* you play.

———

I would like to end this chapter on a slightly more personal note, in part a confession, in part an expression of perplexity. Like many others, I've had a lifelong love affair with sports (although "relationships," as we know, are sometimes rocky and require some effort to maintain). I've been an athlete, coach, fan, team general manager, and university athletic board member. I know something about sports from the inside. It is from this perspective that I wonder why Weiss says some of the things he does. How could anyone say, for example, that the athlete "plays less than most other men do"; that "a man is normally most a man only when he stops playing and tries to do some justice to his responsibilities"; and that the "athlete is rarely playful"?[42] The answer is obvious to me. Weiss is really an outsider; he has no first-person experience upon which to base his theory. The paradox of his whole theory is that he wants to understand the reality of the participant's immediate experience, but the only standpoint from which he can view sport is as a spectator, a curious philosopher whose only access to what he is trying to explain is an abstract stance. It is as if the aesthetician had no aesthetic sensibility. It is from this abstract stance that Weiss focuses on what seem to be the more negative aspects of athletic activity and persistently asks why athletes would go through so much pain, fatigue, risk, and self-denial. He concludes that they must be admirable young men, pursuing ideality.

> Athletes usually submit themselves, often with enthusiasm, rarely with reluctance, to long periods of training . . . At times they risk injury, and in some cases death. Fatigue is a familiar. Sooner or later every one of them comes to know that he is preparing himself for defeat, and perhaps humiliation . . . Why? . . . Why are they willing to risk making their inadequacies evident, instead of enjoying the struggle of others from afar, or instead of plunging into a game without concern for how they might fare. Why do they subject themselves to the demands of a severe disciplining? Why are they so ready to practice self-denial or to sacrifice their interest in other pursuits to prepare themselves for what may prove disastrous?[43]

Here is a genuinely puzzled man who can see this type of human experience only from the outside, and what he sees is wholly negative. Therefore, the experience must be undergone because of a goal or an ideal; a "that-for-the-sake-of-which." His view of sporting experience must be teleological.

I have already argued that Weiss's conception of the "athlete" is limited; the category does not describe the participant's experience on the broadest scale. "Athlete" is simply not the exclusive tool used to conceptualize the experience of the participant in sport. But even the "athlete"— in Weiss's sense—experiences an intrinsic enjoyment of which Weiss seems to have no notion. From the inside of the experience described by Weiss and lived by the athlete, there is a joy, a heightened sense of being that is an ineradicable element of the experience and may be difficult to explain to the nonathlete or nonparticipant. In this sense, athletic activity is self-contained and intrinsically enjoyed. This is often why an athlete, even when her abilities are on the wane, cannot give up her sport. This may be why the nonathlete, with no realistic chances for attaining anything like "excellence," continues playing.

My concluding point is this: Weiss, or any philosopher of sport, can hardly adequately understand "why people engage in sport" without living through it. Perhaps a hint of mysticism is called for here. I find it interesting that Dr. George Sheehan, a once popular "philosopher" of sport and running, a man whose philosophical gifts could hardly match Paul Weiss's, offers a keener insight into sporting experience than Weiss's extended theory. In his engaging and aphoristic style, Dr. Sheehan says the following:

> The intellectuals who look at sport start with the assumption that it must serve something that is not sport. They see its useful functions of discharging surplus energy and providing relaxation, training for fitness and compensation for other deficiencies. What they don't see is that play is a primary category of life which resists all analysis.
>
> Play, then, is a nonrational activity. A supralogical nonrational activity in which the beauty of the human body in motion can reach its zenith. Just as the supralogical feast of Christmas confirms man's unique value and destiny. So the intellectuals are probably as upset with play as the theologians are with Christmas. Men having fun is as mystical and supralogical as the Word made flesh.[44]

I would not go so far as to say that play cannot be described or analyzed; I have done just that. Yet I am inclined to endorse a part of Sheehan's mysticism. For the notions of sport as competition, leisure, instrument of socialization, character builder, and all the rest can never capture the element of joy or fun when people play, as they inevitably do.

What is the importance of thinking about the nature of sport, or, in particular, attempting to think about the relationship of sport and play? Is this merely another trivial academic enterprise? I don't think so. The way we talk about things determines the emotional hue of our thinking; our words affect our choices and our actions. If we decide to call an object an "artwork" rather than a piece of "pornography" or an "obscenity" it will affect our attitude toward the thing. Engaging in arguments about concepts like "art," "pornography," and "obscene" has public and private consequences. In a like manner, it matters how we talk about sports. It matters whether we insist on talking about sports primarily in relation to competition, excellence, winners and losers, and the like, or whether we associate sport with playfulness, irony, and joy. It matters whether we use the language of intrinsic value (autotelicity) or the language of instrumentalism because of the way such language is used in the rhetorical atmosphere of debates about sports and other important human values: education, virtue, equality, economic health, entertainment, and so on. Developing these suggestions must be done elsewhere. For the time being, it is enough to direct our attention to the neighborhood of sport as play.

Although I have stressed the importance of play as a corrective to Weiss's emphasis on sport as the pursuit of bodily excellence, I do not deny that sport is a competitive activity. The language of competition, the pursuit of excellence, meeting challenges, and the desire for winning seem often to exclude the language and values associated with play, and such exclusion has consequences. My arguments in this chapter should be placed in the relevant context, as reminders about the internal qualities of sport as a playful activity. It's interesting that moments of tragedy occasion comments about keeping sports in "proper perspective"—after all, we're talking about "games." Such comments were commonly heard after the terrorist attacks of September 11, 2001, then . . . forgotten? Sport is competitive play, and there's no doubt that the tension and pressures associated with competition, meeting challenges, and the pursuit of victory contribute to our interest and even our fascination with sport. Yet these elements arise in a world of play, as I have stressed in this chapter. These themes arise in later chapters as I discuss the narrative qualities of sport, the moral possibilities associated with participation in a practice, and various ethical issues that arise in sports participation. But the initial emphasis on play is an essential aspect of the discussion that follows.

2 The Freedom
of Play

Paul Weiss's seminal book on philosophy of sport is motivated by the curiosity expressed in the following questions:[1] What is the attraction of sport? Why the widespread interest? Why are so many involved? To answer these questions we must say something about what sport really is and what it offers to those participating in it. Weiss believes that its benefits are primarily bestowed on the young, since such goods are available to young people in ways that other important goods, like intellectual and moral virtue, are not. According to Weiss, sport is attractive because it provides opportunities to attain excellences specific to our physical or bodily being. The Olympic athlete represents what sport is all about.

The view that Weiss defends is obviously not irrelevant, but it is certainly questionable whether his view adequately answers such questions. As I have previously argued, Weiss seems to approach sport as an outsider; consequently, he underestimates the power of the category of play to address his questions. He seeks understanding as an unbeliever, but he lacks the believer's intimate acquaintance with the relevant experiences that reveal and sustain the believer's relationship to the object.

Now consider the following plaintive yet hopeful introductory remarks from Michael Novak's *The Joy of Sports*. He describes one ordinary Monday evening in New York, riding the subway home to Long Island, when he realizes that it is Monday night, which means *Monday*

Night Baseball will be on television. But this was to be an even more special Monday night treat, because the Dodgers were to play in that night's game. Suddenly his day was transformed as the Dodgers injected some new meaning into an otherwise dull and ordinary day. That night the Dodgers lost, Novak suffered, and his wife couldn't have cared less. Yet Novak is a reflective man, and he wonders:

> How could I be forty years old and still care what happens to the Dodgers? How could I have thrown away three hours of an evaporating life, watching a ritual, an inferior dance, a competition without a socially redeeming point? About the age of forty, almost everything about one's life comes into question. There is so little time to grasp and hold, it slides through fingers like the sand. It seems important now to concentrate. And so I asked myself: Is it time for sports to be discarded? Is it time to put away the things of childhood?
>
> Quietly, I knew the answer. What I had just seen was somehow more important than my other work, was deeper in my being than most of what I did, spoke to me of beauty, excellence, imagination, and animal vitality—was *true* in a way few things in life are true. My love for sports was deeper than any theory that I had. The reality is better than its intellectual defense.[2]

Like Weiss, Novak wonders about the attraction of sports. He immediately affirms it, yet questions the value of a theory that would explain the attraction. I understand what Novak is saying here. I don't love the Dodgers, but I still seem to care about some of these "inferior dances." But there is another important perspective related to, and probably presupposed by, Novak's love for the Dodgers. Many people do consistently throw away hours and hours of an "evaporating life" watching these spectacles; what interests me further is not simply that people cannot give up witnessing these "rituals" and "inferior dances," but that many cannot give up their active participation in them. I suspect that people somewhat younger than Novak start to wonder as their body tells them something that they hardly care to consider. They still love playing their games or participating in sports, but, like Novak, they wonder whether these childlike or adolescent activities are to be left behind with all of the other relics of youth. The point remains the same: age and experience force one to reflect on part of life that youthful unreflectiveness often neglects. The believer, both participant and spectator, may want to understand. Novak says: "Faith in sports, I have discovered, seeks understanding. I cannot forever split my life in two, half in love with sports, half in love with serious thought. Life seeks unity."[3] The reality may be better than its intellectual defense, but such a defense is important nonetheless.

I believe that the most plausible interpretation of sport involves the notion of play. For our purposes let's assume that a plausible case has been made for the notion that sport is grounded in play. The play theory has strong intuitive appeal. We might begin with the provisional insight that from the standpoint of the person who participates in sports, this activity appears to be a form of play. But what is play? The claims made in the name of sports are ambiguous, disparate, and more often than not, exaggerated. We ought to be able to evaluate these critical judgments; and if participating in sports is a form of play, then an understanding of the nature of play is essential for our understanding of sport. Is play childish, frivolous, and something to be outstripped in maturity? Is play "separate" from ordinary reality? Is it "unreal"? Or does our play reveal something about who we are? Most important, what is the attraction of sport, if we understand it as a form of play? If play is essentially related to freedom, and sport is an expression of play, then sport will be experienced as liberating. In the rest of this chapter I combine phenomenological and speculative comments that might help to clarify the meaning and significance that sport often has for people who participate in it. One may see in sport, as Weiss did, primarily the negatives that must be faced squarely and transcended: exhausting training, risk of injury and failure, self-denial and self-sacrifice, and the possibility of public humiliation. No wonder that one might come to believe that the attraction of sport could only be explained by the possibility of being good, achieving excellence, and attaining victory in competition. However, what is missing in this picture is once again associated with play. Why sport? Physical excellence? Competition? Winning? Why not—the experience of freedom?

In *Homo Ludens,* Johan Huizinga's classic study of the play element in human culture, he first suggests that the proper standpoint from which to understand play is the standpoint of the player himself. It is from this standpoint that the inadequacies of biological and psychological theories can be seen most acutely. We might call this the phenomenological standpoint, and a description of the player's standpoint necessitates a return to the arena of first-person lived experience. According to Huizinga, the problem with these other theories is that they assume "that play must serve something which is *not* play, that it must have some kind of biological purpose."[4] In the spirit of phenomenology, Huizinga suggests that we should bracket this assumption and return to "the question of what play is *in itself* and what it means for the player."[5] "We shall try to take play as the player himself takes it: in its primary significance.["]6 From this standpoint, what can be said about the nature and significance of play?

As we have seen in the previous chapter, it is often argued that an essential element of play involves freedom. Play is, quite simply, a free activity. Huizinga, Callois, Novak, and even Weiss agree on this.[7] But what exactly is meant when we say that play is a free activity? For that matter, what is a free activity? Is it simply an activity that is freely chosen by the individual? But the play of children is problematic in this respect. Do children always *choose* to play? Weiss's explication of what Caillois means by calling play "free" is very instructive.

> In referring to play as free, Caillois means that it is voluntary, dependent on the individual to begin and terminate. This, however, is not a necessary feature of play. Children can be sent out to play; they can be made to play in games against their desires or express intent; they can be made to end their play. Play, though, must be freely accepted even when it is not freely entered into or freely ended; it is free in the sense that it is carried on by the player only while he desires to engage in it. Made to play, he nevertheless plays only while he willingly does what he must.[8]

Whether the player voluntarily begins to play—and, admittedly, he usually does—the important feature of the activity is that while it is being undertaken, the player identifies with what he is doing. At the heart of play is a strong sense of affirmation on the part of the player, and this affirmative "yea-saying" spirit is an essential part of the player's stance. This also accounts for the sense in which play is often deeply enjoyable or pleasurable. The clue that leads one to think that he has just been playing is a very simple utterance: "That was really fun!" When some other person is puzzled concerning why you have perhaps expended so much time, energy, and even occasional pain to pursue an activity—when your only answer is "Because it was fun!"—you have probably been playing. From the standpoint of the lived experience of the player, this appears as an irreducible and essential element of his activity. To say that this element is irreducible is to insist that one has reached a phenomenon of human experience requiring no further explanation. This also suggests that the activity is engaged in for its own sake. Recall Huizinga's emphasis on this very element: "Yet in this intensity, this absorption, this power of maddening, lies the very essence, the primordial quality of play."[9] "The *fun* of playing resists all analysis, all logical interpretation . . . It is precisely this fun-element that characterizes the essence of play."[10] Thus the freedom of play involves the way in which one affirms, embraces, or identifies with the activity, and it also involves the concomitant enjoyment that arises out of this identification. As a spectator, it might be difficult to believe that the sweating, straining faces of pick-up basketball players express some deep sense of enjoyment and identification; but from the standpoint of the lived experience of the players, there is little doubt about this point. The freedom of play involves identification. A further reflection on this aspect of play will also shed light on other supposedly "essential" characteristics of play, as described by Huizinga and Caillois, because at times play is also described as "non-serious," "unreal," "make-believe," and "separate."

In his book *On Being Free*, Frithjof Bergmann has presented an insightful and elegant rethinking of the notion of freedom.[11] His treatment is extremely suggestive in relation to thinking about the nature of play. Bergmann examines a number of different and conflicting views of freedom in the attempt to find some common structure that might reveal the ultimate presuppositions of any notion of freedom. For example, he examines at length Dostoyevsky's exemplar of freedom, the Undergroundman. The Undergroundman thinks that a free act is one that "offends reason," and freedom "demands that rationality be violated."[12] A free act is described as an act of "sheer caprice, performed in total independence, in rebellion against every consideration of advantage or of reason."[13] Whether we are critical of the position or not, the important question now is to understand why the Undergroundman holds such a view. Bergmann asks: "What is the experience presupposed by this idea of freedom?"[14] The answer is quite clear: "The affirmation of the Undergroundman that one must act contrary to reason to be free presupposes that he experiences his rationality as something other than himself."[15] Thus, the Undergroundman does not identify even with his own thoughts; the demands of rationality are experienced as coercive forces dictated by order and society. An act of self-identification is presupposed by his view of freedom, and it is the Other, not his authentic self, that speaks to him in the guise of rationality. What it means to be free depends upon how the Undergroundman conceives of his "real" or "true" self.

Likewise, when other theories of freedom are examined this same structure is revealed. The Platonic view of freedom, contrary to the Undergroundman's irrationalist position, holds that we are free only when we follow the dictates of reason; we are unfree when our actions are enslaved by and conform to the demands of the passions. On this view a free act is one performed according to reason. If we once again ask how a person experiences his reason if he holds the Platonic view (or a version of it), the answer is again obvious. Reason is not a coercive force; rationality is experienced as an expression of one's authentic self, and what Bergmann calls "identification" is presupposed by the theory. Bergmann offers "a kind of definition" after examining yet a third conception, and the definition is, I think, a metatheory, a theory about theories of freedom. This is an attempt to understand what it might mean to say that some activity is free. "An act is free if the agent identifies with the elements from which it flows; it is coerced if the agent disassociates himself from the element which generates or prompts the action. This means that identification is logically prior to freedom, and that freedom is not a primary but a derivative notion."[16] This means that the condition for calling an act free is some conception of the self, because freedom is really self-expression.

Furthermore, Bergmann argues that freedom is not merely the having of choices, absolute independence, nor the absence of constraints.[17] One of the most interesting examples he offers to reinforce the idea that freedom is best understood in terms of identification—instead of choice— is his own "choice" to become a philosophy teacher.

> For a long time I strongly resisted becoming a teacher of philosophy. One compelling—although in retrospect embarrassing—reason for this was my image of professors in general, and more that of professors of philosophy, was very uninviting. I must have seen them somehow as spun into white cocoons, secreted by their thinking, through which they only rarely gave a sign of life. So I chose a series of quite different professions, but was forced again and again—of course by something in me, but by something which opposed my will—to return to philosophic thinking. After exhausting myself like a hooked fish, I finally reached the point of saying "Other men have to live with even worse defects," and began to teach. So there is certainly a sense in which I did not choose philosophy. And yet nothing was as liberating to me as this resignation. There is now more exhilaration in this aspect of my life than in any other, and a part of me was set free through this capitulation.[18]

Choice is neither a necessary nor a sufficient condition of a free act. As Bergmann concludes, "An act can be free even if I did not 'choose' it (if it expresses what I really am), and an act can be unfree even if I did 'choose' it (if I do not identify with the thought that moves me toward one of the alternatives)."[19]

We shall not follow Bergmann through the next part of his theory of freedom. At this point in his argument he advances a theory of the self in order to show what it would mean to think of freedom as the performance of actions that are authentic expressions of the self. It is now possible to connect the idea of play as a free activity with Bergmann's notion of freedom as identification. As Bergmann admits, the notion of a "self" is a difficult and elusive one, but as the self forms and is formed, we come to realize and experience the way in which some of our actions conform to what we "really" are. There is a natural sort of conformity between what we are and what we do, and when we do whatever naturally expresses what we are, there is a sense of liberation. Bergmann expresses it this way: "Freedom for us is the expression of what we are, of the qualities and characteristics we possess, but in an unpretentious sense: it is the expression of qualities with which we identify."[20] Freedom is a "matching":

> Our outward life has to match our identity or our self if we are to attain freedom. We have to achieve something like geometrical congruence, a mutual fit, a kind of attunedness, like a harmony between two tones. There should be a basic sense of ease, as when two gears spin without friction in a prearranged synchronization. The usual stress on the difficulty of freedom . . . should begin to have some slight ring of melodrama and pathos, and just the reverse side should make itself felt: the absence of strain, the collapse of tension, the lightness of freedom, glorious as that of *pure play* (emphasis mine).[21]

It is with Bergmann's last remark that we rejoin our original object of reflection, and the point of his theory of freedom for our purposes should be clear. If play is a free activity, and freedom involves identification, then play deeply expresses what I am. Far from being unimportant or frivolous, the free activity of play expresses some aspect of my self that I take to be "real" or "authentic." This way of thinking about play and freedom is enlightening. For example, play is usually opposed to "work," and this dualism immediately suggests characteristics of play that are misleading. According to this view, the child involves himself with play until he grows up or matures. Then the adult is thrust into the "real" world of everyday reality. Now the person must become "serious" about his responsibilities, give up his phantom world of play, and involve himself with the more "important" aspects of living. The work ethic is proclaimed as the sacred ethic of life. But instead of thinking about play in relation to childish irresponsibility, conceive of play as a free activity, a natural outflow of the self, whether child or adult. That is, think of play as an activity expressive of some real part of a self and it becomes apparent that people should play more, not less. Those times when we *feel* most free, less tense or strained, and most lighthearted are times in which we are involved in something like a playful activity. We should also like our vocation to be something that tangentially approaches the play experience, for our vocation would then be in liberating coincidence with our true selves.

If we conceive of the free activity of play in this way, it would seem that the best of all possible worlds would embrace an ethic of play. This interpretation of play would make sense of Michael Novak's remark:

> Play, not work, is the end of life. To participate in the rites of play is to dwell in the Kingdom of Ends. To participate in work, career, and the making of history is to labor in the Kingdom of Means. The modern age, the age of history, nourishes illusions. In a protestant culture, as in Marxist cultures, work is serious, important, adult. Its essential insignificance is overlooked. Work, of course, must be done. But we should be wise enough to distinguish necessity from reality. Play is reality, work is diversion and escape.[22]

What should be added here is that "work, career, and the making of history" are "essentially insignificant" if they do not express the real self, that is, if they are unfree.

If I consider the way in which teaching philosophy is for me more like play than work, it makes sense to think of it as an activity I would do even if I didn't have to work; it is an activity I would choose to do because it expresses what I am. But what specifically is expressed in teaching philosophy? What is it that I am identifying with? In other words, what am I speaking of when I speak of my "self"? Certainly part of the self that is expressed in this activity is my inclination to be reflective, curious, and questioning. Philosophical thinking and its expression in philosophical conversation involve the free play of ideas, the imaginative and energetic interplay of point and counterpoint, and the tension of reflective potentiality directed toward resolution—all in ways that seem quite natural and liberating in relation to what I take myself to be, as a rational, inquiring self. But my self-interpretation involves more than this. Let us return to play and sport.

We must ask the following: What aspects of the self are expressed in sports, by virtue of which people deeply identify with this play experience? For a person in love with sports the answer to this question might be long and complex, because the elements involved in participating in sports are extremely varied. But whatever the answer, we know that some or many aspects of sports are consistent with some basic part of the participant's being. For example, if Weiss is correct, sports are attractive to young people primarily because they offer the person the opportunity to become good at some physical activity. Other people might identify with taking up challenges, testing limits, or becoming particularly adept at the strategic thinking associated with game playing.

In light of these reflections, consider the very simple activity of running or jogging. The runner often testifies to a very basic satisfaction that arises from this activity. We can think of running as a form of play.[23] It is, I shall suggest, a very "pure" form of play, in the sense that it is not organized by formal rules. If we think of running as a free activity expressing some sense of what a self takes itself to be, with what does the runner identify? Here I am not just talking about the competitive runner, the athlete, the runner of marathons. Why does the ordinary runner run? The pursuit of good health is certainly part of the answer; but from my own experience and after talking with runners and reading what others say about their experience, I think this is only a small element. Some speak of the enjoyment involved here as a pleasant diversion from ordinary reality. Yet this is quite misleading; once again, it is as if this playlike activity is a momentary escape from the "real" world. This *is* extremely important. The first moment of this activity is a kind of "separation" from the activities and concerns of ordinary social life. This first movement from the complexity and confusion of ordinary social life to another aspect of one's being is something with which, no doubt, the runner deeply identifies. Thus the element of "diversion," "escape," or "reprieve"—however one might describe this—is part of the meaning and significance of this experience; but these elements must not be misinterpreted.

The second moment of the activity involves an immediate participation in the activity, and something basic is revealed here, something with which the runner identifies. To put it simply, it feels good to run—at least if a person is in shape. Like children at school who are released at recess to run and jump on the playground, the runner experiences the energy and vitality associated with spontaneous physical exercise. Children engage in frolic, the least formal variety of human play, according to Kenneth Schmitz. Frolic "is usually intense and brief and tends to dissipate itself with the outburst of energy that makes it possible."[24] In this sense, running may not be about merely "staying in shape" or "losing weight" or "looking good." Of course, running may be instrumentally valuable; as such, it is a means. As play, however, it is more like frolic, an end in itself. As Schmitz adds, frolic "is an immediate and unreflective expression of a kind of animal joy, a kicking off of the normal patterns of behavior, purposeless and without constraint."[25] In this outburst of energy there is an unconstrained and "purposeless" expression of a self's physical presence in the world. For the runner there is simplicity and a tremendous sense of physical well-being.

Frolic is the least formal variety of play because it is not guided by rules. It has no goal other than energetic spontaneity. Yet it is easy to see, on the playground and in sport, how unconstrained physical affirmation becomes directed toward an object or purpose when rules are created. The batter explodes out of the batter's box; the wide receiver goes long; the fast break results in a quick basket. Weiss was right, of course, to stress the physical nature of sport. But this emphasis need not rule out the notion that sport may be experienced as liberation insofar as a self may deeply identify with the animal joy of physical activity removed from the everyday world of instrumental values.

Recall how Huizinga summarizes the formal characteristics of play as

> a free activity standing quite consciously outside "ordinary" life as be-ing "not serious," but at the same time absorbing the player intensely and utterly. It is an activity connected with no material interest, and no profit can be gained by it. It proceeds within its own proper boundaries of time and space according to fixed rules and in an orderly manner.[26]
>
> Play is a voluntary activity or occupation executed within certain fixed limits of time and place, according to rules freely accepted but ab-solutely binding, having its aim in itself and accompanied by a feeling of tension, joy and the consciousness that it is "different" from "ordi-nary" life.[27]

Huizinga argues that play is nonserious in the sense that it is separate from ordinary reality, even though the activity of play can be engaged in very seriously. I agree that play is separate from ordinary reality in a gen-uine sense; for example, in the case of running. But this sense of sepa-rateness should not be misunderstood. First, this does not mean that play is unreal or unimportant. As a free activity, play expresses some sense of what a self is; play attests to some aspect of one's "real" or "true" self. In this sense, it is a very real activity. In addition, separateness need not entail the fact that play is a rule-governed activity, "executed within certain fixed limits of space and time." I think running is a suggestive counterexample, as are activities like dancing and swimming.[28] Roger Caillois also agrees with Huizinga—wrongly I believe—that play is always separate, "circumscribed within limits of space and time; defined and fixed in advance;"[29] uncertain, because the "course cannot be determined, nor the result obtained beforehand;"[30] "governed by rules," or "make-believe," "accompanied by a special awareness of a second reality or of a free unreality, as against real life."[31]

Both Caillois and Huizinga fail to make an extremely important distinction that play in its *primary* sense is what might be called "pure" play. Here there is no play-world within which play is performed; in its primary meaning play is not "separate" in the sense that it is rule-governed and enclosed within fixed boundaries of space and time. Here play is simply a free and immensely enjoyable activity, pursued for its own sake with an element of self-consciousness that might be termed "lightness." But play has the tendency to take on these characteristics that Huizinga and Caillois describe. When play becomes intentional—"impure" if you like—that is, when play involves the playing *of* a game, a play-world is constituted by rules and boundaries of space and time.[32] It is for this reason that sport as play is sometimes thought of as unreal, make-believe, and separate. But as a form of play, participation in sports is still a free activity that expresses something with which a self identifies. Part of what the person identifies with in sports is the continued renewal of the sense of his or her physical being. Yet the experiential situation becomes much more complicated when play becomes intentional, because now the person is also involved with goals, rules, challenges, and other people. This is the point at which the moral aspects of sport arise, and some persons' love of sports certainly involves the way in which tension, excitement, build-up, resolution, victory, imagination, and perfection are involved in each unique sporting situation. Yet the important point remains: even when play becomes organized and separate from ordinary reality by virtue of its play-world, it is still profoundly real to the participant who engages in this joyous, free activity. The lover of sports need not apologize for his love affair. If this were required he might as well be required to apologize for what he is. We can only insist that he love the *right* things, the best in sport—but that would require a long and very different kind of argument.

———————

To understand the freedom of play as identification is to see that in playful activity some important reality of the self is affirmed. The freedom of play is the freedom to engage in self-affirmation. But there's obviously more to the freedom of sport and play than the exuberant and joyful affirmation of a self's bodily presence in the world. Surely an important part of the experience of freedom in sport is related to the notion that sport *is* separate from reality in some important sense. The freedom of sport is also a freedom *from*, not simply a freedom *to*.

It might be helpful to think of the relevant issues using categories borrowed from aesthetics. One prominent aesthetician has distinguished isolationist and contextualist views of art and aesthetic experience.[33] These categories describe the metaphorical distance or space between "real life" and the sphere of aesthetic experience or art. For example, Bell's formalism, Bullough's "physical distance," and an "art for art's sake" aesthetic would be isolationist views of art and the aesthetic. Tolstoy's expression theory, Dewey's aesthetics, and socialist realism would be examples of contextualism. Is art simply about itself? Or does art represent, express, or dramatize fundamental human concerns?

The distinction between isolationism and contextualism might be used to understand and evaluate various kinds of emphases offered in interpreting and even justifying participation in sports. The emphasis on excellence, competition, character building, and winning usually places sport in close relation to life. One coach is quoted as offering a paradigmatic expression of the contextualist view of sport: "Football is not a matter of life or death; it's more important than that."[34] Or consider another well-known coach's remark: "Show me a good loser and I'll show you a loser." On the other hand, as I have suggested, the play theorist (Huizinga, Caillois, and others) tends to stress the separateness of the play-world, its isolation from the so-called real world. Sometimes the language used to describe the world of play seems interchangeable with descriptions of aesthetic experience: magic, disinterestedness, enchantment, captivation. The emphasis is put on the secludedness of the distinctive order characteristic of this realm of experience. The play world seems to have its own values, its own telos, its own spatial and temporal boundaries, and, in general, its own possibilities apart from everyday life.

This isolationist language may be overdone, and the distinction between ordinary life and the world of play may be overdrawn. But the distinction discloses something I take to be true and important. When we play our physical games (sports) we engage in humanly and arbitrarily constructed activities that have been created simply for the purpose of engaging in them. Hitting, kicking, and throwing balls, for example, are trivial human activities from an instrumentalist point of view, yet doing such things, and attempting to do them well in the context of the formal constraints of games, frees us from the usual concerns and frustrations of everyday life. There is an element of illusion or unreality when we play these games. When we play we must remind ourselves, as we sometimes do—usually when we confront failure or defeat—that "It's only a game." It is not really serious, like real life, although we engage in play with utmost playful seriousness. The contextualist is often a realist with respect to sport, one who can only view sport as an extension of life and its basic concerns—competition, struggle, winning and losing, honor, prestige, economic rewards, and so forth. Yet the emphasis on play as the ground of sport stresses an antirealist viewpoint. Any worldly values are always filtered through the unworldly, unreal, playful character of the play world removed from worldly concerns. Part of the magic of the world of our national sports like baseball, football, and basketball arises when we bracket our ordinary concerns. We place the "real" world in abeyance and minimize the intrusion of work, obligation, and suffering. It is often the inappropriate overintrusion of the worldly that diminishes our experience of play. It is the spirit of distance or detachment that preserves the wonderful character of the play world and the experience of freedom we find there.

We should not interpret the realist versus antirealist debate about sport and life as an "either-or," as if we must choose one or the other when thinking about appropriate behaviors and attitudes in relation to sport. I believe the fundamental paradox associated with the experience of sport relates to this very issue. At the heart of sport is the ambivalent recognition that sport is both serious and nonserious, real and unreal, authentic and pretend, essential and superfluous.

3   Sport, the Aesthetic, and Narrative

From Paul Weiss's relatively early and legitimating reflections in *Sport: A Philosophic Inquiry* to more recent ruminations in books and scholarly publications, numerous philosophers have been fascinated by the fascination of sport. For example, in his recent book, *Philosophy of Sport*, Drew Hyland again wonders about the "significant and apparently transcultural appeal" of play and sport.[1] I won't attempt to catalogue the various attempts to understand why so many of us are attracted to sport, especially sports that involve the playing of games. Like many people, I've wasted a good part of my life playing and watching these games, and I've given up being ashamed or apologetic about it. But I still want to *understand* the attraction, as any reflective human being should. I suppose one could read the writings of Hyland (a former college basketball player), George Will, or Bart Giamatti as wholesale rationalizations in defense of triviality. But there must be something "deeper" going on here. Or so we think. What could be deeper?

According to my students (and, of course, many others), the deeper attractive realities of sports relate to competition, victory, and the pursuit of excellence. Each semester, at the beginning of my classes, I ask my students to write a paragraph telling me something about themselves. Invariably the most common response expresses a strong interest in sports. Their responses cross the boundaries of race, sex, class, religion, and region. (After all, ESPN is as committed to equality and democratic viewing as is MTV.) Whenever I have the occasion to ask them to explain their attraction, the responses are as predictable as they are obvious. Perhaps I shouldn't be so harsh. Surely part of the nature and attractiveness of sport does involve the intense and often satisfying experiences involved in competing, striving for victory, and becoming better. But such a view of sport is partial; it leaves out too much of the joy. It makes sport sound too much like winning a war or closing a big business deal. It robs sports of its magic and its imaginative appeal, and it impoverishes the rich vocabulary that can be used to reveal sport's possibilities. Previously I've tried to make the case for the view that sport is a form of human play. A play theory of sport is more phenomenologically adequate in showing the attractive possibilities of sport and in showing what sort of attitudes and comportment are appropriate when engaging in playful activity. The play theory of sport seems to me to be a more powerful explanation of the attraction experienced by the player. However, it's not obvious that the people who view sport, the fans (in the broadest sense), are attracted in the same way as the player.

I want to suggest another fruitful response to the question concerning the appeal of sports. I begin with an intuition, and I hope to develop the intuition and its implications more fully. Consider the notion that one of the significant elements in the fan's love of watching games like baseball, football, and basketball has something to do with the way in which sport structures experience and represents it to us. We can see here a close relationship between the kinds of experiences associated with art and the experiences of watching games. Perhaps the aesthetic element plays an important role in the fan's love of the game. Furthermore, in certain kinds of aesthetic experiences we are captivated by our involvement in another temporally articulated world. In the world of the aesthetic object we are taken up by an alternative context of meaning and significance, so much so that these very involvements seem to give us not only a momentary reprieve from the ordinary world, they also help give sense to our lives. If such a response concerning the appeal of sports is enlightening with regard to the fan's experience, I believe it also discloses something important about the participant's experience. Two central notions emerge from these reflections. First, sport provides the occasion for intrinsically interesting experiences, and insofar as it does, is aesthetically valuable. Second, sport also provides contexts of meaning for people, narratives that become existentially valuable for selves seeking a sense of meaning in life.

To work toward these conclusions, let's begin with an alternative account of human experience. Against the backdrop of the view of experience described by Sartre in his early novel *Nausea*, the aesthetic and narrative possibilities of experience emerge more sharply.

Nausea[2] is the purported diary of a young man, Antoine Roquentin, whose life is undergoing fundamental changes. Antoine is writing a biography of a minor nineteenth-century historical figure while he attempts to understand the recurring revelatory experience denoted by the title of this existentialist novel. Antoine's nausea supposedly reveals the brute facticity of being, the utter contingency of himself and all other things, a contingency concealed by various philosophical, religious, and practical strategies. To exist is simply to be there, superfluous (*de trop*). One shows up on the scene and must realize that any attempt to understand human nature in terms of some kind of rational necessity is to falsify what it means to be. Sartre's novel is a sustained reflection on the theme of contingency. For our purposes, however, it is Antoine's related remarks on adventure that are most significant, for the feeling of adventure, he insists, relies on the imposition of narrative structures that falsify the basic contingency of experience.

Prior to returning to the fictional Bouville to use the library for his historical researches, Antoine had traveled widely. The pathetic little "humanist," the Self-Taught Man, systematically reading all of the books in the library in alphabetical order, envies Antoine's adventurous past. This *autodidacte* wants to pursue adventures after he has finished his own instruction. As they talk, the Self-Taught Man's adoring interrogations occasion Antoine's reflective denial of the possibility of adventure, because he realizes he has lost the sense that adventurous events can make moments of life special or particularly meaningful. He attempts to understand and explain this loss of meaningfulness.

Antoine says: "I had imagined that at certain times that my life could take on a rare and precious quality. There was no need for extraordinary circumstances: All I asked for was a little precision" (*N*, 37). The "precision" would be constituted by a series of events with a "beginning." "The beginnings would have to be real beginnings. Alas! Now I see so clearly what I wanted. Real beginnings are like a fanfare of trumpets, like the first notes of a jazz tune, cutting short tedium" (*N*, 37). Antoine believes that when one experiences an adventure, the experience of time is altered. "Each instant appears only as part of a sequence," unlike the daily routine of life. The felt sense of a "real beginning" is dragged forward by a sense of immanent direction in the experience, like the notes of a melody. A sense of fitness shapes each developing moment. Antoine summarizes his analysis of adventure:

> This is what I thought: for the most banal event to become an adventure, you must (and this is enough) begin to recount it. This is what fools people: a man is always a teller of tales, he lives surrounded by his stories and the stories of others, he sees everything that happens to him through them; and he tries to live his own life as if he were telling a story. (*N*, 39)

Antoine expresses here the notion that our stories attempt to give some narrative shape to our otherwise fragmentary and amorphous experience. But he now denies that stories capture the true nature of our experience. Storytellers are condemned to falsify experience, which has no such narrative form. Storytelling is just another mode of self-deception; it is the attempt to hide from contingency. "But you have to choose: live or tell" (*N*, 39). Live or tell! Truth or storytelling—you can't have it both ways. "Nothing happens while you live. The scenery changes, people come in and go out, that's all. There are no beginnings. Days are tacked on to days without rhyme or reason, an interminable, monotonous addition" (*N*, 39). Antoine realizes that life is just one damn thing after another, with no internal coherence, no direction, no unity.

One can attempt to transform the past by telling about it, but the structure is imposed, a projection in which the end artificially transforms the nature of events: "As if there could possibly be true stories" (*N*, 39). This model of projection, the imposition of structures on the events of experience, is clearly explained in Antoine's following comments. (Note, here, as in other parts of the book, the Humean character of his reflections.)

> This feeling of adventure definitely does not come from events: I have proved it. It's rather the way in which the moments are linked together. I think this is what happens: you suddenly feel that time is passing, that each instant leads to another, this one to another one, and so on; that each instant is annihilated, and that it isn't worth while to hold it back, etc., etc. And then you attribute this property to events which appear to you *in* the instants; what belongs to the form you carry over to the content. You talk about the amazing flow of time but you hardly see it. (*N*, 56–57)

Such reflections should be disturbing to a biographer, and it is easy to understand why Antoine gives up his writing project. But what does he do after he realizes that stories falsify? Direction is puzzling; contingency is inescapable. He no longer has the luxury of seeking adventures. "I wanted the moments of my life to follow and order themselves like those of a life remembered. You might as well try and catch time by the tail" (*N,* 40). Antoine's future is only hinted at in the book, but his salvation will have something to do with the necessity he perceives in the unfolding character of songs. Of course, he's not a musician, but he embraces an ontology of art that allows for the salvational qualities of the experiences of composer, performer, and perceiver. Works of art don't "exist" like the brute facticity of contingent beings in the world. In the artwork, there is a felt necessity that transcends the contingency of ordinary life. Perhaps he would write a book:

> Another type of book. I don't quite know which kind—but you would have to guess, behind the printed words, behind the pages, at something which would not exist, which would be above existence. A story, for example, something that could never happen, an adventure. It would be beautiful and hard as steel and make people ashamed of their existence. (*N,* 178)

Sartre's narrator leaves us with a provocative but somewhat dreary view of life. On the one hand, life would make sense if all or parts of it had an immanent, storylike character. If life is just one damn thing after another, it's going nowhere; it's not even a tale told by an idiot, since it is not a tale at all. No wonder Antoine wanted the moments of his life to have the order of a story. We do often experience parts of our life as essentially storyless. On the other hand, must we agree that such structures are added only in retrospect, reflectively modifying, transforming, and thus falsifying a mere dissociated sequence of events as the sequence is represented or reflectively reenacted? Antoine hints that one might find salvation in the experience of aesthetic necessity, "above existence," but he leaves no doubt that ordinary life is without such order. Is there an unbridgeable gap between ordinary experience and the narrative reconstruction of it associated with our stories and our other aesthetic transactions? I don't think so. To show this we should look at another account of experience.

One of the main problems with Antoine's view of experience is that his own diary belies the general account his diary expresses. Obviously, the form of a diary might be an appropriate way to express the fragmentation that he describes. His diary was found, supposedly, among his papers. Does it begin? Only in the sense that there is a first entry, but there is no "real beginning." The reader merely shows up at a point in which the diary is in process, not that this date is of any particular significance. Neither is there some specific "end" to transform the sequence of events. In the final entry we find that Antoine will drift into indeterminacy, his future hinted at yet shrouded in uncertainty. But the life described in the diary is no undifferentiated flow. Antoine recounts a series of situations and events: lunch with the Self-Taught Man; the meeting with his former lover, Anny; the final tragic scene when the Self-Taught Man is caught flirting with a young boy and chastely caressing the boy's hand. It is this last scene, especially, that is expressed with tautness and suspense. The situation unfolds with dramatic necessity. When the Corsican smashes the Self-Taught Man's face and the little humanist retreats in humiliation, his abstract love of humanity nullified by the realities of real human hatred and disgust, it's not that Antoine's telling has transformed the experience. The narrative has disclosed the immanent development of the situation.

Life is not necessarily like Antoine's description of it: it has "no beginnings. Days are tacked on to days without rhyme or reason, an interminable, monotonous addition." I think of my own life as a teacher. For many years at least part of my life has been structured by the rhythms of an academic calendar (an academic "season," in the language of baseball). My life, in part, consists of semesters, courses, and classes. Parts of my life stand out from the general flow of experience. For example, most teachers can recall an especially excellent and pleasurable course, and within such a course certain days in which the class discussion developed in an exciting and wonderful way: perhaps a new line of inquiry, novel comments, an interesting new argument, effective Socratic direction, the material coming together in an unsuspected way leading to a satisfying conclusion. Such an experience is integrated and fulfilling. Contrast that with courses and classes in which there is no smooth development; there are starts and stops, gaps and edges, and there is no sense of completion or satisfactory end. Contrast the alluring and satisfying character of the good class with the unappealing quality of the bad class. Our lives are not simply "one damn thing after another" in one undifferentiated flow of experience.

John Dewey has described this with acuteness in *Art As Experience*.[3] "For life is no uniform uninterrupted march or flow. It is a thing of histories, each with its own plot, its own inception and movement toward its close, each having its own particular movement; each with its own unrepeated quality pervading it throughout" (*AE*, 35–36). Dewey speaks of the difference between experience in general and having *an* experience, when "the material runs its course to fulfillment. Then and only then is it integrated within and demarcated in the general stream of experience from other experiences" (*AE*, 35). I have given as an example of *an* experience my own experience as a teacher, but such possibilities are pervasive in life. Dewey mentions such possibilities in relation to finishing a piece of work, solving a problem, eating a meal, writing a book, having a conversation, and playing a game. He offers an extended description of an experience of thinking to show when it is possible that an experience is "so rounded out that its close is a consummation and not a cessation. Such an experience is a whole and carries with it its own individualizing quality and self-sufficiency" (*AE*, 35).

Dewey stresses two important features of an experience. First, there is a temporal structure of connection within the experience. There is a structure of organization and growth: "inception, development, fulfillment" (*AE*, 55). "In such experiences, every successive part flows freely, without seam and without unfilled blanks, into what ensues" (*AE*, 36). Such experiences are temporally integrated. The second feature is somewhat more difficult to understand phenomenologically. There is a felt unity within an experience, "constituted by a single *quality* that pervades the entire experience in spite of the variation of its constituent parts. This unity is neither emotional, practical, nor intellectual, for these terms name distinctions that reflection can make within it" (*AE*, 37). In some experience, one of these elements may dominate and reflection can apprehend such dominance. If one recalls an experience of philosophical reflection, the intellectual elements would predominate, but Dewey insists that the experience as lived would be emotional as well. "No thinker can ply his occupation save as he is lured and rewarded by total integral experiences that are *intrinsically worthwhile*" (*AE*, 37, emphasis mine).

Dewey insists that every experience so constituted as *an* experience has "esthetic quality." Aesthetic experience proper, for example, the creation and experience of works of fine art, differ from predominantly intellectual and practical activities in the dominating interest, intent, and materials. But here as elsewhere, Dewey wants to deny what he sees as a pernicious dualism. He denies the radical separation of the aesthetic and the nonaesthetic. In practical activity ("overt doings") and in intellectual activity ("thinking") there are latent aesthetic possibilities. Even in *an* experience of thinking, "the experience itself has a satisfying emotional quality because it possesses internal integration and fulfillment reached through ordered and organized movement. The artistic structure may be immediately felt. Insofar, it is esthetic" (*AE*, 38). I believe Dewey calls such a quality of an experience "esthetic" for two related reasons: because the quality is felt or perceived in an immediate acquaintance and because such a structure is intrinsically satisfying or valued. In fact, Dewey believes that art involves the intention to make objects whose sensuous qualities are immediately enjoyable to perception because of the aesthetic structure he describes.

The upshot of Dewey's analysis of the aesthetic is to alter the normal view that aesthetic experience is different in kind from acting and thinking. He attempts to show that "the esthetic is no intruder in experience from without, whether by way of ideal luxury or transcendent ideality, but that is the clarified and intensified development of traits that belong to every normally complete experience" (*AE*, 46). It is striking to read Dewey's account of "an experience" with sport in mind, since the description captures so sharply the experiences of viewing (and playing) sports. Consider a baseball game. The game is initiated by a real beginning, not merely an accidental first occurrence associated with clock time. The first inning is internally related to all future occurrences in the game; events that occur later invest early moments with novel significance, and earlier moments become meaningful in relation to later moments (a kind of hermeneutic circle). The pitcher attempts to establish his fastball, probes the weaknesses of certain hitters, and attempts to gain a sense of the umpire's strike zone. Fielders position themselves according to their judgment of the swing and strength of the hitters; they must remember previous at bats. Coaches learn and respond as the game proceeds. The pitcher has a poor move to first; the catcher's arm is strong but his release is slow and his feet are plodding. The pitcher never throws breaking balls when he's behind in the count. A decision is made to steal second base. And so on. The game involves "overt doings," but these practical activities are invested with strategic meanings. Each moment is pregnant with future possibilities as the game develops. If the game is a good one, the action is tense and occasions excitement and suspense. From the fan's perspective, attention is intensely focused on the actions, decisions, and meanings inside the world of the game. If one knows baseball well, the complexity of a particular game is quite amazing. An entire book might be written describing *one* game![4] The teleology within the development of the game finally leads to a consummatory moment when victory or defeat makes the experience complete. In Dewey's language, the game has constituted *an* experience, an integral experience with aesthetic quality.

Dewey describes a mundane practical activity: a stone rolling down a hill toward a resting place. But he imaginatively adds an interesting possibility. Suppose the stone is self-conscious:

> Let us add, by imagination, . . . the ideas that it looks forward with desire to the final outcome; that it is interested in the things it meets on the way, conditions that accelerate and retard its movement with respect

to their bearing on the end; that it acts and feels toward them according to the hindering or helping function it attributes to them; and that the final coming to rest is related to all that went before as the culmination of a continuous movement. Then the stone would have an experience, and one with esthetic quality. (*AE,* 39)

Let's change Dewey's example slightly. Suppose that the stone is a self-conscious leather ball filled with air, but it allows others to act in order to achieve its final resting place, and those others are interested in its movement. Together, the ball and other self-conscious beings make some arbitrary decisions in order to make possible intrinsically enjoyable actions and experiences. They decide to construct a goal, allow the ball to be advanced only by kicking, place boundaries on the space within which the ball can be advanced, the time it takes to have opportunities to kick the ball into the goal, and the number of players who will either attempt to make a goal or keep others from kicking the ball into the goal. The players, interested in such activities, would have an experience. Likewise, if we let others watch and if these self-conscious beings were knowledgeable about the rules of the activity and interested in the outcome, they would also have an experience with aesthetic quality.

Why would people be captivated or fascinated by watching such activities? One reason, I believe, is the contrast they would find between the satisfying structures of *an* experience and the typical experiences of ordinary life. Recall Antoine's interpretation of human experience: life is merely a series of events leading nowhere. Things happened to him, but with no apparent meaning that related these events to one another. Life can be like that. Again, to use Dewey's language, this is to see life as an aimless succession of events. We drift, toward nothing or nowhere in particular. The drift of aimlessness leads to boredom. At the other extreme, parts of our life may be so ruled by a kind of order or structure that each moment seems to succeed the previous one in mechanical determination. Here the paradigm example would be factory work in which some task is repeated over and over, activities strictly determined by time, tightly governed rules and technical expertise. Aesthetic interest, constituted by acute attentiveness, anticipation, tension, and teleologically directed captivation, is contrasted with the boredom of aesthetic looseness and the oppressiveness of aesthetic constriction. Moments of experience are aesthetically interesting when integration is mediated by novelty; unity in development is colored by uncertainty; initiations are fulfilled by consummatory moments, not mere endings. Dewey is right to insist that it is incorrect to distinguish sharply between aesthetic experience associated with art proper and supposedly ordinary nonaesthetic experience, simply because so much of our experience consists of one of these two poles: loose succession with no internal development and consummation or mechanical succession.

> There exists so much of one and the other of these two kinds of experience that unconsciously they come to be taken as norms of all experience. Then, when the esthetic appears, it so sharply contrasts with the picture that has been formed of experience, that it is impossible to combine its special qualities with the features of the picture and the esthetic is given an outside place and status. The account that has been given of experience dominantly intellectual and practical is intended to show that there is no such contrast involved in having an experience; that, on the contrary, no experience of whatever sort is a unity unless it has aesthetic quality. (*AE*, 40)

If Dewey is correct, experiences of sport and in sport, like the experiences associated with reading books, listening to music, going to movies, and so on, can be seen as attempts to replace aesthetically impoverished ordinary experiences with experiences that have aesthetic quality. Of course there are differences, but it is the Deweyan similarities that I want to stress. These similarities offer a plausible explanation of at least part of the attraction of sport.

Let me end this section with some brief related remarks that confirm the association I have suggested. Monroe Beardsley's well-known notion of aesthetic value depends heavily on Dewey's description of aesthetic experience.[5] Beardsley says that, among other things, aesthetic experiences are intense, unified (they "hang together"), and internally complete, in the sense that they are differentiated from the "general stream of experience." All of this is quite familiar to us after having looked carefully at Dewey's account. Beardsley adds that the characteristics of aesthetic experience are found in other experiences but they are combined differently. He even mentions playing games, in which we enjoy activities having "no practical purpose." But according to Beardsley, "it seems not necessarily to be an experience of a high degree of unity. Watching a baseball or football game is also generally lacking in a dominant pattern and consummation, though sometimes it has these characteristics to a high degree and is an aesthetic experience."[6] Beardlsey's comments confirm the notion that sport offers aesthetic possibilities. However, these possibilities may be more available to those whose interests in and knowledge of the sport are keen, just as the aesthetic possibilities of a work of art are more available to the sensitive and knowledgeable consumer of art.[7]

———————

As we have seen, one way to respond to Antoine's phenomenology is to think about the concept of the aesthetic in Deweyan terms. But recall that Antoine specifically uses the language of narrative and story. As storytellers we are condemned to falsify our experience. Sartre's narrator wanted the moments of his life to be ordered, like a story, but that would merely be a life remembered, not lived. However, the aesthetic structure of an experience is not merely imposed. There are "real beginnings," in sport and elsewhere in life. What Dewey calls the aesthetic structure of a developed and integrated experience, rounded out and differentiated in the general stream experience, could also be described as a narrative. As Dewey has said, life consists of histories, with different plots, rhythms of development, distinctive "emotional" qualities, and consummatory moments. Life consists of stories we *live*, not simply artificially reconstruct in reflection.

Alasdair MacIntyre has stressed the role of narrative in life, in the context of a criticism of the modern conception of a self who is unable to be the bearer of the traditional virtues.[8] For our purposes, a narrative conception of selfhood will be another significant ground for the attractiveness of sport. Briefly, MacIntyre criticizes modernist conceptions of life that either attempt to explain human action atomistically or radically to separate the individual from the social roles he inhabits. He shows that action can be adequately explained only by referring to an agent's intentions, and these intentions are themselves embedded in "settings" that have histories. (Settings may be practices, institutions, or other situations.) To explain what a person is doing is to refer to narratives within which individuals live and act. An act of gardening may be a way of sustaining the family, helping a marriage, or attaining a more healthful personal life. "Narrative history of a certain kind turns out to be the basic and essential genre of the characterization of human actions."[9] Narrative interpretation makes action intelligible by placing it in a historical context.

MacIntyre insists that even such a common and familiar type of situation as a conversation must be understood in terms of narrative. Conversations "have beginnings, middles, and endings just as do literary works. They embody reversals and recognitions; they move towards and away from climaxes."[10] Likewise, human transactions in general have a narrative structure: "battles, chess games, courtships, philosophy seminars, families at a dinner table, businessmen negotiating contracts."[11] He concludes that "both conversations in particular then and human actions in general are enacted narratives."[12] He is quite clear that Antoine's view of life is simply a false picture typical of modernity.

> It is now becoming clear that we render the actions of others intelligible in this way because action itself has a basically historical character. It is because we all live out narratives in our lives and because we understand our own lives in terms of narratives that we live out that the form of narrative is appropriate for understanding the actions of others. Stories are lived before they are told—except in the case of fiction.[13]

What do we make of MacIntyre's narrative conception of selfhood in relation to the possibilities associated with sport? Perhaps MacIntyre is right that narrative is the essential way we make sense of life. Of course, there is a complex relationship among the various narratives we live as individuals. MacIntyre speaks of narratives being "embedded" in one another. A person may be a mother, wife, friend, teacher, scholar, poet, and amateur chef, all embedded in one life. But whether it's merely an aberration of modernity or an inevitable part of any human life, individuals often appear to lose the sense that important parts of their life or life in general have any narrative structure. Marriages fail and important friendships fade. Flowering careers are displaced by unemployment, health is replaced by disease and suffering. Families disintegrate and communities or small groups are wrecked by dissension. It is often quite difficult to see where all of this, or even discrete parts of it, could be going. MacIntyre's account of the narrative structure of human life is tainted by nostalgia, as if fragmentation is merely an accidental historical condition.

Richard Lischer has expressed a halting pessimism in the face of attempts to make story pervasive in life. In his useful article, "The Limits of Story,"[14] he expresses a middle way between MacIntyre's optimism and Antoine's deep and abiding pessimism that narratives falsify our life. Arguing against theologians and preachers who have embraced the primacy of story, Lischer believes that parts of our life are indeed shapeless and storyless, that "story falsifies those vast and deep non-narrative domains of human life."[15] Narratives impose a structure on a disordered life and "may provide the sense of order so desperately needed *or* they may appear transparently palliative to those whose experience has resisted the broom that sweeps in one direction."[16]

We may experience our life or parts of our lives as essentially storyless. And when we do, it is natural to seek out new stories, or return to areas of experience that offer the meaningful possibilities of story. I can think of no area in modern life (except watching television, I suppose) that offers more possibilities for storylike experiences than sports. Certainly viewing sports and being a "real fan" may appear to be more "transparently palliative" than reading our scriptures or praying to our gods. Nonetheless, it seems to me that the ways in which people identify with the narratives associated with sports are important strategies for finding a sense of meaning and concern in an otherwise anarchical life. I don't want to appear to be saying that the only role that sports play in the life of individuals is therapeutic, keeping the wolf of despair at bay. For the psychologically fit as well as the despairing, sport is there. But if our gods are dead, our politics shallow, our cultural life thin, our work alienated, and our relation to the world overly technological, we may need the atmosphere of play and narrative more than ever. (The overcommercialization of sport may be cause for despair as well.)

Lischer offers apt comments on the storyless places in our lives:

> They exist wherever episodic complications have stagnated and cease to develop with any organic connection toward new episodes and new complications. Life continues as a series of unrelated episodes, as in a collection of short stories by many authors, or it proceeds by a series of "slices" or scenes, as in a cabaret show or picture gallery. An objective thread of identity may persist, but to those caught in this kind of life, the "I" known long ago in Act One has become a stranger. Indeed, if one is to make sense of such a life, it will not be by casting it into acts and rationalizing its plot but by rediscovering the continuity of identity throughout the confusion of broken plots, botched lines, and embarrassing nonsequiturs.[17]

Think about these comments in relation to the games we played in childhood and the games we still care about as adults. (I use baseball only as an apt example. There may be nothing particularly "special" about our national pastime as a source of certain kinds of storylike experiences.) For many who played baseball as a child, it meant really caring about something, about hopes and dreams, special moments, enduring relationships, magical situations, and joy. It also meant having heroes, collecting baseball cards, listening to and watching games, sometimes heated conversations, and, yes—fathers playing catch with their sons. So one grows up and gets on with life. Winter comes to a close, days get longer, and spring rolls around. It's baseball season again! At least there may seem to be one thing in life that makes sense in its captivating and alluring qualities. The unity of a life may reappear as spring training begins. If "episodic complications have stagnated" in one's life, and have ceased "to develop with any organic connection toward new episodes and new complications," there are still available the narrative experiences of sport. To watch a baseball game is to move from ordinary life to a realm of experience in which episodic complications are alive with possibilities, organically developing in a teleologically directed movement. But a game may be "embedded" (MacIntyre's term) in a series, and a series may be embedded in an entire season. If we think about major league baseball, the narrative possibilities that we may identify with and vicariously experience are practically endless. For each game, each inning, even every pitch and at bat, is embedded in a complex historical setting. Players, coaches, teams, and leagues have careers, statistical relationships abound, and strategic maneuvers are omnipresent. To love baseball is to immerse oneself in a world of transparent meanings, efficacious actions, heroic deeds, and admirable excellences. It is to identify with the story of a game, a team, a career, and even one's own life. If there is a need for story in our lives, as there was for Antoine, one may momentarily keep the wolf at bay by being a fan. And the distance between the transparently palliative experiences of the fan and "real life" may be closed by sustaining an internal relationship to sport by playing or coaching.[18]

Recall that Antoine's diary ends on a somewhat hopeful note. He says he may write a book, create a story "which would not exist, which would be above existence." His ontology of art is the basis for an act of transcendence, beyond the contingency of the ordinary, as if participation in the structure of a story would give some hope of salvation. Although I've insisted that ordinary experience has aesthetic and narrative possibilities, the experience of sport is not quite ordinary. If Antoine can be saved by or through art, "above existence," the storylike experiences of sport are also insulated, in some sense, from real life, and that is why sport is such a fecund arena for these possibilities. This is the point at which sport as aesthetic and sport as narrative naturally reconnect with sport as play. Recall Huizinga's famous account of play.[19] Play is not ordinary or real life; it is a free activity standing outside of ordinary life, in which a distinctive order reigns. Kenneth Schmitz has also emphasized the notion of play as "suspension of the ordinary," the world of play as a "distinctive order," and sport as rule-governed activity grounded in the spirit of play.[20] We are now in a position to see the peculiar order of the world of play in aesthetic and narrative terms. Since people find aesthetic quality intrinisically satisfying and since people need stories in order to experience life as having some shape, pattern, or end, it is natural that so many people would be drawn to sport—not merely because of a thirst for victory, a desire to make the other submit, a love of violence, or a need to be excellent. Lovers of sport need not be apologetic about their appreciation of the aesthetic nor their need for story in life.

4 *Play and the Absurd*

One of the most interesting aspects of the relatively recent discussions of play and sport is the way philosophers have shown, in their descriptive and speculative reflections, how fundamental aspects of human existence are revealed in the experience of play. These elements are lived by the player and made manifest to the spectator. One thinks first of the classic discussions offered by Huizinga, Caillois, and Eugen Fink, which describe such themes as freedom, spontaneity, joy, the transcendence of the ordinary, the lived experience of space and time, illusion, mystery, and imagination.[1] Building on these seminal discussions, other thinkers have added breadth and depth to these insights. For example, Kenneth Schmitz has stressed the fact that when we play we freely decide to suspend the ordinary concerns of everyday life, and in doing so, we open ourselves to new possibilities of "meaning, freedom and value."[2] Drew Hyland offers a Heideggarian analysis of play and suggests, contrary to Heidegger, that the extension of play that we find in sport offers the opportunity for an authentic experience of friendship and community.[3] Joseph L. Esposito thinks that play should be characterized essentially as an encounter with possibility,[4] while Keith Algozin finds the most fascinating element of play and sport related to the person's desire, in the midst of the confusion and uncertainty of ordinary life, for completeness in the transparency of activity whose meaning is fully illuminated in an internally related context of significance. That is, Algozin views the play of the athlete as "unalienated activity," effecting a momentary sense of completion in an otherwise incomplete life.[5]

I cite these examples not from any desire to offer an exhaustive list of "fundamental aspects of human existence" revealed in play and described by these thinkers. This brief list is meant merely to be suggestive. There is no simple answer to the question of why sport fascinates. One *can* view the activities and experiences associated with play and sport as childish and insignificant diversions from "real" life. One *can* view players as entertainers and sport as trivial amusement. But I believe that such views tend to impoverish the richness and complexity of the phenomenon of human play. Central themes of mythic import are constantly "played out" in the play worlds that we create and in which we participate. These themes are available for appreciation by anyone who perceives the play event.

Experience, as Dewey says, is ongoing, fleeting, and complex. We can at times stand back from this continuous process when we attempt to understand the immediacy of life by reflecting upon our experience. Likewise, it appears that art has the power of ordering the experience of a self interacting with the world, transforming it into a more articulate structure for our examination and appreciation. And sport, whether the great spectacles viewed by thousands or the minor event viewed by only a few, also has this power to transform ordinary experience into a more limited and orderly structure. Concerns become more focused, activities are invested with clear meanings, and central aspects of life shine forth with more clarity. I wish here only to suggest tentatively that at least the viewing of sport has much more to do with the sphere of the aesthetic—broadly considered—than we might think when only considering the classical beauty of grace and form in human movement. When the event becomes the object of our appreciative gaze, elements of otherwise ordinary experience are demarcated and magnified, just as in our experience of reading literature or viewing a painting. Courage, resolution, competition, will, cunning, tacit knowing, perseverance, struggle, victory, physical excellence, defeat, pain, friendship, community, exceptionality, character, joy, freedom, spontaneity, creativity, rootedness, and place—all may be revealed for our appreciative gaze as the players live these moments of their singular histories. Sport dramatizes some of the essential elements that constitute our existence.

I also want to say something about the nature of play—especially the kind of play associated with contests—and its broader import in the life of human beings attempting to understand themselves and endeavoring to get on with life. It is not as if my discussion will depart radically from those thinkers I have already cited, and it is not as if I want to falsify other positions. Rather, I want to contribute to an understanding of the complex phenomena at issue, perhaps like the reader who gives yet another interpretation of a great text by offering another way of reading it. My way of "reading" this text may at first appear to be strikingly odd. To associate play and the absurd may seem to be misguided, for, it might be argued, the absurd is associated with frustration, paradox, and even despair. To speak of some situation as absurd, or to speak of life itself as absurd, may be the expression of desperation or the recognition of something negative and unreasonable. On the other hand, play appears to have the "coloring" of joy, as Fink says, and Huizinga certainly emphasizes the sheer exuberance and fun of the spirit of play. Play seems to be something positive and life-affirming. Let us first consider a famous image of absurdity.

Consider Sisyphus, condemned by the gods to the eternal drudgery of ceaselessly and strenuously pushing a huge stone to the top of a hill, only to see it roll back down, where he must retrieve it and continue his endless toil. The punishment inflicted upon Sisyphus is not absurd or meaningless simply because he is condemned to lead a life of endless toil. Here is an image of a being, with a human heart and human desires, confronting a future in which any desire contrary to the desire to push rocks must be eternally frustrated. What is absurd, perhaps, is the incongruity between human purposiveness and necessary frustration. As Camus interprets the myth, Sisyphus is the image of a being whose whole being "is exerted toward accomplishing nothing."[6] This is activity that has no telos; no goods come about, no external justification invests it with meaning. Richard Taylor also argues that the toil is meaningless because "nothing ever comes of what he is doing, except simply, more of the same . . . the work is simply pointless."[7]

Now consider *homo ludens:* for example, the pick-up basketball player or the aging tennis player. Is *homo ludens* Sisyphus? Is his play absurd, like the pointless toil of Sisyphus? Admittedly, there is a sense in which nothing comes of the playing. This is the essential aspect of play that Caillois called "unproductive." As he argues, there may be an exchange of money involved—playing games of chance, for example—but no goods are created by the activity. The labors of Sisyphus result in no stone edifice being constructed; the activity of the player results in nothing tangible being produced. As Caillois puts it,

A characteristic of play, in fact, is that it creates no wealth or goods, thus differing from work or art. At the end of the game, all can and must start over again at some point. Nothing has been harvested or manufactured, no masterpiece has been created, no capital has accrued. Play is an occasion of pure waste: waste of time, energy, ingenuity, skill . . . As for professionals . . . it is clear that they are not players but workers. When they play, it is at some other game.[8]

Just as the abilities, interests, and desires of Sisyphus must be eternally wasted in pointless activity, there is a common intuition that the person who spends much of his time playing games is absurdly wasting his "time, energy, ingenuity, skill" in the pursuit of pointless and adolescent tasks.

Caillois' remarks are also suggestive on another point. Sisyphus' labor must inevitably lead to boredom because of the endless repetition of his activity. Likewise, the game begins, it is momentarily played out, and it ends. Nothing comes of it, yet it will begin again, over and over, in the playful life of the player who continuously seeks to pursue this pointless repetition. Nothing comes of his play—except more of the same. Thus it is not prima facie implausible to compare play and the absurd toil of Sisyphus. However, even in light of what has just been said about the seemingly pointless, unproductive, and repetitive aspects of play, I think it would be a mistake to construe the absurdity of play in terms of the image of Sisyphusian labor. The differences are more striking than the similarities.

First, recall that Sisyphus is condemned and sentenced by the gods. We are to regard his laboring as wholly involuntary. But this stands in stark contrast to the phenomenon of play. As we have seen, play is characterized by freedom. Typically, the player freely decides to play, and this very freedom associated with the phenomenon of play suggests a variety of other central aspects. Because the player freely chooses to play, he must identify with his activity. He must see it as very much his own sort of doing, unlike activities that are alienated and seem to be foreign to the one who engages in them. Play is never constrained or forced, else the activity wouldn't be play.

Moreover, although we have admitted that play is in some respects as unproductive as the toil of Sisyphus, certainly that doesn't mean that play is as meaningless as Sisyphus' toil. Although nothing comes of play, the free decision to play suggests that one desires to engage in the activity; it is a good. But it is good not by virtue of any goods that it brings into being; we have already denied that this is the case. Play is activity that is intrinsically valued. In fact, thinkers such as Robert Osterhoudt have suggested that play is less a description of concrete activities than a way of viewing and living a variety of activities:

> Play is therefore of a different order than concrete activities as such: it is effectively a way of regarding these activities. It is a quality of concrete activity by which the activity(ies) to which it is "attached" (or in which it inheres) is intrinsically valued, or valued in-and-for-itself, and so voluntarily engaged, of an extraordinary or supra-mundane and disinterested character, and aesthetically ordered.[9]

In this broader meaning, play might even describe activities we would normally not associate with play—like teaching, for example—if one might choose to engage in the activity regardless of external constraint or utility. Also related to this intrinsic valuing of play is the joy, exuberance, happiness, and fun of play. Certainly this aspect of play experience is quite different from the supposed response of Sisyphus to his abject toil.

Furthermore, we have said there is no "end" to the toils of Sisyphus. His activity is pointless repetition, unproductive like the play of humans. But we must be careful not to equivocate here. While Sisyphus' labor and play may be unproductive in one sense—thus having no "end"—there is certainly an end associated with much of human play that we do not find in the image of Sisyphus. When the player in sport chooses to play, he voluntarily commits himself to the rules of the game in which he is playing. The rules describe the proper end(s) of play and also prescribe the only acceptable means by which the end may be brought about. Within a game there is a telos at the center of all the activities associated with playing it. Activities take on a clear meaning by virtue of the rules internal to the game. A world of transparent meaning comes about. Something is at issue, players freely commit themselves to goals and prescribed behavior, and something gets settled. These play activities are purposive insofar as they are oriented toward the ends internal to the play world, and they lead toward a consummation. There is no real consummation in the activity of Sisyphus; although he momentarily reaches the top of his hill, nothing really gets settled because no "end" has been at issue. This consummatory aspect of play gives meaning to the activities that lead toward the end in view. Play is a striving, a quest with purpose, ending in fulfillment. (Remember that we are talking about game playing, especially.)

Thus play is a free activity, intrinsically valued and therefore meaningful, joyous, or happy, ending in a consummation or fulfillment. If play is absurd, it must not be absurd by virtue of an exact analogy with the absurdity of Sisyphus' plight, for the analogy is obviously an imperfect one. Absurdity must not exactly be meaninglessness. Consider Richard

Taylor's remarks: "Meaninglessness is essentially endless pointlessness, and meaningfulness is therefore the opposite. Activity, and even long-drawn-out repetitive activity, has a meaning if it has some culmination, some more or less lasting end that can be considered to have been the direction and purpose of the activity."[10]

But I think play is absurd, and one final comparison between Sisyphus and homo ludens might be helpful in leading to an altered view of the absurd and its relation to play. Unlike Sisyphus, the player deeply identifies with the activity in which he freely decides to participate. Attitudes, here, are of greatest importance, for suppose that Sisyphus wanted to do what he is, in fact, doomed forever to do by necessity.[11] We should think that his activity would then be like the bliss of heaven rather than the torment of hell, for his activities would be in perfect conformity with his desires, and each moment would be the experience of immediate gratification. What makes Sisyphus the image of an absurd life is the gap between his desires and the reality of his activity; he is burdened by attitudes absurdly inconsistent with his situation. It is difficult to conceive of something "objectively" absurd, because the absurd seems to be a function of our wills, desires, or interests. The player throws himself joyfully into an intrinsically valued activity, and therefore his play seems different from the endless toil of Sisyphus. Yet there is also a tension between his own attitudes and the reality of playful activity. Unlike Sisyphus, the player regards and lives his activity *as if* it were truly significant and meaningful, but, like Sisyphus, he realizes that his play really does come up empty. Nothing comes of it, and he knows that his play isn't *really serious*. We need to examine this tension more closely, but first we must more closely clarify the concept of the absurd.

———————

Recall Camus' description of the absurd. For Camus, the absurd resides neither within the person alone nor within an irrational world. The absurd arises in the relationship between the person's desire for understanding, unity, and the Absolute, and a reality that will not divulge any ultimates. The absurd for Camus is really a brand of epistemological skepticism, and his early philosophy is the attempt to work out the existential implications of this Archimedean uncertainty. He is a failed Cartesian who wants to ground his life only on the basis of certainties, yet must finally draw out the honest consequences of recognizing that the only certainty is the absurd: "The absurd is born of this confrontation between the human need and the unreasonable silence of the world. This must not be forgotten. This must be clung to because the whole consequence of a life can depend upon it."[12] Although Camus' description of the absurd may be limited, insofar as he insists that the key to the necessary absurdity of life rests upon the contingent desire "to know" in some ultimate sense, his analysis is very suggestive. The absurd arises in the incongruous clash between our aspirations and the reality we confront.

Thomas Nagel has attempted to clarify the concept of the absurd and show how life as a whole is absurd. "In ordinary life a situation is absurd when it includes a conspicuous discrepancy between pretension or aspiration and reality."[13] An absurd situation might be called an instance of "local" absurdity. Obviously there are a variety of situations in life that often meet this description, based on the particular contingent desires and aspirations of people. But Nagel's claim is much stronger; he thinks life is "globally" absurd:

> If there is a philosophical sense of absurdity, however, it must arise from the perception of something universal—some response in which pretension and reality inevitably clash for us all. This condition is supplied, I shall argue, by the collision between the seriousness with which we take our lives and the perpetual possibility of regarding everything about which we are serious as arbitrary, or open to doubt.[14]

How, according to Nagel, is this seriousness necessarily undermined?

> We cannot live human lives without energy and attention, nor without making choices which show that we take some things more seriously than others. Yet we have always available a point of view outside the particular form of our lives, from which the seriousness appears gratuitous. These two inescapable viewpoints collide in us, and that is what makes life absurd. It is absurd because we ignore the doubts that we know cannot be settled, continuing to live with nearly undiminished seriousness in spite of them.[15]

Perhaps Nagel's analysis is more akin to Camus' discussion of the absurd than first appears, because, although Nagel doesn't simply focus on the mind's desire for understanding, there is still in his elucidation the notion that the absurd is generated by skepticism. For Nagel, we do and must live our lives with utmost seriousness, yet we have the power to disengage ourselves in reflection from the immediacy of living and recognize that the very hinges upon which our life turns are themselves arbitrary and nonderivative. The very contingency of any belief we take as ultimate undermines the seriousness of life. Reflective detachment provides the permanent possibility of fueling a doubt that is more real than the abstract Cartesian methodological procedure. Once again, Nagel argues:

But this is precisely what provides universal doubt with its object. We step back to find that the whole system of justification and criticism, which controls our choices and supports our rationality, rests on responses and habits we never question, that we should not know how to defend without circularity, and to which we shall continue to adhere even after they are called into question.[16]

What is the upshot of this recognition of the absurd? Just as Camus wanted to draw out the consequences of the absurd in the life of the absurd hero, Nagel also thinks such a recognition has profound implications for our basic attitude toward life. This skepticism will certainly not force us to abandon our fundamental hinges or beliefs, but, according to Nagel, "it lends them a peculiar flavor . . . we return to our familiar convictions with a certain irony and resignation."[17] Our seriousness would be mediated by an ironic sense of our own limitations and an unconvinced retreat from dogmatic claims of ultimacy. An ironic sense of detachment never allows the world to be too much with us. Such an attitude recognizes that Promethean scorn, Sartrean despair, or religious dogmatism are equally invaded by a spirit of seriousness that either denies our finitude, romantically thinks that the situation can be other than it is, or hopes that life can be magically transformed by defiance.

We are now ready to consider play once again.

Play is a momentary reprieve from the burdens of ordinary or everyday life. We work, help others, study, pay bills, raise children, buy things, go to church, and generally get on with life as best we can. But when we play we momentarily step out of everydayness as we participate in a play world with its own meanings and prescriptions. The freedom of play suggests that we voluntarily bracket our ordinary and pressing concerns as we take a stance outside the practical affairs of life. Recall that Huizinga described this as one of the essential characteristics of play: "Play is not 'ordinary' or 'real' life. It is rather a stepping out of 'real' life into a temporary sphere of activity with a disposition all of its own."[18] Echoing Huizinga's position, Kenneth Schmitz thinks that this constitutes the very essence of play. "The essence of play comes into existence through a decision to play. Such a constitutive decision cannot be compelled and is essentially free. Through it arises the suspension of the ordinary concerns of the everyday world. Such a decision does not simply initiate the playing but rather constitutes it."[19] Thus one might see the positive aspect of play as the transcendence of worldly constraint in the free projection of alternative possibilities.

This stepping out of the ordinary lends a peculiar flavor to play, for it is a withdrawal from those things normally associated with the "seriousness" of life. Like the make-believe play of children, there arises a sense of "unreality" associated with the play world. As Huizinga says: "This 'only pretending' quality of play betrays a consciousness of the inferiority of play compared with 'seriousness,' a feeling that seems to be something as primary as play itself."[20] Yet this *as if* quality of play does not mean that the activity is engaged in with an uncaring attitude. On the contrary, play is undertaken with "utmost seriousness, with an absorption, a devotion that passes into rapture and, temporarily at least, completely abolishes that troublesome 'only' feeling."[21] A certain abandon goes along with the freedom of play. So we arrive at a curious dialectic within the experience of play, between the serious and the non-serious. We play our games with abandon and intensity as if nothing mattered more than making this basket, winning this game, overcoming this challenge. Yet this attitude of seriousness is undermined by the reflection that insists that it is "only a game," with something less than world-historical import or even the more limited importance of job, success, and material well-being. In this sense, play is "unreal," or only partly real, as Eugen Fink's ontology of play suggests, when he says that "play is a magical creation in the world of play . . . The world of play is an imaginary sphere."[22]

This means that there is a basic absurdity at the center of play. Recall that the absurd involves "a conspicuous discrepancy between pretension or aspiration and reality." The player must at one and the same time embrace the seemingly contradictory attitudes that his play world is a fiction, his commitment to the arbitrary rules of his game is utterly gratuitous; yet he must play *as if* it really mattered, because his decision to play necessitates such commitment. Without commitment, he isn't really playing; with commitment he must act *as if* his play really mattered, even though it doesn't. Without pursuit of victory, the play of contests is reduced to mere frolic and the spirit of the play world is lost. Remember that for Nagel the absurdity of life as a whole, global absurdity, involves the fact that "we always have available a point of view outside the particular form of our lives, from which the seriousness appears gratuitous." This situation is precisely seen in play, because of the bracketing of the ordinary and the creation of a play world with its own internal aspects of meaning, space, and time. The "always available point of view" outside the play world is, of course, the standpoint of the ordinary world that generates the criteria for what we take as "really serious."

Whenever we say "it's only a game" we acknowledge this ability to de-tach ourselves from the immediate participation in play, yet this doesn't mean that we will not play "seriously" in the future, just as the recogni-tion of the absurd doesn't mean that we will henceforth fail to take any-thing in life seriously. Therefore, to speak of play as absurd describes this structure or dialectic. The absurdity of play describes the incongruous collision between the single-minded aspiration of the player and an on-tology of play that undermines the seriousness of the pursuit. Regardless of whether Nagel is right about life as a whole, the local absurdity in-volved in game playing is apparent.

There is, consequently, something deeply ironic about the attitude of the player. He must attempt to balance aspiration and reality in a pre-carious way. To become too serious about his play would negate the iro-ny. The paradigm for such an abuse of the ironic stance of the player is the famous remark, "Winning is not the most important thing: it's the only thing." Yet equally abusive would be another famous dictum about sport, "It's not whether you win or lose, but how you play the game," as if play were merely the instrument of moral education. Finally, it would also abuse the irony of the play attitude to emphasize entirely the intrin-sic value of play to the exclusion of a serious pursuit of an end—"It's not whether you win or lose, but *that* you play the game." All of these are only partial truths that overemphasize one side of the dialectic. Play is serious, but unreal. You must have it both ways.

But one might wonder whether this attitude is significant in a broad-er sense, and whether this ironic stance of the player might be akin to the attitude described by Nagel occasioned by a recognition of global ab-surdity.

All of this talk about the "real" seriousness of life as opposed to the "unreality" of play might be questioned. Once we return to the ordi-nary concerns of life we are left with the dualism that first undermined the seriousness of play. We have two standpoints: one within the play world, the other in everyday reality. But from the standpoint of ordi-nary reality it is hard not to turn our nostalgic gaze back upon our play. We now recall the standpoint within the play world, where actions have clear meanings, goals are delineated, challenges are taken up, activities are consummated, exuberance and joy are experienced, freedom prevails, and friendships and community are uniquely encountered, and we might begin to wonder what really counts in life. Life is lived more intensely, more joyously, in play; players do not want to give up their games. Now, perhaps, we might experience the undermining of the ordinary, or what we normally take to be "really serious," and our entire dialectic is turned upside down. Are we not inevitably led to the position expressed by Michael Novak, which we have encountered in our previous discussions?

> Play, not work, is the end of life. To participate in the rites of play is to dwell in the Kingdom of Ends. To participate in work, career, and the making of history is to labor in the Kingdom of Means. The modern age, the age of history, nourishes illusions. In a protestant culture, as in Marxist cultures, work is serious, important, adult. Its essential significance is overlooked. Work, of course, must be done, but we should be wise enough to distinguish necessity from reality. Play is reality, work is diversion and escape.[23]

The original ontology of play is now reversed, and a new standard of reality is established. The ethic of work and the serious is now taken to be as arbitrary as the rules of the games we play. Yet I think it is important not to overstate the case for this revised ontology of play. In a world of human suffering, it is difficult to conceive of every ethic as an arbitrary construction. Yet much of our work ethic appears from the standpoint of life-affirmative play drab and lifeless. Now the ordinary and the play world inevitably play themselves off against one another, with each making a claim to ultimacy, yet both appearing as arbitrary. The play world produces a skepticism about the ethic of the serious and the ordinary, while the original claim of seriousness made by the ordinary is impossible to negate. What must be our response to such dialectical vertigo?

Recall Nagel's position that "philosophical skepticism does not cause us to abandon our ordinary beliefs, but it lends them a peculiar flavor . . . we return to our familiar convictions with a certain irony and resignation." In this ironic attitude resides the superiority of the attitude of play. Play is absurd from the standpoint of what we normally take to be serious. Yet even this absurdity can be undermined by an altered ontology of play that describes play as what is most important. We can take up either of these incongruous standpoints; play or "real life" may be taken as absurd. But it is the attitude of play that is consistent with this topsy-turvy skepticism. In life, as well as in play, we must pursue our goals *as if* what we did really mattered, knowing full well that we are also precisely that person who can take a standpoint from which such seriousness is undermined. Our life, in a sense, is unchanged, but, as Nagel says, "We then return to our lives, as we must, but our seriousness is laced with irony."[24] Our life, I would say, is laced with the spirit of play. Play becomes the fundamental attitude of life. Life is to be played. The irony of *homo ludens* adds detachment and lightness to life, and we are better off for it because we are immune to the despair of *homo gravis*.

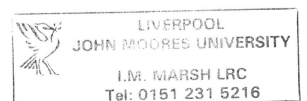

5   Sport and the View from Nowhere

"Isn't football the toy department of life?" famous television journalist Mike Wallace asks, with that cynical, disarming smirk, his accusatory gaze fixed on yet another pitiful subject. But we feel no sympathy for this subject. Famous, passionate, obsessive football coach Bill Parcells glares back, his mouth framed somewhere between a grimace and smile: "It may be to you, but not to me. It's my life."

Mike Wallace represents the reflective gaze of objectivity, ruthlessly calling a spade a spade—or, in this case, wondering how a grown man could take a mere game so seriously. He is the quintessential outsider, reminding us of the folly of our immature attractions. On the other hand, Bill Parcells is the quintessential insider, resisting Wallace's cynical attempt to reduce to triviality the sport participant's devotion. Perhaps Wallace was being ironic, yet Parcells seemed incapable of sensing any irony at all. It was an interesting moment, one rarely experienced in the constant chatter about sports in our culture. The ultimate value of sport was questioned. What is interesting, however, it not the apparent conflict between believer and unbeliever in which each seemed momentarily unable to understand and enter into the world of the other. What is more interesting is when the conflict arises in the consciousness of a single human being. What happens when we judge our most cherished attachments to be trivial or without overarching significance? In particular, what are the implications when the passionately committed sports participant comes to believe, as he might, and perhaps should, that sports do not really matter?

Part I: Nagel's Problem

In a number of well-known papers, many of which have been collected in *Mortal Questions*,[1] and in *The View From Nowhere*,[2] Thomas Nagel has analyzed a single problem that reappears in a variety of perennial philosophical disputes. Early on he spoke of this as the problem of "subjective and objective"[3]: the conflict or opposition between two very different viewpoints we can take toward our selves and our experience of the world. On the one hand, we experience life from a particular perspective, dragging along the contingencies of particularity as we make our way through the world. On the other hand, we can step back from our immediate involvement in life and take a new viewpoint that includes the original, more particular perspective. The possibility of transcending one's subjective viewpoint and seeing it from a larger perspective appears to be a permanent possibility for a complex reflective being. As we will see, this possibility occasions a number of puzzling personal and philosophical questions.

Nagel later speaks of objectivity as the "view from nowhere" and systematically explores this problem in the book by the same name. The problem is "how to combine the perspective of a particular person inside the world with an objective view of the same world, the person and his viewpoint included" (*VN*, 3). Nagel's distinctive approach to the philosophical problems associated with freedom, knowledge, ethics, the metaphysics of mind, and the meaning of life generates both metaphilosophical conclusions and broader notions about basic attitudes toward life and death. In most cases, Nagel neither offers a solution to these perennial philosophical problems nor engages in therapeutic attempts to dissolve our worries. In fact, he shows why our worries are both real and seemingly intractable. He attempts to show why we find these issues so perplexing and how we might live in the face of such uncertainties. If he's right, philosophical understanding resides in proper perplexity: "Certain forms of perplexity—for example, about freedom, knowledge, and the meaning of life—seem to me to embody more insight than any supposed solutions to these problems" (*VN*, 4).

Like Nagel, I find it natural to view the human situation in terms of the opposition between these two standpoints, and I identify with the need to investigate strategies for reconciling them. But I wish to focus on an area of life that Nagel has ignored, at least in his published work. Like many people, involvement in sports has been a significant part of my life since childhood. But as a philosopher I have found this involvement puzzling and not easy to understand. Nagel's approach is quite helpful in understanding the sources of the forms of perplexity associated with thinking about sports participation. His way of looking at things has important implications for our attitudes toward life in general, not simply our attitudes toward sport. This is because reflections about sport are related to arguments about what matters in life. Worries about sport naturally involve worries about the value of these activities, and questions about the value of sports participation lead inevitably to questions about the foundation of our idiosyncratic attachments in life. Why do we care so much about certain apparently trivial activities? Isn't meaning in life intimately related to the pursuit of worthwhile projects? Yet the notion of worthwhileness is difficult to pin down. One of the sources of philosophical interest in reflecting about sport is found right here: philosophical thinking about sport leads to questions about what in fact matters to us, why it matters, and how we might, in principle, show what should matter to us.

I would like to deepen our understanding of the implications of Nagel's approach when applied to sport. I borrow from him the basic structure and some remarks about its analysis. But the spin will be my own, as well as the way I apply it to sport. Once I have clarified the structure in the next section, I show how the opposition between our immediate involvement in sport and a more detached view of this involvement occasions the problem of reconciling these viewpoints. Strategies arise for avoiding the conflict—none of which succeed. Finally, I show that there are certain attitudes toward sport that are more appropriate expressions of the paradoxes that arise, because we can and should view sports activities in two very different ways. Moreover, these attitudes have important moral implications for participation in sports.

Part II: Subjectivity and the Objectivity

Let us return to the idea of subjectivity versus objectivity and begin our discussion with two common examples from ordinary life. Suppose a teacher is supervising two small children playing together, when one child becomes aggressive and mean. The teacher intervenes, stops the hurtful behavior, and offers the expected moral lesson. "Would you like it if someone did that to you? How would that make you feel?" The moral lesson involved is interestingly ambiguous. The teacher might be suggesting a Kantian inconsistency argument, such that if you think that other people have a reason not to hurt you, then you would have the same reason not to hurt anyone else. Here an impersonal, more objective, reason is supposed to replace a personal desire as a motive for action. Or, the teacher might want the child to engage in an imaginative projection into the perspective of the other person, asking the child to consider how the other feels as the object of mean behavior. Such a new perspective might generate compassion or sympathy for the other person. In either case, the child is asked to step back from her personal stance and take a new perspective in which this more personal perspective is included. The child is asked to consider that all people have feelings, or all people have reasons not to be hurt, so she must consider herself as simply one person among all persons, with no special or distinctive status.

For our second example, consider a parent whose child is a substitute on a high school basketball team. The child badly wants to play, is miserable on the bench, and feels unfairly treated. When the parent feels terrible because the child isn't playing, the perspective is one step away from a subjective viewpoint that is wholly self-preoccupied and ignores other persons altogether. But we often say that the parent needs to judge relative abilities more accurately—to have a perspective that is less tainted by subjective concerns.

From these two ordinary examples it is easy to extract the structure that gives rise to numerous perplexities. From the more subjective viewpoint our perspective is conditioned by the specific aspects of being a particular human being. Here the specific and contingent aspects of individuality shape our experience: our particular desires, needs, perceptions, sensations, goals, values, and so on. But we have the capacity to step back from the subjective and gain a new perspective that includes the subjective in it. As Nagel says, to gain "a more objective understanding of some aspect of life or the world, we step back from our initial view of it and form a new conception which has that view and its relation to the world as its object . . . we place ourselves in the world that is to be understood" (*VN*, 4).

It may seem odd to begin the clarification of objectivity with an example from moral education, since so many people would mistakenly characterize the whole area of morality as subjective. However, the example is instructive. The distinction between subjective and objective is not simply a distinction between a scientific view of things—whatever that means—as the paradigm of objectivity, and all other perspectives as inevitably soiled by subjectivity and its contingencies. The opposition may at first have the appearance of an "either-or" where objectivity means a factual, scientific perspective, subjectivity means a value-laden perspective, and science always wins the epistemic game. However, this is mistakenly oversimplified. In various places Nagel points out that the distinction between internal and external views is a "matter of degree" (*VN*, 5), a "polarity" (*MQ*, 206), in which the distinction is "relative" (*MQ*, 206). "A view or form of thought is more objective than another if it relies less on the specifics of the individual's makeup and position in the world, or on the character of the particular type of creature he is" (*VN*, 5). In our first example, we might see the moral point of view as more objective than the original personal and aggressive perspective, because it is the standpoint from which a particular person can consider the interests of *all* sentient beings (including herself) when she acts. Of course, we might come to see the moral viewpoint of particular persons as merely expressions of their own contingent selves, especially in regard to possible cultural or linguistic prejudices involved. A sociological or anthropological explanation of morality and its attendant relativism would be more objective than some philosophical theories of morality, especially if a philosophical theory, like intuitionism, for example, seemed to express the biases of more personal attachments. In any case, the movement away from subjectivity toward a view that attempts to transcend the specifics of the individual should be seen as a possible step-by-step process along a continuum.

The second example suggests another important issue involved in clarifying the basic structure. When the parent steps back from the situation and attempts to perceive accurately the relative basketball abilities of the child, this new, more objective perspective seems to offer a more accurate view of things. Here objectivity is a way to understand how things are, and an objective understanding of the situation generates beliefs and attitudes that render the more subjective perspective as a source of mere appearances. This broader perspective includes these personal judgments and feelings, and explains them. There is no problem, in one sense, of what to do with the more subjective viewpoint, since it has been corrected— although the residual psychological aspects may still be difficult to deal with. This analysis may lead us to think of reality as "a set of concentric spheres, progressively revealed as we detach gradually from the contingencies of the self" (*VN*, 5).

Thus the second important element in the analysis of the internal-external dynamic: while the distinction is relative, when we abstract from the personal we seem to be headed in the direction of truth. This is because increasing objectivity seems to be the attempt to approach the way the world is in itself and not just in relation to some individual. Because the development of objectivity seems truth-guided, the objective viewpoint may appear to dominate any relatively subjective viewpoint, and it may exert certain "pressures toward a more external viewpoint" (*VN*, 208).

A third important element involved in coming to understand the distinction between subjective and objective is that the development of objectivity delivers a new way of seeing the world as a whole. Objectivity has metaphysical implications, since it seems to assume that the way things are is ultimately "a conception of the world which as far possible is not the view from anywhere within it" (*MQ*, 206). The fundamental distinction is a matter of degree, often truth-guided, and offers a view of the world that attempts, in principle, to be centerless.

Yet if the situation were so simple, there would be no problem associated with the distinction between subjectivity and objectivity. That is, there would be no problem of combining the two perspectives, since the point of developing an increasingly objective view of life would be to give up appearances in favor of a true, more objective understanding of reality. But there is a problem, or, rather, there are a number of problems, because it isn't clear that it's always more truthful to negate the subjective in whatever way seems appropriate for a more objective way of understanding. Consider our first example of moral education. It may be true that a social scientific account of morality, as simply a set of rules conventionally agreed upon, is objective in some sense, but it doesn't appear to be a true account of morality, for a variety of reasons.[4] There are other possible objective or scientific explanations of our moral life (e.g., biological explanations), but, prima facie, they seem to leave behind, in their explanations, our immediate sense of some things being "really" right or wrong, good or bad. It is always possible that the subjective sense of moral value conflicts with an objective account of morality as a set of conventionally accepted rules; for example, when the nineteenth-century abolitionist in America embraced the notion that it is really wrong to own another human being, regardless of the social approval involved in slavery. Here a conflict arises. "The opposition between subjective and objective can arise at any place on the spectrum where one point of view claims dominance over another, more subjective one, and that claim is resisted" (*MQ*, 206).

There is nothing distinctive about the way this problem arises in ethics, as a theoretical reflection on our moral life. As Nagel insists, the "internal-external tension pervades human life, but it is particularly prominent in the generation of philosophical problems" (*VN*, 6). To give just two examples: from the inside of life, I seem to be an agent who performs free actions and for whom autonomy means the ability to do otherwise. However, when I step back from my actions and see them as events or processes with causal explanations, and I see my self not as some mysterious immaterial nugget but as the locus of various causally pro- duced biological and psychological processes, agency seems to vanish.[5] Likewise, from the internal viewpoint, I seem to have privileged access to my own irreducibly subjective mental states. I am directly aware of tastes, sounds, feelings, and so on, and I assume that there's "something it's like" to be a particular human being.[6] When I step back, however, and see myself as a part of nature, it's not clear how dualism could be true, in part because it has so little explanatory power when contrasted with various forms of materialism, and in part because the interaction between immaterial mental processes and brain processes would be so mysteri- ous. In both of these examples, the objective perspective confronts some- thing that resists its reductive or eliminative impulses. As Nagel remarks, "The trouble occurs when the objective view encounters something, re- vealed subjectively, that it cannot accommodate. Its claims to compre- hensiveness will be threatened. The indigestible lump may either be a fact or a value" (*MQ*, 210). In the philosophy of mind and the freedom- determinism debate, the objective viewpoint can't accommodate certain "internal" facts about the self as an agent, whose existence seemingly can't be reduced to a set of complex physical processes. In ethics, our sense that certain values are real or true or justified resists the objective attempt to expel them from the "furniture of the universe,"[7] or the attempt to view them as subjective fictions rather than rationally respectable rea- sons for action.

For our purposes, the way the objective threatens our *values* is most important, and the threat is not simply a scientific one. Let's consider this and then turn our attention toward sport. When people decide what to do in life—or what kind of person to be—their goals may be relatively personal. I may save my hard-earned money for a vacation in Cancun. But I may also consider the fact that my desires for rest and relaxation on the beach are relatively unimportant when I contrast my situation with the plight of people who are starving, homeless, or oppressed. I could give my money to a service organization or spend my time directly help- ing others. From the standpoint of overall good, I could develop other- directed motives that recognize the triviality of my concerns in relation to some larger moral perspective. In ethics there are enormous problems that arise on the continuum from subjective to objective because moral judgment seems to force one from a more self-centered, personal, even egoistic viewpoint to a more impersonal viewpoint that is other-directed.[8] Yet how do we legitimately integrate our personal concerns into an acceptable moral outlook?[9] Some ethical theories, such as those that appeal to individual rights or individual well-being, are more agent-centered than the outcome-centered emphasis found in consequentialism; hence they are more subjective, in a sense, than the appeal to overall good as the determining criterion of moral action. Furthermore, if the development of objectivity in ethics is driven by the desire to "get outside of ourselves," there are no obvious final resting stops in the movement from the personal to the relatively impersonal to the extremely impersonal or even centerless view. For the consequentialist (utilitarian), the pursuit of overall good trumps personal goals, as well as appeals to individual rights, special obligations, and perfectionist ends.[10] (Obviously, it's not clear that consequentialism is therefore the most acceptable ethical theory because it is most objective.) But consequentialism may be transcended in a more objective philosophical reflection. Any justification of value may be skeptically undermined:

> Objectivity itself leads to the recognition that its own capacities are probably limited, since in us it is a human faculty and we are conspicuously finite beings. The radical form of this is philosophical skepticism, in which the objective standpoint undermines itself by the same procedures it uses to call into question the prereflective standpoint of ordinary life in perception, desire, and action. Skepticism is radical doubt about the possibility of reaching any kind of knowledge, freedom, or ethical truth, given our containment in the world and the impossibility of creating ourselves from scratch. (*VN*, 7)

We are left with a very perplexing situation. Sometimes the objective standpoint offers a truer way of understanding the world. When we transcend our prejudices and presuppositions, we are able to see the way our particular nature distorts our perspective. The success of science constitutes a powerful testament to the belief that objectivity should be our ideal for understanding reality. But the movement toward objectivity has problems in both directions. In the direction of subjectivity, it leaves behind some—or much—of what it means to be a particular, highly specific human being, whether it be autonomy, mind, or meaning. It seems to lead to reductionism. At the other extreme, in the direction of the most "centerless" form of objectivity, the attempt to recognize our epistemic limitations may inevitably lead to a skepticism or nihilism that undermines both objective knowledge and any values to which we are personally attached. How do we decide where the legitimate claims reside in the continuum from subjective to objective, from the internal to the "view from nowhere"? How do we determine a method for sorting out the truth-claims of personal metaphysical and axiological appearances, impersonal moral demands, scientific models of explanation and reduction, along with various arguments offered by both local and global skeptics?[11]

Part III: Sport and Conflicting Perspectives

As I have suggested, the problems associated with sports participation are related to the problem of the meaning of life—at least insofar as the problem of the meaning of life arises because we have the capacity to step back from our immediate involvement in life and take a detached viewpoint from which our life seems not to matter much at all. We struggle to get through school, get a good job, raise a family, worry about the bills—for what end? As Nagel has said: "From far enough outside my birth seems accidental, my life pointless, and my death insignificant, but from inside my never having been born seems nearly unimaginable, my life monstrously important, and my death catastrophic" (*VN*, 209). From the outside, from the view from nowhere, my life seems to be an accidental and insignificant moment in the entire scheme of things; my attachments as well seem as accidental as my life, objectively insignificant from the standpoint of a skeptical reflection that denies the ultimate justification of value.[12]

Now if it is difficult to follow Nagel to the furthest reaches of objectivity from which the problem of the meaning of life arises, it is certainly not difficult to see the way in which the path toward objectivity threatens some of our cherished attachments in life. I am most interested in the sports participant for whom sport matters in a relatively significant way. For such a person, sport is an important part of life. Think especially of players and coaches at all levels of play and at all ages. From the inside of this involvement, nothing seems to matter more than what happens in their respective sport. Participants spend countless hours at practice, worry about improvement and execution, and often think the fate of the world—*their* world—depends on who wins the game. There is often a pervasive spirit of *seriousness* when participants engage in sports. Players are praised for the intensity of their competitive seriousness. From the internal viewpoint, life often seems to present itself at its subjectively best—or worst—in sports. Internally, experience is enhanced when structured by the rhythms of games, contests, and seasons. Sports participation seems to give life some dramatic or narrative shape as the pursuit of athletic success unfolds. However, subjective attachment to sport is only part of the picture, precisely because we are complex, reflective beings who can step back from our particular involvements and scrutinize them.

How does a more objective view of an individual's involvement in sport arise? For some, the development of objectivity is natural and commonplace; for others, it may take failure, tragedy, or suffering to occasion a broader perspective. In many cases, the movement toward a more objective view of sport is expressed in comparative judgments. Consider the obvious and commonplace examples. The young player strikes out with the bases loaded and the team loses the Big Game. Someone attempts to console the distraught young person: "It's only a game." Death or illness in the family causes a player to miss a practice or game. Poor academic performance causes athletic suspension. The demands of a job force someone to forgo the big softball tournament. Someone is severely injured in a game. The other stunned players look on and later say: "Something like this shows what's really important." A national tragedy puts sports in "proper perspective." In the movement from subjective to objective, one doesn't have to travel far to see sport as *less* important than other things in life. You step back and compare sport to other parts of your life, you see your involvement in relation to other things that seem to matter, and sport loses. It still seems "important," sometimes overwhelmingly so, but you're not sure why. At this point, the central problem concerning subjectivity and objectivity arises. Recall that the "opposition between subjective and objective can arise at any place on the spectrum where one point of view claims dominance over another, more subjective one, and that claim is *resisted*" (MQ, 206). From the internal viewpoint, sports participation is serious, sometimes all-consuming, and "monstrously" important. But even for people who are not disposed to be very reflective, an objective viewpoint insinuates itself into experience and suggests that sport is relatively unimportant. How are these two viewpoints to be reconciled? How can they coexist? After all, it may be within the same person that the two standpoints clash. The objective viewpoint claims that sport is not important. Subjective involvement resists that judgment and wants to return to its prereflective attachment unaffected by the objective perspective.[13]

The problem increases when the gap between subjective and objective increases. If we want to reflect on our involvement and attempt to understand why sport seems less important than other things in life, we must attempt to understand the nature of sport itself. Here we reflect not simply about the relative importance of our attachments; we want to understand something about sport itself in order to reflect back on the appropriateness of these very attachments. Obviously, much has been written about the nature of sport, but for our purposes, we need only to highlight the essentials. First, it is plausible to assert that sport involves the playing of games. This thesis is associated with Bernard Suits, who argued in an early essay, "I would like to advance the thesis that the elements of sport are essentially—although not totally—the same as elements of game."[14] He later qualifies this thesis by distinguishing between games and performances (like diving and figure skating) because of the apparent differences in the way rules function in refereed games as opposed to the way ideals function in judged performances.[15] However, I agree with Klaus Meier that Suits's earlier view is the more accurate one, because performances are, in fact, rule-governed in the required way, so the minimal qualifications of game playing are satisfied.[16]

What are these qualifications? Here is Suits's original account of game playing:

> To play a game is the attempt to achieve a specific state of affairs (prelusory goal), using only means permitted by rules (lusory means), where the rules prohibit use of more efficient in favor of less efficient means (constitutive rules), and where such rules are accepted just because they make possible such activity (lusory attitude). I also offer the following only approximately accurate, but more pithy, version of the above definition: Playing a game is the voluntary attempt to overcome unnecessary obstacles.[17]

Of course, it is plausible to insist that sports involve other important elements, such as physical skill, institutionalization, or competition. But Suits's original account of sport as essentially involving game playing is already quite suggestive. Consider these activities: Putting a little ball in a small hole in the ground some distance away. Carrying a leather ball to a point many yards away. Hitting a thrown ball with the intention of allowing one to run around in a circle, arriving at precisely the point from which one starts! In Suits's language, the prelusory goal can always be brought about in much more efficient ways than the means permitted by the rules. If I wanted to put the little white ball in the hole in an efficient manner, I could simply walk or run to the hole and place it in the cup with my hand. From the standpoint of ordinary life, games are by their very nature rather silly. Suits recognizes this, but denies the inherent absurdity of games. As he says," in anything but a game the gratuitous introduction of unnecessary obstacles to the achievement of an end is regarded as a decidedly irrational thing to do, whereas in games it appears to be the absolutely essential thing to do."[18] However, Suits rejects the implication that games are thereby irrational or absurd, because "the mistake consists in applying the same standard to games that is applied to means-end activities which are not games. If playing a game is regarded as not essentially different from going to the office or writing a checque, then there is certainly something absurd, or paradoxical, or simply stupid about game-playing."[19] Suits is only half right in saying this. From the internal standpoint of the player, games *are* decidedly different from means-end activities of ordinary life. It is a mistake from the subjective perspective to apply the standard of rationality as efficiency to the realm of game playing. But we can also step back from our game playing and see it from a perspective that does, in fact, judge game playing as trivial, irrational, and absurd. The same person who invests game playing with seriousness, intensity, and concern, can also see it for what it is—from a perspective outside the immediacy of participation. There is no mistake here; or rather, there is a mistake from only a certain point of view. Both viewpoints make legitimate claims, with each resisting the dominance of the other, and this conflict may take place within the awareness of a single player.

Isn't it curious that we engage in such unnecessary and seemingly trivial activities? What could be the end or goal of activities that are inherently irrational by ordinary standards? Once again, Suits's account is suggestive, although I will take it in a direction with which he might disagree. For Suits, if the goal of the activity is to bring about a state of affairs in an inefficient manner, the player must have an attitude that recognizes this but affirms that the activity itself is still worth doing. The "lusory attitude" of the player is "the knowing acceptance of constitutive rules just so the activity made possible by such acceptance can occur."[20] In my judgment, this attitude toward an instrumentally trivial or absurd activity must affirm the intrinsically satisfying or valuable nature of the activity—at least in the genesis of the game or the player's introduction to it. So we are led to the neighborhood of play with this understanding.

The relation of sport and play is a complex and contentious issue, and I don't wish to get side-tracked by this important debate. Suffice it to say that from the internal standpoint many participants identify strongly with Huizinga's original description of play, stressing the freedom and joy of playing, outside of real-life concerns, with utmost seriousness about and absorption in such an intrinsically valuable but superfluous activity.[21] Even college and professional athletes often lament that the "fun" has been taken out of the game and express a certain nostalgia for their original experience of playing sports. For some, the internal standpoint is filled with the radiance of play, whose inherent worth resists objective dismissal.

It is possible to widen the gap between subjective and objective even further. As I have suggested, the arguments about the meaning and value of sport participation are similar to the way in which Nagel approaches the problem of the meaning of life. The difference is simply how far we "step back" from the immediacy of particular involvement in life and where we find ourselves when we land as a result of the distancing made possible by this reflective metaphor. If an objective philosophical reflection finds sport to be trivial and irrational, then, a fortiori, at the furthest reaches of skepticism, whatever values we experience in sport are undermined. Recall "The Absurd," in which Nagel argues that a situation is absurd "when it includes a conspicuous discrepancy between pretension or aspiration and reality" (*MQ*, 13). For example, at fifty years of age a person quits his well-paying job and leaves his family in order to pursue the dream of playing in the NBA. This would be absurd, as would be the single-minded attempt to communicate with plants (Nagel's example), or devoting one's life to collecting as many clipped toenails as possible, at the expense of many things we normally think are constitutive of the good human life—fulfilling work, friendship, and so on. For Nagel, life as such is absurd because it inevitably involves a "collision between the seriousness with which we take our lives and the perpetual possibility of regarding everything about which we are serious as arbitrary, or open to doubt" (*MQ*, 13). From this standpoint, sport is absurd because life is absurd, not simply because our seriousness in sport collides with the recognition that there are many more important things in life than improving one's backhand or winning games.

In any case, the pressures exerted by the reflective movement toward the "view from nowhere" are real and occasion the fundamental problem, which we will call the "problem of coherent attitudes." Nagel is interested in this problem, in general, for any of our attachments in life. We are most interested in how this problem is experienced in one specific area of life: sport. The problem arises because of the claims made from the standpoint of reflective detachment.

> The same person who is subjectively committed to a personal life in all its rich detail finds himself in another aspect simultaneously detached; this detachment undermines his commitment without destroying it—leaving him divided. And the objective self, noticing that it is personally identical with the object of this detachment, comes to feel trapped in this particular life—detached but unable to disengage, and dragged along by a subjective seriousness it can't even attempt to get rid of. (*VN*, 210)

The problem of coherent attitudes is the problem of how to respond to such worries, which Nagel calls the "discomfort of objective detachment." These worries alienate some persons from themselves. Objective transcendence brings with it some inevitable degree of disengagement or dissociation from the original subjective engagement, and the problem is how the objective self rejoins the subjective self. For the reflective sports participant the problem is significant. "Some of us feel a constant undertow of absurdity in the projects and ambitions that give our lives their forward drive. These jarring displacements of the external view are inseparable from the full development of consciousness" (*VN*, 211). From the internal standpoint, seriousness is uncontested. The pursuit of excellence, the exuberance of play, and the satisfaction of victory give meaning to the life of the sports participant. Yet once the self expands to include the external point of view with its concomitant judgments, the objective self returns, reconstituting the activity. If a person now finds, from an external point of view, that a significant part of his life is objectively insignificant, how is he to deal with this? Sport is meaningful and significant. Sport is trivial and absurd. It there a way out of this impasse? Can this inner conflict be eliminated? Are there attitudes that can reduce but not eliminate this opposition?

Part IV: Unsuccessful Responses

The logic of possible strategies in response to the opposition between the subjective and objective in sport is quite clear.[22] One might attempt to deny the subjective importance of sport by wholly affirming the objective viewpoint; one might attempt to deny the objective viewpoint altogether; or one might argue that no "solution" is called for because the whole issue is misguided or unreal. This would be the attempt to dissolve the problem. I don't believe any of these strategies work, but there are more or less appropriate ways to alter our attitudes and behavior such that the extremity of the conflict between objective detachment and subjective engagement is reduced. First, let's briefly consider these unsuccessful ways of dealing with the problem.

The first solution would be to embrace the objective perspective by denying the claims of the internal viewpoint. At its most extreme, this would probably mean a relatively radical negation of sports altogether, depending on one's personal situation: no playing, coaching, watching, or reading. Complete unconcern about the sports world would be the result, or extreme cynicism if one were forced to sustain some uncomfortable relationship with the sports world.[23] Like the person who resolves to give up reading worthless, trashy romance novels in order to spend more time with good literature, the recognition of objective insignificance leads to a rejection of old attachments and new avenues of more worthy involvement. I have certainly known people who seem to embody this viewpoint toward sport, who simply can't see the point of all the mindless, pervasive involvement. In another context, Nagel offers an apt image of detachment: "Watching the human drama is a bit like watching a Little League baseball game: the excitement of the participants is perfectly understandable but one can't really enter into it" (*VN*, 217–18). On the one hand, many people at Little League baseball games certainly need more detachment, since they do seem to be absurdly serious about a trivial event. There ought to be an unmistakable "undertow of absurdity" in the life of an intensely serious Little League coach, or perhaps *any* intensely serious coach for that matter. On the other hand, to use Nagel's image, the problem of subjective and objective in sport is that one is simultaneously observer and participant. It is like sitting in the stands watching the game and judging it to be trivial while at the same time playing or coaching with utmost seriousness, playing or coaching *as if* it really mattered. From the internal perspective, it does really matter to practice and play hard, to try to become better, to compete intensely, and to attempt to win. Subjectively, there's too much good involved in sport to allow objective skepticism to negate it. If there's really joy, fun, camaraderie, and achievement in the experience of sport, the extinction of subjective value for individual participants is misguided. These values need not be endorsed by objective reflection in order to survive.

For the sports enthusiast the other strategy is the more important one to consider. There are always friends willing to point out the flaws in the object of your love, but you may be able to forget or ignore these criticisms if your passion is strong enough. But it is bad faith, or simply dishonesty, to ignore the criticisms altogether. Some subjective concerns survive, in some form, the attempt by the objective to extinguish them. "Playing in a Little League baseball game, making pancakes, or applying a coat of nail polish are perfectly good things to do. Their value is not necessarily canceled by the fact that they lack external justification" (*VN*, 220). This merely means that the subjective self need not succumb to the most extreme pressures of objectivity. But these pressures are real. The objective self is as much a part of a person, in principle, as the more subjective one. The denial of objective insignificance might take various forms. It would be natural to inflate the objective pretensions of certain subjective concerns in order to satisfy the demands of objectivity and reduce the conflict. In a moment, I'll pursue this strategy, but it seems doomed when we consider the value of what so many are concerned with in sports: winning. Another way to avoid the conflict would be to forget the claims of objectivity and simply ignore the deliverances of such an assessment of sport. But this is dishonest. Forgetfulness doesn't negate the legitimacy of the objective assessment of sport. Finally, there are those who seem not to be bothered by the objective insignificance of sport, perhaps because they are ignorant of this standpoint or have not developed the capacity to step outside the immediacy of subjective attachment. But this isn't a solution or strategy that denies the objective; for such people, objective reflection is available as a development in human consciousness—it has merely not developed in relation to an understanding or sport.

The denial of either aspect of the polarity in favor of the other is misguided. The final strategy is to deny the status of the objective viewpoint, not its judgments, by claiming that the objective self is unreal. To experience objective discomfort is, in Nagel's words, "to forget who you are. There is something deranged in looking at one's existence from so far outside that one can ask why it matters" (*VN*, 220). The objection may seem appropriate for the more global problem of the meaning of life than for an objective reflection that remains within it and works its skepticism piecemeal on various aspects of life. But I agree with Nagel that the "view from nowhere," at its most skeptical extreme, is still a part of us, as is any moment on the continuum from objective to subjective. The problem cannot be dissolved by asserting the unreality of objective detachment. As Nagel says: "The objective self is a vital part of us, and to ignore its quasi-independent operation is to be cut off from oneself as much as if one were to abandon one's subjective individuality. There is no escape from alienation or conflict of one kind or another" (*VN*, 221).

So the attempts to solve the problem by avoiding the conflict between the internal and external standpoints are unsuccessful. We must live with the conflict. What this means is that our participation in sports is, or should be, plagued by what I would like to call a kind of "double consciousness" that affirms both perspectives. They must be allowed to coexist. How are we to understand and live with this conflict?

Part V: Playing Ironically

The answer to the problem of reconciling subjective and objective attitudes is to find ways of regarding sporting activities that produce as much harmony as possible between the perspectives. In general, I believe it is possible to develop attitudes that harmonize disparate judgments about certain states of affairs. Suppose you have a dear friend who has hurt you deeply by violating some trust, and you believe that act is very much out of character. Your friendship may survive because of your willingness to forgive, which recognizes both your friend's good character and the pain of the violation of trust. Forgiveness grounds the continuation of friendship, not by forgetting the violation but by recognizing it and overcoming it, although the certainty of the original trusting relationship has been altered.

The appropriate attitude for the reflective sports participant is irony. This is a somewhat unusual way of speaking of irony. What I have in mind refers neither to ironic uses of language nor to the irony of unexpected events. Rather, irony refers to "an attitude of detached awareness of incongruity."[24] Irony is a way to regard sports participation, including the pursuit of athletic excellence and the desire for victory, *as if* it really matters, while at the same time recognizing that it is relatively trivial in the larger scheme of things. Like Nagel's image of watching a Little League game, we become simultaneously a player who is passionately involved and a detached spectator who views the spectacle from a distance. I take irony to be a unifying attitude that is positive, not negative; it is an awareness of the paradoxical nature of sport as competitive play, serious nonseriousness, or nonserious seriousness. Irony is an attitude that embraces the basic incongruity of our devotion to triviality, our celebration of absurdity every time we compete intensely and play games seriously. The ironic competitor, or the athletic ironist, is a person whose engagement is modified by objective detachment and whose detachment is mediated by immediate engagement.

Joel Feinberg nicely describes irony as a "cosmic attitude" appropriate to the human situation in general. His description also fits the athletic ironist's attitude toward sport. Irony is

> a state of mind halfway between seriousness and playfulness. It may even seem to the person involved that he is both very serious and playful at the same time. The tension between these opposed elements pulling in their opposite ways creates at least temporarily a kind of mental equilibrium . . . One appreciates the perceived incongruity much as one does in humor, where the sudden unexpected perception of incongruity produces laughter. Here the appreciation is more deliberate and intellectual.[25]

I also welcome Nagel's suggestion that humility is an attitude that promotes harmony and integration between the internal and the external. Humility is a consequence of the objective perspective on sport (and life). In general, humility works against our tendency to inflate the significance of our personal projects and successes. In particular, humility in the sports world works against the athlete's natural reaction to our culture's glorification of athletic success. Humility for the sports participant realistically deflates the seeming global pretensions of our merely local athletic concerns. Humility is a way to come to grips with our capacity to step back from our participation in sports while at the same time sustaining our commitment. As Nagel says about this attitude:

> Humility falls between nihilistic detachment and blind self-importance. It doesn't require reflection on the cosmic arbitrariness of the sense of taste every time you eat a hamburger. But we can try to avoid the familiar excesses of envy, vanity, conceit, competitiveness, and pride—including pride in our culture, in our nation, and in the achievements of humanity as a species. (*VN*, 222)

Of course, Nagel is talking about humility as a fundamental general attitude in life, but what he says seems particularly pertinent when we think of the excesses of pride, vanity, and competitiveness in sports. Moreover, this also suggests that we are talking about attitudes that have practical consequences in our life. The ironic competitor, who embraces an attitude of humility toward his athletic talents and successes, will *act* differently from the pretentious and arrogant participant who lacks this perspective.

If humility is an appropriate effect of the objective perspective, I believe our subjective involvement is itself doubled-edged, as has been suggested in the discussion of irony. From the internal standpoint, commitment to a particular sport requires a competitive attitude in order to become better and excel. Moreover, attempting to become good in a sport is a source of significant personal satisfaction. Performing well is an important good, internal to the practice of a particular sport.[26] Competition is essential to sport, since it provides the possibility for achieving the internal goods made possible by participating in such a practice. On the other hand, since sport involves participation in activities whose external significance is originally minimal, and whose value is, for the most part, intrinsic to the activity, sport inevitably is associated with play. For most who will never be paid to play or supported in order to promote national pride, "If it ain't fun—it ain't worth it." From this standpoint, it's a mistake to say: "If the point is not to win, what is the point?" The response is: "The point is to play—else why was the game created?" The athletic ironist is a playful competitor whose playfulness reinforces his humility and moderates his competitiveness. This suggests that in the midst of spirited competition, the playful competitor attempts to sustain a certain light-heartedness. If sport is objectively insignificant and participation is absurd, it's more appropriate to participate without gravity or solemnity, to reinforce the possibilities of play with an attitude expressed in a wry smile rather than a grimace of discomfort.

One final strategy of integration is extremely important. Recall that our first example of the movement from subjective to objective was one in which the moral viewpoint was described as a perspective from which one considers how actions affect others as well as oneself. In a broad sense, the development of moral sensibilities and moral character is the attempt to mold a self whose actions and dispositions can be endorsed by a more objective viewpoint. In Nagel's words, "Morality is a form of objective reengagement. It permits the objective assertion of subjective values to the extent that this is compatible with the corresponding claims of others" (*VN*, 222). If, from some relatively objective viewpoint, we insist that sport is, in itself, relatively trivial and insignificant, there is certainly also a standpoint outside of the immediacy of internal attachment that affirms the importance of the moral qualities made possible by sports participation. In sport we must confront the possibility of isolation and failure. Sport is an arena in which courage and responsibility may be developed. Since sport is rule-governed and embodies standards of achievement for those who attempt to become good, players may exhibit an understanding of justice as they respond to their own competitive situation in relation to others. Since they must compete with others who challenge them to become better, they may develop respect for opponents, without whom the achievement of excellence would be impossible.[27] Because sport requires officials to enforce rules, sport offers the opportunity to respect the guardians of order within the game. Since sports develop historically, participants may develop a respect for tradition and past excellence that expresses a certain broadness of appreciation and opens the self to the rich possibilities of historical consciousness.[28] In short, sport is an arena within which it is possible to develop and display the excellence of good moral character, and the development of good character can be endorsed by an objective viewpoint.[29]

Objectivity here is seen as a kind of filter. What is filtered out of sports participation is the objective significance of the supposed end of games, winning, and the external value of athletic excellence itself. What is objectively retained as significant is the moral atmosphere of sports participation: possibilities for developing sportsmanship, excellence of character, and the important attitudes that are essential to good character in sport. Sportsmanship involves attitudes of respect for opponents, teammates and team, coaches, officials, and the game itself.[30]

As Nagel says about various forms of morality, they involve to some degree "a position far enough outside yourself and other people to reduce the importance of the difference between yourself and other people, yet not so far outside that all human values vanish in a nihilistic blackout" (*VN*, 222).

This position should not be misunderstood. It's not as if the only justification of sports participation is the old character building argument. From the internal viewpoint, sport is significant because of the personal satisfactions and values involved, whatever they are. From a more objective standpoint, sport is insignificant and the collision between our seriousness and its objective insignificance makes our participation absurd. From the most extreme objective vantage, the view from nowhere delivers a judgment of global insignificance on our life. Yet one way to bring a degree of harmony to the opposition between subjective and objective is to see the way in which "morality as objective reengagement" reduces the opposition. This means that developing attitudes associated with sportsmanship is an appropriate way to respond to the paradoxical nature of sport.

Part VI: Can the Good Competitor Be Detached?

There is one final important question. I have recommended a certain attitude, or a set of attitudes that should be embraced by the sports participant who wants to respond truthfully to the nature of sport. The sports participant—the athlete, player, coach—should embody irony, humility, playful competitiveness, and the respectful attitudes of sportsmanship. But all of these attitudes are the result of a detachment from the kind of unreflective immediacy characteristic of intense involvement in sports. Wouldn't these attitudes tend to dull the competitive edge? Doesn't sport require complete involvement, passion, and a commitment to excellence and winning that are incompatible with the detached, ironic stance that I have described? Aren't irony, humility, playfulness, and respectful attitudes incompatible with the very nature of sport as competitive, as a contest whose ultimate goal is winning and defeat of the opponent?

Let's call the position from which this criticism comes the "Kierkegaardian competitor." Recall that Kierkegaard recommends faith as an infinitely committed relation of subjectivity to an objectively uncertain object.[31] For Kierkegaard, the very nature of faith excludes the possibility of an objective reflection that could endorse it through the pursuit of arguments or rational support. Likewise, the Kierkegaardian competitor recommends complete involvement and dedication to the internal goals of sport, such that any reflective detachment would be contrary to the proper relation of the "true competitor" to his sport. For the Kierkegaardian competitor, the double-consciousness of the ironic competitor is untrue to sport, just as the tentative religious believer's stance distorts a proper relationship of faith within the subjectivity of the "authentic believer."[32] At its higher levels, sports participation often requires a total passion and dedication incompatible with the doubt of reflective ironic detachment. The "winner" is infinitely committed, says the Kierkegaardian competitor. The ironist "doesn't want it enough," hence, both ultimate success and the most intense forms of sports experience will elude the partially disengaged ironist.

However, I do not think that the ironic competitor is required to engage in sport listlessly or halfheartedly, nor are the benefits of sports participation denied to the reflective participant. An objective perspective is the consequence of the development of self-consciousness about one's life. The problem of finding coherent attitudes toward sport arises because we have the ability to step back from our life and reflect on it. I do not see how the external viewpoint can be denied, since this capability is an essential aspect of what it means to be a person.[33] The ability to step back poses the problem of re-engagement or co-existence, and the attitudes I've recommended are appropriate responses that confront the problem instead of ignoring or denying it. It's not as if the ironic competitor must continually mutter to herself, "Sport is absurd, sport is absurd," as she shoots every jumper or fields every ground ball. The athletic ironist can practice hard and compete intensely; she need not be denied the heightened experiences of sport. Yet her attitudes will make a difference in how she comports herself—how she competes within the constraints of rules, how she relates to others in the sports world, how she reacts to victory and defeat, how she handles her life in sports in relation to the rest of her life, what she expects and what she hopes for, etc. The ironist's attitudes work as dispositions to behave, sources of emotions as covert judgments about aspects of sports experience, and reminders about the very nature of sport.

Absurdity in life arises because of the incongruity between our desires and aspirations, that is, our seriousness, and the reality of the situations within which we find ourselves. Nagel's analysis of the absurd extracts the fundamental structure from various situations in life—the pursuit of a NBA career by a middle-aged man—and generalizes it to apply to life as such. He seems to miss one of the interesting implications of his analysis. Situations are sometimes absurd, life as a whole may be absurd—and *persons* are or can be absurd to the extent that a part of their life is absurd.[34] For example, given certain assumptions about the depth of their commitment and the time and energy expended in the public display of their beliefs, either the priest or the atheist is an absurd person. Moreover, the more extreme the commitment, the more absurd is the person for whom the object of commitment is trivial, futile, worthless, or even nonexistent. Where we have the reflective resources to determine, in some way, the objective insignificance of our attachments, the more extreme the form of seriousness then the more absurd the person becomes. With this in mind, it's hard not to come to the conclusion that the sports world is populated by many absurd persons. In one sense, everyone who is serious about sport is absurd. Yet, based on the analysis I've offered it's possible to reduce, without entirely eliminating, the absurdity of sports participation. The crazed Little League coach or fan, the ruthless, cheating high school or college competitor or coach—even the ex-professional athlete who is suicidal after defeat—all are absurd. Yet if we see sports from an external viewpoint and return to our competitive play with a suitable amount of detachment, the integration of the viewpoints lessens our absurdity and salvages what really matters in sport.

Nagel may be right about life in general.[35] If that is true, the case I've made for how to view sport follows rather obviously. For those who find Nagel's larger position difficult to swallow, it's much easier to see the way in which the "view from nowhere" insinuates itself into segments of our life. For Nagel, the backward step undermines our egocentric self-absorption throughout life. He concludes his discussion of the meaning of life with these remarks: "Our constitutional self-absorption together with our capacity to recognize its excessiveness make us irreducibly absurd even if we achieve a measure of subjective-objective integration by bringing the two standpoints closer together. The gap is too wide to be closed entirely, for any who is fully human" (*VN*, 223).

For the reflective and honest sports participant, it's better to approach sport as absurd than to deny our reflective judgments or to give up the joys of sport. "It is better to be simultaneously engaged and detached and therefore absurd, for this is the opposite of self-denial and the result of full awareness." Our situation is comic, not tragic, and deserves an ironic smile as we reflect on the foibles of human existence. Better to be absorbed and absurdly preoccupied than to miss out on all the fun.

PART TWO

Sport and Ethics

6 *Sportsmanship*

A movement in contemporary moral philosophy is attempting to return our attention to thinking about the centrality of virtue in the moral life. Until recently the language of virtue had seemingly fallen into disfavor in twentieth-century philosophizing about moral matters. We heard much talk about the naturalistic fallacy, verificationism, the expression of attitudes, prescriptivity, universalizability, the principle of utility, and the like, but little talk about *being* a certain kind of person, having certain dispositions or characteristics that we have always thought to be central to living life in a civilized moral community. In the move toward thinking about lived moral experience, philosophers began talking about issues of pressing social concern, such as abortion, euthanasia, and war. The mistaken impression occasioned in our students and in the community may have been that the return to relevancy, to "real" moral concerns, involved the necessary connection between applied ethics and social ethics. Again, one wonders what happened to the texture of individual moral experience, moral discourse, and moral education, where we stress the importance of friendliness, compassion, fairness, truthfulness, and reliability. Perhaps an important part of applied ethics involves trying to understand individual virtues; for example, what do we mean or what are we recommending when we speak of aspects of the virtuous life such as compassion or boldness?

In this context I believe it is relevant to think about the virtue of sportsmanship. Sports have a prevalent place in American cultural life, as well as in numerous foreign countries. Spectator sports set attendance records, yet crowd behavior is often atrocious. More adults participate today in sports with differing degrees of seriousness. Vast numbers of young people play sports, coming of age morally as they devote a large amount of time to their athletic endeavors. Impressive claims are made about the role of sports in the development of character and how important sports are as a preparation for later competitive life. It should be important to understand what it means to be a good sport. Parents often stress to their children the importance of being a good sport, but it is not apparent what that means.

It is helpful to start with a few examples before turning to the main arguments of this chapter. The paradigm case of a bad sport is the cheater. Consider a high school basketball game. At the end of a close game, a flurry of activity takes place beneath the basket. A foul is called and the coach sees that the referees are confused about who was fouled. He instructs his best foul shooter to go to the free throw line to take the shots although he knows, as does his team and most of the crowd, that another player, a poor foul shooter, was actually fouled. The wrong player makes the free throws and his team wins.[1] In this case the coach has cheated. He has instructed or encouraged his players to cheat, and we would say he is a bad sport or, in this instance at least, whether acting out of character or not, he has acted like a bad sport.[2] He has displayed poor sportsmanship.

Why is the cheater a bad sport? What is wrong with cheating? The answer is not difficult to find. Two teams agreed to play the game of basketball, defined by certain rules that constitute what it means to play basketball. By cheating, the coach intentionally broke a rule, thereby violating the original implied agreement. In this sense, cheating is a kind of promise breaking or violation of a contractual relationship. Notice that the moral reason that explains the wrongness of cheating is not unique to playing basketball; an ordinary moral rule has been broken. In the language of virtue, the coach has been found lacking in trust and integrity. He has attempted to gain an unfair advantage by breaking a rule. Perhaps being a good sport is simply an extension of being a good person—in one sense, this is an obvious truism—and the meaning of the virtue of sportsmanship is not unique to the activity in question.

Consider some other examples. The intent to injure would usually be a serious moral violation, but acting in such a way that one *might* injure an opponent is often morally ambiguous. Think of a hockey player fighting or a pitcher in baseball throwing one "under the chin." Should one yell at an opponent in hopes of rattling him? Certainly how one responds to defeat or victory is often thought to be an important part of sportsmanship. Should one ever refuse the traditional handshake after the contest? What about running up the score on an opponent or refusing to give credit due to an opponent who has defeated you? In such cases our judgments are more ambiguous and our explanations less obvious. Certainly no rule is violated when one team runs up the score on another, or when a tennis player continually whines, complains, throws his racket, interrupts play, and questions calls. But we want to say this type of behavior is bad form, somehow inappropriate because it violates the nature of what sport is about.

Is there some essential meaning of the virtue of sportsmanship? How can we unify our concept of sportsmanship? Are some aspects of it more central than others? In this chapter I attempt to respond to these questions. First I critically discuss James Keating's views. Keating first published his analysis of sportsmanship in 1964, and it has become a standard part of the literature in philosophy of sport.[3] Later, he published a revised version of his original paper.[4] Because of the significance and influence of Keating's seminal work, it is appropriate to begin our reflections on ethics in sport with a consideration of the framework within which he attempts to understand sportsmanship. Moreover, his fundamental distinction between sport and athletics is still very much with us; it is often either explicitly or implicitly used to reinforce the notion that the behavior and attitudes appropriate for playful, recreational activities are quite different from the norms and responses appropriate for participation in the deadly serious world of competitive athletics. Keating has offered an important framework within which to initiate an understanding of sportsmanship, just as Weiss's seminal work provided a useful starting point for reflecting on the nature and attraction of sport. I do not believe that Keating is correct in radically separating sport and athletics, and to the extent that this type of view is still prevalent when people talk about sport and what is and is not appropriate behavior in sports, a correction is needed. The chapter is not wholly critical, however. Emerging from the friendly engagement with this type of approach to sport and sportsmanship will be a positive view that attempts to preserve the precarious balance between the seriousness of competition and the nonseriousness of playful activities.

Keating's paper is a valuable resource for a number of reasons, not the least of which is his overview of the many and varied claims made about the nature of sportsmanship. Some have made extraordinary assertions about the importance of this notion, as if it is *the* most important virtue in American cultural life. The interpretations of the essence of sportsmanship have included numerous other virtues: self-control, fair play, truthfulness, courage, endurance, and others.[5] Keating attempts to unify our understanding by providing a tidy scheme that shows which virtues are essential and which are of only accidental importance. His argument is simple and compelling. Sportsmanship is the conduct that is becoming to a sportsman, or one who engages in sport, so we simply have to understand what sport is. Here we have the crux of the argument, because the term refers to "radically different types of human activity."[6] Keating could not be more emphatic stressing the extreme separation of sport as playful activity and sport as competitive athletic contests. On three different occasions he speaks of them as "radically different types of human activity," and at one point says that "a drastic change takes place" when we move from playful activity to athletics.[7]

What, more precisely, is the distinction? Taking hints from dictionary definitions and etymology, Keating argues that "sport" refers both to the pleasant diversion of play and to spirited competitive athletic contests. To understand the true meaning of sportsmanship, we must carefully distinguish conduct and attitude appropriate to play and conduct and attitude appropriate to athletics. "In essence, play has for its direct and immediate end joy, pleasure, and delight and which is dominated by a spirit of moderation and generosity. Athletics, on the other hand, is essentially a competitive activity, which has for its end victory in the contest and which is characterized by a spirit of dedication, sacrifice, and intensity."[8]

Thus the virtues of the player are radically different from the virtues of the athlete. Insofar as the activity determines the conduct appropriate to it, the player should conduct himself with an attitude of "generosity and magnanimity," keeping in mind his obligation to maximize the pleasure of the event and reinforce the ludic character of the activity. Play is essentially cooperative. On the other hand, the athlete is engaged in a competitive struggle whose end is exclusive possession of victory. In the words of G. J. Warnock, this is a situation in which things have the "inherent tendency to go badly"[9] unless moral restraints are put on the rigors of competition. "Fairness or fair play, the pivotal virtue in athletics, emphasizes the need for an impartial and equal application of the rules, if the victory is to signify, as it should, athletic excellence."[10] In athletics, generosity and magnanimity are misplaced, as they supposedly are in other areas of life that are essentially competitive. Your opponent expects only that you fairly pursue your self-interest, not that you are to be interested in his goal, for you cannot be. Victory is the telos of the activity and an exclusive possession. Once the contest ends, the athlete, like the victor or vanquished in war, should face victory or defeat with modesty or a strength of composure.

Since Keating's view of sportsmanship depends so heavily on the sharp distinction between sport as playful activity and sport as athletic competition, we should look more closely at that distinction. How does Keating arrive at it? He begins by citing Webster's definition of sport as "diversion," "amusement," and "recreation." However, since so many sporting events (he mentions, among others, the World Series, the Davis Cup, and even a high school basketball tournament) would be inaccurately described in these terms, there must be another important sense given to this notion. Etymologically, the English forms of the word "athlete" suggest the centrality of contest and the struggle for excellence and victory, so "sport," he concludes, must refer to "radically different types of human activity." Although there might already be something misleading about placing such emphasis on etymology and dictionary definitions, the distinction ultimately is a phenomenological one. We should look at lived experience for the basis of the distinction, for play and athletics are radically different "not insofar as the game itself or the mechanics or rules are concerned, but different with regard to the attitude, preparation, and purpose of the participants."[11] Now curiosities arise, of a logical, psychological, and moral nature.

Consider one of Keating's own examples, a high school basketball tournament. Suppose Team A is coached by Smith, who views sport as little short of war. The opponent is the enemy, who must be hated in order to produce maximum intensity and effort. Practices and games are pervaded by a spirit of overarching seriousness. He yells at his players and at referees. He never lets up because he views sport as real life, or, if not quite like real life, of great importance as preparation for the harshness of the "real" world. There is a certain ruthlessness in his pursuit of victory, and anything goes, short of outright cheating, although even here he is inclined to think that it's alright if you don't get caught. For example, he wouldn't hesitate to run up the score if it might enhance his team's rating and its future tournament seeding. He expects no less from his opponent.

On the other hand, Team B is coached by Jones, whose whole approach to basketball is fundamentally different. He is also a spirited competitor who instills in his player-athletes the value of excellent performance, victory, and fair play. However, he never forgets that basketball is a game, an arbitrary construction of rule-governed activities invented in order to make possible an intrinsically satisfying activity.[12] For Jones there is always something magical about the world of basketball, with its special order, its special spatial and temporal rhythms. It is set apart from the concerns of ordinary reality. To play and coach basketball is to engage in joyful activities, and the pleasure is increased by improving skills, being challenged to perform well, inventing strategies, and achieving one's goals. He sees the opponent not as an enemy but as a friendly competitor whose challenge is necessary to enhance the pleasurable possibilities of his own play. He realizes it is difficult to sustain the spirit of play within spirited competition, but that is his goal. His seriousness about the pursuit of victory is always mediated by an awareness that basketball is "just a game," valuable for the moment, whose value consists primarily in the intrinsic enjoyment of the activity. Fun is an essential element in his understanding of sport.

Are these two coaches engaged in fundamentally different human activities? The example suggests that Keating's distinction is plausible. In one sense, the coaches' attitudes are so dissimilar that we want to say they are engaged in different activities. But the most important question here is moral, not psychological. I see no reason to take Smith's attitudes as normative. Although the picture of Smith may appear to be overdrawn, it is undoubtedly a correct description of the understanding and attitudes some people have regarding sports. However, it doesn't follow that their attitudes are correct. Keating's argument is logically curious. Recall that play and athletics have been characterized as being radically different with regard to attitudes, but later he states that "the nature of the activity determines the conduct and attitudes proper to it."[13] Without further clarification, this appears to be circular and uninformative concerning how our original attitudes toward sport should be formed. I would say that Smith has an impoverished view of sport, an impoverished experience of sport, and it is just such views and attitudes that tend to generate unsportsmanlike behavior in sport.

There are two main problems with Keating's analysis, vitiating his account of sportsmanship. First, because he takes his understanding of play simply from Webster's definition of sports as "diversion," "amusement," and "recreation," he fails to describe adequately the nature of play so as to understand how sport could be seen as an extension of play. Second, and probably because of his limited clarification of play, he incorrectly ascribes a false exclusivity to the psychology of the player and the athlete.

The player and the athlete are to be radically distinguished supposedly on the grounds that they differ with regard to attitude, preparation, and purpose. The previous example made such a distinction plausible but failed to show why one set of attitudes should be normative. In numerous other cases, however, the distinction is difficult if not impossible to make, precisely because the attitudes of the participants are mixed. Consider an ex-college basketball player engaged in a pickup game. Is this person a player or an athlete? What virtues should characterize his conduct? On Keating's model it would be difficult to say. Suppose the basketball player intends to play well, puts out maximum effort, competes hard, pursues victory and attempts to play fairly. Why? Because he still loves the game; he still enjoys the competitive play, the very feel of the activity. Each game is a unity, the development of a totality with its own finality. Something is at issue, and this is an arena in which the issue at hand will be decisively resolved. He finds the dramatic tensions satisfying, as well as the frolicking nature of running, jumping, and responding to the physical presence of other players. He enjoys the sheer exuberance of the experience. He is serious about his play because such seriousness enhances the activity and heightens the experience. He is serious because the internal logic of the activity demands the pursuit of victory and he both loves and respects the game of basketball. Yet he realizes that in a profound sense, his seriousness is misplaced. It doesn't really matter who wins the game, although it does matter that the festivity occurs. Such an attitude toward the pursuit of victory acts as an inner negation of his original seriousness and produces moderation. One might go on here with an extended phenomenological account, but the point is already clear. His attitudes and purposes are extraordinarily complex. He is simultaneously player and athlete. His purpose is to win the contest *and* to experience the playful and aesthetic delights of the experience. His attitudes are at once both playful and competitive, and these color his relationship with his fellow participants. He sees his opponent as both competitor and friend, competing and cooperating at the same time. These are the attitudes that guide his conduct.

Such a fusion of attitudes and purposes may be unsatisfying to some, but I think such a picture of the player-athlete is a truer one than the one offered by Keating. His radical distinction between play and athletics is an excellent example of what Richard Taylor calls polarized thinking. In the context of showing how such thinking leads to metaphysical puzzlement or confusion, Taylor says the following:

> There is a common way of thinking that we can call *polarization,* and that appears to be the source of much metaphysics. It consists of dividing things into two exclusive categories, and then supposing that if something under consideration does not belong to one of them, then it must

belong in the other. "Either/or" is the pattern of such thought, and because it is usually clear, rigorous, and incisive, it is also often regarded by philosophers as exclusively rational.[14]

Such sharpness and precision are sometimes bought at the expense of truth, for reality is far too loose a mixture of things to admit of such absolute distinctions, and sometimes, both in our practical affairs and in our philosophy, we are led into serious errors, which are fervently embraced just because they seem so clearly to have been proved.[15]

Keating offers only one extended example to show what his polarized view of sportsmanship would look like in practice, and his conclusions are odd.

It is the contestant's objective and not the game itself which becomes the chief determinant of the conduct and attitudes of the players. If we take tennis as an example and contrast the code of conduct employed by the player with that of the athlete in the matter of officiating, the difference is obvious. The player invariably gives the opponent the benefit of any possible doubt. Whenever he is not certain, he plays his opponent's shot as good even though he may believe it was out. The athlete, however, takes a different approach. Every bit as opposed to cheating as the sportsman, the athlete demands no compelling proof of error. If a shot seems to be out, the athlete calls it that way. He is satisfied that his opponent will do the same. He asks no quarter and gives none. As a result of this attitude by comparison with the player, the athlete will tend toward a legal interpretation of the rules.[16]

I have played tournament tennis and find this example not only unconvincing, it is simply inaccurate in some respects. It bears little resemblance to my own experience and that of those with whom I play. First, based on Keating's model, it would be impossible for me to know whether I am a player or an athlete in the context of my tennis playing. I should say I am both, since I compete for victory, but also find great fun in the activity and recognize my opponent as a partner of sorts. Moreover, the conventions of tennis render Keating's example misleading and of little value in helping us to understand sportsmanship. If one is not certain that a ball is out, one plays it. Only if one is sure the ball is out is it to be called out. If a call is made but disagreement arises, a let is called and the point is replayed. Giving the benefit of the doubt to the opponent isn't generosity here; it is simply recognizing the relevant conventions. Actually, Keating's description of the so-called "athlete" sounds suspiciously like an example of bad sportsmanship, since such a person's zeal in the pursuit of victory ignores the unwritten rules of playing without officials and tends to destroy the spirit of play. A more playful spirit would mediate against a zealousness that fuels inappropriate conduct and ignoring the rules.

The other main problem with Keating's view of sportsmanship is his account of the nature of play and its relationship to sport. Such a topic demands an extended treatment, and I have attempted to do this in the previous chapters. Briefly, the most accurate and inclusive phenomenological accounts of experience in sport are those that focus on the nature of play and which show, either explicitly or implicitly, that sport is a formal, competitive variety of human play. I agree with Kenneth Schmitz when he says that "sport is primarily an extension of play, and that it rests upon and derives its central values from play."[17] Huizinga's classic account of play stresses that it is an activity freely engaged in when someone metaphorically "steps out" of ordinary life and becomes absorbed in an alternative world of play, with its own order and meaning, constituted by its own rules, experiential rhythms, traditions, tensions, and illusory quality. He also stresses the element of fun as essential. He sums up his account in the following passage:

> Summing up the formal characteristics of play we might call it a free activity standing quite consciously outside "ordinary" life as being "not serious," but at the same time absorbing the player intensely and utterly. It is an activity connected with no material interest, and no profit can be gained by it. It proceeds within its own proper boundaries of time and space according to fixed rules and in an orderly manner.[18]

Schmitz strengthens the analysis of play by distinguishing four types: frolic, make-believe, sporting skills, and games.[19] The movement from frolic to sport is a continuum from less formal, spontaneous, animal-like behavior to more formal activities guided by rules, in which knowledge, preparation, and understanding are called for. In all forms, Schmitz, like Huizinga, stresses the movement from the ordinary to the world of play by a free decision to play. "Such a constitutive decision cannot be compelled and is essentially free. Through it arises the suspension of the ordinary concerns of the everyday world."[20] This decision constitutes an act of transcendence beyond the natural world, in which a new totality is opened and experienced with a sense of exhilaration and celebration. Schmitz compares the transcendence of play with religion and art. Also akin to Huizinga's account, Schmitz stresses, especially for the more formal varieties of play, the new order of the world of play with its new forms of space, time, and behavior. It is a "transnatural, fragile, limited perfection . . . delivering its own values in and for itself, the freedom and joy of play."[21] Finally, it is a "distinctive mode of being. It is a way of

taking up the world of being, a manner of being present in the world
... whose existential presence is a careless joyful freedom."[22]

The problem for the play-theorist of sport is how to connect such a
striking description of play with sport. Many think, as Keating seems to,
that this account necessarily excludes essential elements of sport, including the striving for excellence and good performance and contesting for
victory. But the strength of the play theory of sport is the way in which
it can provide both a rich phenomenological account of the experience
of play within sports and an explanation of the prominence and appropriate value of good performance and victory. No one would deny that
the pursuit of victory is essential in sport; after all, a contest is not mere
frolic. But why *do* so many engage in sport? Why do we create our games
and begin and continue to play them? The critics of sport give us an
important perspective here when they wonder why so many people become obsessed with things like hitting a ball with a wooden club, throwing a ball into a hoop, or smashing a little ball around expansive fairways.
They can understand why children, lacking maturity and experience,
could enjoy the exuberance of such activities. But grown people? Compared with suffering, friendship, and possible catastrophes because of
deep-rooted human conflicts, playing games and treating them with utmost seriousness seems silly. Bernard Suits brings this out well in attempting to define game playing:

> It is generally acknowledged that games are in some sense essentially
> non-serious. We must therefore ask in what sense games are, and in
> what sense they are not, serious. What is believed when it is believed
> that games are not serious? Not, certainly, that the players of games
> always take a very light-hearted view of what they are doing. A bridge
> player who played his cards randomly might justly be accused of fail-
> ing to play the game at all just because of his failure to take it serious-
> ly. It is much more likely that the belief that games are not serious
> means what the proposal under consideration implies: that there is
> always something in life more important than playing the game, or that
> a game is the kind of thing that a player could always have reason to
> stop playing.[23]

The important insight here is that the nonseriousness at the heart of play
is based on the recognition that there are more important values in life
than the value of improving sporting skills and winning games. A correct and wise attitude concerning sport would place these values in an
appropriate hierarchy. Suits goes on to deny such nonseriousness as the
essence of game playing on the grounds that one could take a game so

seriously as to consider it supremely important, taking over one's whole life and forcing one to avoid other duties. But his point is psychological, not moral. Undoubtedly someone *could* have such an attitude, but he ought not. Suits sees this clearly. "Supreme dedication to a game . . . may be repugnant to nearly everyone's moral sense. That may be granted; indeed insisted upon, since our loathing is excited by the very fact that it is a game which has usurped the place of ends we regard as so much more worthy of pursuit."[24] Suits concludes his attempt to define game playing by arguing that when we play a game we accept the arbitrary way in which means are used to achieve certain ends—for example, in golf our goal is not just to put the ball in the hole but to do it in an extraordinarily limited way—because we simply want to make the activity possible.[25] Evidently, such activity, without external practical ends, must be intrinsically satisfying.[26]

This analysis leads us to a point where we can see the paradoxical attitudinal complexity of the player-athlete. We might distinguish between internal and external seriousness. The activity of playful competition calls for pursuit of victory. As Suits suggested, if someone isn't serious in this sense he might be accused of not playing the game at all. On the other hand, there is an external perspective from which the internal seriousness of competition is mediated by an awareness that the activity is a form of play, infused with its own values and qualified by the values of life outside the play world. The activity engaged in is both competition and play, serious and nonserious. This is the understanding of the activity that gives rise to a more adequate understanding of sportsmanship. The spirit of play may be absent within sport, but it ought not to be if, as has been argued, sport is intimately and in some sense originally related to the playful activity of game playing. Once again, Schmitz offers helpful comments.

> Sport can be carried out without the spirit of play. Nevertheless, in the life of individuals and in the history of the race, sport emerges from play as from an original and founding posture. Sport is free, self-conscious, tested play which moves in a transnatural dimension of human life, built upon a certain basis of leisure . . . There is certainly a return to seriousness in the discipline of formal sport. There is training, performance and competition. But the objectives of sport and its founding decision lie within play and cause sport to share in certain of its features—the sense of immediacy, exhilaration, rule-directed behavior, and the indeterminancy of a specified outcome.[27]

Let us turn now to a positive account of the virtue of sportsmanship.

In my view, instead of a rigid and precise distinction between play and athletics, we must be content with a fuzzy picture of the fusion of these activities, a picture in which edges are blurred and paradox is retained. Keating's view embraces tidiness at the cost of truth. Still, we want to ask, What is the essence of sportsmanship? I tend to think that the question is misleading and the phenomenon is dispersed in our experience in innumerable particular instances. We ought to be hesitant about attributing to this notion an abstract unity that is not found in experience. Wittgenstein's admonition that we ought to be suspicious of such talk and appeal to particular cases is well taken here, as always. However, if we view sport as an extension of human play, competitive play, we can offer an understanding of the virtue of sportsmanship that will be somewhat more satisfying intellectually, although it will not always generate easily purchased moral recommendations. This shouldn't surprise us.

Keating is right to see that we must understand sportsmanship as conduct arising from our attitudes, and he is correct in attempting to describe the attitudes appropriate to sport. He is simply incorrect about the attitudes. If sport is understood as an extension of play, then the key to sportsmanship is the spirit of play. Within the arena of competition the spirit of play should be retained. It would be helpful to think of this in Aristotelian terms. Recall Aristotle's description of virtue:

> By virtue I mean virtue of character; for this pursues the mean because it is concerned with feelings and actions, and these admit of excess, deficiency and an intermediate condition. We can be afraid, e.g., or be confident, or have appetites, or get angry, or feel pity, in general have pleasure or pain, both too much and too little, and in both ways not well; but having these feelings at the right times, about the right things, toward the right people, for the right end, and in the right way, is the intermediate and best condition, and this is proper to virtue. Similarly, actions also admit of excess, deficiency and the intermediate condition.[28]

In fact, Aristotle's description of the virtuous person reinforces my previous attempt to ascribe a certain psychological complexity to the player-athlete. The courageous or brave person, according to Aristotle, is neither excessively fearful, else he would be a coward, or excessively confident, else he would be foolhardy and rash.[29] He feels appropriately fearful, which moderates his confidence, and he feels appropriately confident, which moderates his fear. His virtuous acts are expressions of such moderation and a result of experience and habit. Likewise, the good sport feels the joy and exuberance of free, playful activity set apart from the world, and he feels the intensity of striving to perform well and achieve victory in the context of playing fairly according to the rules and traditions of his sport. Sportsmanship is a mean between excessive seriousness, which misunderstands the importance of the spirit of play, and an excessive sense of playfulness, which might be called frivolity and which misunderstands the importance of victory and achievement when play is competitive. The good sport is both serious and nonserious.

Many, if not most, examples of bad sportsmanship arise from an excessive seriousness that negates the spirit of play because of an exaggerated emphasis on the value of victory. Schmitz has a superb comment on such exaggeration:

> The policy of winning at all costs is the surest way of snuffing out the spirit of play in sport. The fallout of such a policy is the dreary succession of firings in college and professional sport. Such an emphasis on victory detaches the last moment from the whole game and fixes the outcome apart from its proper context. It reduces the appreciation of the performance, threatens the proper disposition towards the rules and turns the contest into a naked power struggle. The upshot is the brutalization of the sport. And so, the sport which issued from the play-decision, promising freedom and exhilaration, ends dismally in lessening the humanity of players and spectators.[30]

Such exaggeration of victory goes hand in hand with the way we view our relationship to our opponents. The spirit of play moderates, not negates, the intensity with which we pursue victory and introduces a spirit of friendship and cooperation in what would otherwise be a "naked power struggle."[31] Thus, the good sport doesn't cheat, attempt to hurt the opponent, or taunt another. A certain lightness of spirit prohibits uncivil displays of temper, constant complaints to officials, and the like. Throughout the activity, self-control and kinship with others are necessary to maximize the possible values of the play world.

What does all this mean in more particular instances and over a wider range of examples? Once again Aristotle is helpful. First he insists that it would be misguided to expect an extreme degree of exactness, clarity, or precision in our present moral inquiry. We should expect a degree of precision appropriate to the inquiry, and in ethical theory, "it will be satisfactory if we can indicate the truth roughly and in outline."[32] In addition, when speaking of moral virtue we seek the mean "relative to us." Virtue is not alike to all people in all situations. Terrence Irwin comments:

Aristotle warns against any misleading suggestion that his appeal to a mean is attended to offer a precise, quantitative test for virtuous action that we can readily apply to particular cases—as though, e.g., we could decide that there is a proper, moderate degree of anger to be displayed in all conditions, or in all conditions of a certain precisely described type. The point of the doctrine, and of Aristotle's insistence of the 'intermediate relative to us,' is that no such precise quantitative test can be found.[33]

To see the virtue of sportsmanship as a mean between extremes is not to be given a precise formula for interpreting whether acts are sportsmanlike, but to be given an explanatory and experiential context within which we can learn and teach how we ought to conduct ourselves in sports. From the standpoint of teaching and moral education, an appeal to exemplars of this virtue will always be useful, for they show us what it means to be playful and cooperative in our sport experience. I cannot see that the moral philosopher is required to do more.

7   On Cheating in Sports

Perhaps I'm old-fashioned, unrealistic, or engaging in empty romanticism, but I can't accept the notion that, somehow, cheating in sport may be acceptable. Like most people, I take the proscription on cheating to be a central part of sportsmanship. However, some have questioned this. It has even been held that cheating might be interesting, become a part of the very "structure" of sport and, the incompatibility thesis notwithstanding, that cheaters *can* play the game. These theses have been defended in interesting and persuasive ways by some contemporary thinkers.[1] But they can't be right, can they? Surely something has gone wrong here.

We have in this instance another puzzling interplay between intuitions and philosophical arguments. On the one hand, philosophical argumentation often forces us to examine certain "obvious" intuitions of common sense. For example, recent discussions in applied ethics have forced people to reexamine the unreflective moral acceptance of eating animals.[2] On the other hand, it's not clear that we should always give way to philosophical arguments that conflict strongly with intuitive notions that are very difficult to give up. Philosophical arguments may force us to rethink conventionally accepted notions, and for that we must be grateful. But I agree with Thomas Nagel, in the preface to *Mortal Questions*, when he says, "Given a knockdown argument for an intuitively unacceptable conclusion, one should assume there is probably something wrong with the argument that one cannot detect—though it is possible that the source of the intuition has been misidentified."[3]

It is certainly part of the conventional moral wisdom in sports that cheating is wrong, period. What I mean by calling such a view "conventional" is neither difficult nor obscure. Most parents teach their children that it is wrong to cheat; most coaches teach their players that victory is tainted if one must resort to cheating to overcome the opponent. Sport has something to do with character, and playing within the agreed-upon framework of restrictions underlying sport is expected of a good person. In fact, it is at least prima facie outrageous—which probably only reiterates that it is not conventional—to hold that cheating might in some sense be acceptable in sport. But it is much more difficult to sustain the conventional thesis than one might expect. Recent skeptical arguments have shown that. If I am going to defend conventional wisdom, I fear I'm going to sound, well, "conventional," and for that I apologize. It's an unexciting, boring task, but someone must do it. I also fear that I'll sound too much like other conventional pundits, whom I won't consult, but that is to be expected as well.

What is it that causes us to think that cheating is just dead wrong? As usual, it's helpful to start with some examples. In fact, if I'm right the kind of examples we start with and where we go with them are key elements in the attempt to detect what's wrong with the arguments offered by skeptics about cheating. Start with examples in which our use of "cheating" and "cheater" seems natural. (I'm not assuming that ordinary language is the final authority here, but such appeals are helpful.) We often refer to a person as a cheater if he knowingly fills out his income tax form incorrectly, to his advantage. The term "cheater" seems most at home, curiously, when we think of card games. (Perhaps that's a cultural fact because of old Hollywood westerns in which the "bad guy" invariably cheats at cards.) Think of playing cards with a small child who is so concerned with winning that she tries to sneak a look at cards in the stack or barely looks at the next card to be drawn before deciding whether she should take it. What is morally objectionable in these examples?

In the case of the tax-cheat we want to say that he is attempting to make himself an arbitrary exception to the sort of civil obligations that hold for everyone. In this regard it's difficult not to think of Kant and his insistence on the universalizability of moral principles. Living in the community involves taking on the obligations related to social life, and these obligations hold for every person in the community. No exceptions. The cheater seems to want the benefits associated with citizens paying taxes, but he seems also to want to hold an unfair advantage when it comes to paying his fair share. He appears to expect things from others, yet inconsistently exempts himself from those same expectations for no apparent reason.[4] The cheater at cards is in the same boat. What she wants is an unfair advantage. Surely the rules of the card game apply to everyone who plays, but she exempts herself from these prescriptions because she is so obsessed with the goal of winning. She must attempt to deceive because if found out she would be rebuked. We also suppose that in the case of card games each player expects the other to play by the rules.

One more important point: If we are playing cards with a child and we discover he is cheating, we immediately stop the game and explain the issues. (Hasn't this happened to many of us?) From the standpoint of principle, the lesson involves following agreed-upon rules. From the standpoint of character, the issue involves dishonesty and deception. More important, it is a matter of integrity and development of a mature judgment about the relative worth of winning at a game of cards and the kind of person you are in your relations with others. Thus, based on these examples it is reasonable to assume that the concept of cheating will have a great deal to do with breaking rules, the intention to gain an unfair advantage, deception, and issues of character.

When we move to sport-related examples, it is interesting that the most obvious instances of cheating are hardly matters of strategy, as the skeptics sometimes suggest. For example, if a sport requires you to keep score, as most do, then the participants must keep the score fairly. If they don't, that's cheating and it's wrong, period. This can happen, for example, in golf, player-refereed tennis matches, and pick-up basketball games. If a sport or a particular context of some sport has strict eligibility requirements for the players, then playing illegal participants is cheating. In sports in which umpires or referees of some sort are required to ensure that certain rules are not violated, then the hiring of biased officials who give one team an unfair advantage would be a clear instance of cheating. In sports in which equipment is required and there are restrictions on the kind of equipment allowed, using equipment proscribed by the rules would be cheating. For example, using a corked bat in baseball or substituting illegal implements in field events would be cheating. Examples from these general categories could be multiplied.

Now, what do these paradigm cases of cheating have in common? In all cases there is the intention on the part of players, coaches, or interested personnel to gain an unfair advantage by altering certain conditions of competitive equality. Usually this will be done in a deceptive manner since you would not want your competitors to find out. This is often done in relation to central rules of the game that define who can play, how the score is kept, how the contest is officiated, and what sorts of equipment are allowed in playing. These factors constitute the core meaning of our concept of cheating in sports. It's no wonder that conventional wisdom believes we have to hold the line against such behavior. What is at stake is another kind of integrity—the integrity of the game. At its core, cheating proscribes behavior violating elements without which we simply can't have the game in question. So it's also appropriate to conclude that the central meaning of cheating in sports disallows the cheater from winning since he has violated the most basic elements that are constitutive of the game in question.

The unfairness in question derives from the very nature of sport, in which rules are developed that limit the way in which the specific ends of the sport are brought about. Recall Bernard Suits's well-known account of game playing. "To play a game is to attempt to achieve a specific state of affairs (*pre-lusory goal*), using only means permitted by rules (*lusory means*), where rules prohibit use of more efficient in favor of less efficient means (constitutive rules)."[5] Suppose we play golf together. If you are required to use only your golf clubs to put the golf ball in the hole and I am allowed sometimes to use my hand to place the ball in a more strategic place on the course, and if I gain some advantage in doing so, then your situation in relation to mine is prima facie unfair or unjust. Unless there is some morally relevant difference between your situation and mine in this context, or we have agreed to change the rules, the difference in treatment with regard to how we achieve our goals is unjustified. Our play is based on shared expectations, implied agreements. As William Frankena has said, "The paradigm case of injustice is that in which there are two similar individuals in similar circumstances and one is treated better or worse than the other."[6] Here unfair advantage arises because the noncheater's competitive situation is worse, for no good reason.

In sport, the rules of the game create what I would like to call the "prescriptive atmosphere" associated with playing the sport in question. This atmosphere both prescribes and proscribes. It defines the acceptable means in which the goals of the game may be brought about. It defines an atmosphere of competitive expectations in which the participants may gain a competitive advantage, and perhaps win, only in the context of an underlying equality expressed in the rules. The obligations in question are deontological, based on the assumption that playing a sport means we have agreed to compete in a relatively specific and delimited way in pursuit of victory. The problem of course is that the prescriptive atmosphere is only partly constituted by the central, explicit rules of the game in question. This point is crucial for an understanding of cheating, and it leads to the most difficult questions associated with the issue. Again, it is helpful to look at some examples. I will focus on examples from baseball since these will be useful in relation to arguments in later parts of this chapter.

Some years ago a famous ex-major-leaguer became head baseball coach at a southern university. To gain a competitive advantage he attempted to shape his team to the peculiarities of his home baseball field. He usually had six to eight left-handed hitters in his lineup to accommodate the short (315 feet) right-field fence, but strangely enough, not all of his left-handed hitters were power hitters. Some were smaller players with great speed. Now consider two things the coach did to gain an advantage over his opponents. First, it was revealed that the right-field fence was considerably shorter than advertised—barely over 290 feet. Second, after one of his little speedsters had beaten out a routine grounder to short, an irate opposing coach demanded that the distance from home to first be measured. It was measured at 88 feet! (One can only imagine the scene at the ballpark that day!) Did the ex-major leaguer cheat?

Let us assume that he intended to deceive his opponents concerning the distance to the right-field fence. I do not consider that cheating. His opponents could obviously *see* how short the fence was and could change their lineup accordingly. It was dishonest, therefore morally suspect, but not an act of cheating. On the other hand, shortening the distance to first base by two feet fundamentally changes the game of baseball. (Were they still playing baseball?) This is a change that would not be noticeable immediately, hence one would expect that the coach who knew about the shorter distance would have a considerable advantage. (He would put more speed in the lineup and instruct his infielders to play shallow.)

This example generates many of the sticky issues associated with the notion of cheating because the prescriptive atmosphere of certain sports is not always precise. Baseball has a rich tradition, and the customs associated with baseball allow many actions that might appear to the outsider to be inappropriate. Sparky Anderson allowed the Tiger Stadium grass to grow high. Maury Wills and Lou Brock had to steal bases running on watered-down base paths. A good, aggressive base runner is taught to go out of the base path to break up double plays. Stealing signs is a well-developed art in baseball. Many hitters dig up the chalk line in the batter's box and position their back foot, *illegally*, out of the box. Pitchers are taught to throw inside to establish a more intimidating presence on the mound. And, primarily at the professional level, pitching coaches develop and teach the most artful techniques of making the baseball do unexpected things. All of these things are "part of the game," a part of the historical existence of baseball. That is why they do not constitute cheating. In some cases there are penalties associated with behavior, comparable to actions like holding by offensive linemen in football or setting an illegal screen in basketball. But the prescriptive atmosphere of the sport, the ethos if you will, sanctions such behavior and generates expectations that your opponent will attempt to use these strategies to gain an advantage.[7] There is nothing unfair about this, however. To learn the sport, to know the game, is to come to understand such strategies and how to deal with them.

Compare the prescriptive atmosphere of baseball to the ethos of golf. For example, a golfer can rub the front face of his driver with clear Vaseline to keep the ball on the face of the club slightly longer for better control. In amateur tournaments a player is allowed only fourteen clubs in his bag, but some have secretly added an extra club. Some players have substituted a slightly smaller European golf ball in tournaments, for longer drives and easier putting. In re-marking a ball on the green it is sometimes possible to mismark the ball by a few inches. Are these actions cheating? Yes, I believe one can answer without hesitation, because the prescriptive atmosphere of golf is so clear in this regard. Golf is a game of honor. Perhaps because there are so many chances to cheat, the ethos of golf has developed a stringent atmosphere; it is considered scandalous to attempt to get away with such things. In any case, these golfing examples seem once again to support the thesis that cheating involves the attempt to gain an unfair advantage since the cheater's opponent will be competing under conditions that are unjustifiably dissimilar to the cheater's.

On the other hand the ethos of baseball seems, in certain respects, more tolerant. All sorts of subtle illegalities are not only accepted but recommended as suitable strategy. The kinds of actions I have mentioned, such as stealing signs or doctoring a baseball, have become historically embedded in the game. How do general practices become part of the prescriptive atmosphere of a sport? I know of no way to give a tidy and satisfying answer to this question. The ethos of baseball is not so vague and open-textured that it is impossible to make judgments about what is and is not cheating. But the prescriptive atmosphere is subject to change and it is probably subject to the kind of social and cultural pressures that also affect the moral atmosphere of a society. Perhaps we should think of certain moral judgments concerning cheating as analogous to aesthetic judgments concerning the value of an artwork or whether some object ought to be considered an instance of the concept "art." In these cases we appeal to informed judges with knowledge of the tradition, who make decisions based on the relevant criteria associated with

the concept of art or the notion of aesthetic value. With regard to judgments concerning cheating we must decide, based on the central explicit
rules and the traditions of the sport that outline certain latent agreements, what sort of behavior is reasonably expected in the pursuit of
victory. As Aristotle warned, we shouldn't expect mathematical certainty in our judgments; neither should we despair and suppose that the
prescriptive atmosphere of sport is so amorphous that "anything goes."
Good judgment is possible.

So far I have concentrated on what I've called, perhaps metaphorically, the "core" of our concept of cheating, and for good reason. Any
contemporary philosopher, whether he or she has read Wittgenstein or
not, recognizes the difficulty posed by the task of definition. If a philosopher has the temerity to attempt to define some concept in terms of
necessary and sufficient conditions, such boldness is usually answered
by the inevitable counterexamples. That's because our concepts *are* probably open, or elastic, or historically unstable, as many have pointed out.
Depending on your favorite metaphor, however, the change or the indeterminacy often occurs at the boundaries of the concept, and only a radical conceptual revolution or historical development could force us to
change our minds about paradigm examples. We know that Rembrandt
and Beethoven created artworks, that Christianity and Islam are religions,
that capricious infliction of suffering both raises a moral (as opposed to
a nonmoral) issue and is morally wrong. And we know these things de-
spite the fact that "art," "religion," "morality," and "moral wrongness"
may not be susceptible to definition in terms of necessary and sufficient
conditions. I believe that the same could be said for cheating in sports.
Once we have recognized this point, we are better situated to make valid conclusions in relation to the problem of the difficulty of defining
cheating.

At least three different questions are relevant in our discussion and
in the evaluation of the arguments offered by skeptics about cheating.

1. The definitional question—whether some behavior *x* is an example
   of cheating.
2. The moral question—whether, if some behavior *x* is an example of
   cheating, then *x* is wrong.
3. The incompatibility question—whether, if some behavior *x* is an example of cheating, then the person performing *x* is logically disal-
   lowed from playing the game.

I think the analysis so far shows that cheating usually involves the attempt
to gain an unfair advantage over your opponent in a competitive situation

in which equality is normally preserved by certain central explicit rules and latent agreements. With regard to the above questions, the definitional problem will have to be answered in terms of what it means, in specific situations, to gain an unfair competitive advantage. Such a notion will involve an analysis of the relevant rules, explicit or tacit, that come to play in the situation and an explanation of how these produce an atmosphere in which certain behavior can be reasonably expected. One would expect that disagreement would arise in our judgments concerning particulars, but such judgments are in some sense logically unrelated to the moral question and the incompatibility question. For if we decide that some behavior is an example of cheating, then it surely follows that it is wrong and that it disallows the cheater from playing the game. After all, that's what cheating means! I did hedge a bit, because in some cases we may again be thrown back to the puzzling problem of the interplay between our intuitions concerning particular cases and our more general theories that seem to inform our judgments of particulars. Let us now turn more specifically to the interesting arguments we find in contemporary discussions of cheating. Like Keating's seminal article on sportsmanship, the pieces by Oliver Leaman and Craig Lehman have shaped the background against which an examination of cheating often takes place in philosophy of sport. The skeptical views expressed in these articles are also familiar in contemporary discussions of these issues in the sports world, and even on sports-talk radio when people wonder whether cheating can be precisely defined, or whether appeals to unwritten rules (in baseball, for example) are helpful to determine appropriate conduct. Hence, the criticisms that follow, like the criticisms of Keating's view of sportsmanship, are more broadly applicable than one might think.

Oliver Leaman attempts first to show that it is difficult to define cheating in sport and second to show what is morally wrong with cheating. He seems to think the two questions are logically related, since, based on the problem of defining cheating, it is somehow difficult to decide when an unfair advantage has arisen.[8] One would expect to find a number of examples in his article, especially since the definitional question is a central one for him. Surprisingly, he offers few examples. The weight of his conclusions rests on two cases: uncivil and irritating behavior in tennis (intending to upset your opponent) and hockey violence. First, consider the tennis example.

Leaman's discussion forces us to think about cheating in relation to breaking formal rules, violating tacit conventions, and the intention involved, especially the intention to deceive. (I won't discuss the specific definitions he criticizes.) In the tennis example there is no deception involved because the disruptive behavior is apparent to the opponent and anyone watching the match and no formal rules are violated, although the issue of tacit agreement is important. Psychological combat might be perceived as extraneous to the essence of tennis, which is a competition of skill and strategy based on stroke production, placement, velocity, and so forth. Leaman concludes that it is just not clear whether this common behavior in tennis is cheating; therefore it is difficult to define cheating. I want to say two things about this argument.

First, for a reason that is apparent, Leaman picks a borderline or questionable case. But I find the example unconvincing. Consider John McEnroe's well-known behavior when he played professional tennis. It was uncivil, unsportsmanlike, childish, paranoid—in a word, inappropriate. But has anyone ever called McEnroe a cheater? This just isn't an example of cheating, is it? Why? As I have recommended, we ought to look at our core notion of cheating to answer the question. The behavior may be unsportsmanlike, but I don't see anything unfair about it. Psychological strength in combating such tactics is a part of tennis as well as other sports. (Think of a batter in baseball stepping out on a pitcher who works quickly and is in his rhythm or, for that matter, a pitcher who attempts to disrupt the batter by using delaying tactics.) The positive part of Leaman's analysis is his recognition that "latent agreements" are a central issue when we decide whether a person is attempting to place himself in an unfair competitive advantage. Here, however, the fact that such behavior is a part of the game leads to a determinate conclusion.

Moreover, in moving to the question of what's wrong with cheating, the example is used in a logically suspect manner. Leaman argues that the definitional indeterminacy means that it also is difficult to determine when rules are broken or when fair play occurs. Since the cheater still plays, the game hasn't broken down, and "many competitions, especially those with some sort of authority present to regulate cheating, would be more interesting if cheating takes place within it, or if several players try to stretch the rules."[9] Clearly, to show that cheating can be part of the structure of a sport—and an interesting part at that—you need a determinate judgment that some behavior *is* cheating and can or has become an interesting part of the structure of the sport. But Leaman has just argued that our judgments concerning examples of cheating are (often or always?) indeterminate. He seems now to assume what he has just denied. If the tennis example is uncertain, it may not show that cheating is "an option which both sides may morally take up,"[10] since it may not be an example of cheating at all. And if I am right, it isn't. At the least, what Leaman needs is a transparent paradigm case of cheating to support his conclusion, but he has failed to offer one.

I think his argument looks something like this. Suppose I hold that pornography is morally evil since it harms in some way. Suppose a critic argues that it is difficult to define pornography and urges us to consider *The Tropic of Capricorn* or *Last Tango in Paris*. These works have aesthetic value, harm no one, and thus are not morally evil. I can always hold that the critic hasn't supported his conclusions since he hasn't given me examples of pornographic works. My strategy would be to look at *Debbie Does Dallas* and *Deep Throat* to answer the difficult moral questions, since our judgments about these particulars are more clear than our judgments about borderline cases. We need to be sure that the examples are in fact instances of the concept in question. My critic's strategy is to stress the definitional difficulty and then use a determinate judgment—inconsistently, I believe—about a borderline case in order to purchase a questionable moral conclusion.

I should also add that I find Leaman's remarks about the possibly interesting nature of cheating to be irrelevant to his moral conclusion. I assume that "interesting" has something to do with the aesthetic criterion of merit sometimes called complexity,[11] which might be contrasted with the aesthetically monotonous or the boring. No doubt, the kind of murders described by Dorothy Sayers and Agatha Christie are more "interesting" than the ones often found in ordinary life. They are murders nonetheless.

With regard to hockey violence, Leaman argues that hockey training is such that "both the players and . . . the spectators will expect a skillful player to be good at cheating, where this involves breaking the rules when it is most advantageous to his side."[12] I agree. Given the way that hockey is taught and played, spectators and players expect the kind of behavior that Leaman describes. But that is precisely why such behavior is *not* cheating. To draw this conclusion he has simply used an overly simplified version of cheating, "breaking rules," that he has already criticized. He should be (and is) aware that the whole issue of the conventions of the sport is central to what is reasonably expected as "latent agreements." Such expectations are central to what it would mean to attempt to gain an unfair advantage. To admit that players and spectators expect certain behavior suggests to me that the behavior isn't cheating. It may not be admirable or virtuous, but that is a separate issue. Leaman is right that hockey violence is behavior "both sides may morally take up" (in the sense of morality related to cheating); he is wrong that this is cheating. I conclude that the version of skepticism expressed by Leaman has not been adequately supported.

It is natural at this point to turn to Craig Lehman's provocative piece. Although his concerns are somewhat different, his use of a central counterexample to fuel his argument is similar in structure to Leaman's strategy, and the issue of tacit conventions associated with hockey is similar to the conventions associated with Gaylord Perry's spitball.

Ostensibly, Lehman is most interested in the incompatibility thesis: whether one can, from the logical point of view, compete or win by breaking the rules, that is, by cheating. Since rules define the very nature of the game, wouldn't breaking rules entail that the game isn't played at all? Can cheaters play the game? Yes they can, according to Lehman, and there's nothing morally wrong with this. The purists mistakenly suppose a certain "romanticized social context"[13] that demands absolute adherence to rules and ignores the customs surrounding the game.

Lehman's main counterexample to the incompatibility thesis is the fact that Gaylord Perry (among others, I would add) threw a spitball—actually a "doctored" baseball—for many years. Such behavior involved a deliberate violation of the rules of baseball. Lehman asks, "Does anyone seriously want to say that no baseball game is ever played when Perry pitches?"[14] Of course not, but that seems to be entailed by the incompatibility thesis. Hence we are forced to admit that deliberate violations of rules (that is, cheating) do not logically disallow the cheater from playing the game. The incompatibility thesis must be rejected.

Moreover, this counterexample and many more that could be generated (e.g., offensive holding in football) arise because the defenders of the incompatibility thesis appear to ignore the larger social context in which games are played. "The counterexamples all seem to stem from social custom or convenience (i.e., utility). Games are played within a framework of social practices and priorities, and violations of rules must be assessed within this framework to determine whether competition and victory, in the normal sense of the words, have occcurred."[15] Again, custom seems the great guide in life. The spitball is part of baseball; it didn't end with Burleigh Grimes. Gaylord Perry and Don Sutton probably will not be the last Hall of Famers who made a living throwing such pitches. "Perfect adherence to every rule"[16] is not required in order to compete and win. Who would want to take exception to this conclusion?

I fully agree with Lehman on one central point. Perry was playing the game. Lehman is surely right about that. But I contend that he wasn't cheating. If the incompatibility thesis requires strict adherence to rules as a necessary condition of competing and winning, then Lehman has falsified the incompatibility thesis. But deliberate violation of rules isn't necessarily cheating, in my view, precisely because of Lehman's additional points that attempt to explain why Perry was playing the game. The same arguments that show why Perry was in fact playing, also show why he wasn't cheating, since the conventions or customs, however you want to put it, allow for the possibility of such behavior. After all, attempting to throw spitballs is part of the game. Lehman hasn't shown that cheaters can play the game.

I have argued that cheating essentially involves the intent to gain an unfair advantage. What we need to ask in any specific context is this: What would it mean to place the other in an unfair competitive advantage? The tacit conventions of a sport broaden the range of permissible behavior beyond mere strict adherence to the rules and create an atmosphere in which expectations arise. These expectations, it seems to me, are crucial for understanding cheating. Lehman has concluded that cheaters *can* play the game only because he has equated cheating with deliberate violations of rules, but that's too simple. With regard to throwing doctored baseballs, it's not as if every pitcher is encouraged to do this. After all, if a player is caught he can be ejected. But "loading one up" is part of the history and the ethos of professional baseball. The risks are clear to everyone. Throwing a spitball is more like setting a moving pick in basketball (not cheating) than playing an illegal player (cheating).

Again, I agree with Lehman that "between the extremes of angelic obedience to rules and destruction of a game by wholesale violation of its rules"[17] is the locus of the actual playing of sports. I hold, however, that the avoidance of cheating does not demand angelic obedience to rules, as Lehman seems to assume. In fact it may not even rest in the mean between the extremes, since we can violate a variety of rules, strategically or otherwise, and still play the game. Cheating lies in the extreme described by "destruction of the game," because it involves such central violations of the game, as defined by written rules and customs. Perry's spitball didn't violate the integrity of baseball. Notice also that, as in the cases of McEnroe or the hockey thug, it's somewhat unusual to speak of Gaylord Perry as a cheater. I don't think I'm stipulating in a trivial way the meaning of cheating. Lehman himself explains, parenthetically, that he is consulting the "conventional meaning" of certain phrases and "the ordinary meanings of words."[18]

With regard to Lehman's moral conclusions, it should be obvious why he wouldn't be bothered by the kind of "cheating" exemplified by Perry's spitball. He associates the proscription on cheating with angelic obedience to rules, to ensure that such behavior would not interfere with the purpose of the game, the test of skill. I agree that speaking of *the* purpose of a game is oversimplified and the purposes of the game must include the customs generated in its historical development. That is why we must admit that avoiding cheating doesn't require angelic obedience to rules.

By accepting Lehman's emphasis on custom to help us decide what is appropriate behavior or what is tacitly agreed upon, has the definitional question become "insoluble," as Leaman argues,[19] because of the vagueness of the notion? I don't think so. As I have said, the judgment concerning what is appropriate and what is impermissible (cheating) will not always be clear-cut. The issue of reasonable expectations will involve a judgment of practical wisdom, informed by experience and knowledge of the tradition. Consider baseball again. Anyone who knows much about baseball will realize that stealing signs, breaking up double plays by going out of the base path, getting as deep as possible in the batter's box (that is, trying to get your foot *out* of the batter's box), watering down base paths, and throwing brushback pitches are "part of the game." I am not a prude when it comes to what is permissible or impermissible in sport. When I played and coached I could never have been charged with being morally priggish. But it seems to me that the critics' arguments either strip the meaning from our concept of cheating or make it more indeterminate than it really is. If a college baseball coach hires a prejudiced umpire, knowingly plays an ineligible player, or orders his players to disable the opposing star player, he's a cheater. He is ruthless and cares nothing about the integrity of athletic competition.

Leaman and Lehman have argued persuasively that deliberately violating a written rule is not necessarily morally wrong, may be part of the game, and does not entail that one is not playing the game. However, by including in the analysis of cheating a reference to the customs or shared latent agreements surrounding a sport, what I have called the prescriptive atmosphere of a sport, we must conclude that they have not been able to show that cheating can be equated with "deliberately violating a written rule." Because cheating involves the attempt to gain an unfair advantage over your opponent by violating the agreements underlying the game, cheating is morally impermissible, can never be part of the game, and disqualifies the cheater from competing and thus winning.

———————————

Some will have the not-so-vague feeling that I've begged the whole question by the way I've set up the problem and analyzed the concept of cheating. After all, if cheating essentially involves attempting to gain an unfair advantage, then it's clear that cheating must be morally wrong. The critics offer counterexamples to show why cheating is permissible and then I simply agree that the behavior in question is permissible but I deny that it's really cheating. Am I simply stipulating in a trivial manner a meaning of cheating that leads directly to my conclusion?

In a sense, I admit that that is what I've done, but I think there is good reason for it. After all, I'm defending conventional wisdom. Another way of saying this is to say I'm analyzing our ordinary understanding of cheating, and it seems to me that the critics have failed to consider examples of cheating at all. It is often said that cheating is comparable, for various reasons, to lying. However, the prohibition against lying seems less stringent than the prohibition against cheating. For example, our concept of lying admits the distinction between a justified lie, a "white" lie, and a more egregious lie. Compare this to our concept of murder. Murder involves *unjustified* killing. We may argue about whether a certain act is murder or manslaughter or justifiable homicide, and our arguments involve appeals to intention, motive, and character. If we decide that an act of killing is murder, then we know it's wrong. In this sense, I believe that our concept of cheating is more like our concept of murder than our concept of lying.[20]

Our arguments about cheating in sport usually involve arguments concerning whether the behavior is or is not cheating, assuming that if one can show that it *is* cheating, in the way I have argued, then one will have shown the behavior is wrong. I have not trivially stipulated what cheating means; I have described what we mean by cheating. And that explains, finally, why the conclusions offered by Leaman and Lehman are so jarring to our intuitions. Cheating can't be right, can it?[21]

8 Sportsmanship
and Blowouts

As a player and a coach, I've been on both sides in blowouts, games in which a team won by a lopsided score. If my team was crushed, I felt worse than I would have had our team been more competitive. If I was fortunate to be on the winning side, I attempted to be gracious in closing out the game and relating to opponents after the game. I assumed that such graciousness was an important part of sportsmanship. As a player, I learned to be gracious. As a coach, I've insisted that my players behave this way. In contrast, attempting to "run up the score," to beat an opponent as badly as possible, was, I thought, a clear example of bad sportsmanship. Silly me. If Nicholas Dixon is right in his article "On Sportsmanship and 'Running Up the Score'"[1] I have been fundamentally misguided by the acceptance of a common but mistaken part of the moral framework of the sports world.

There are others who have rejected this piece of supposed moral wisdom associated with the language and traditions of sportsmanship. The most notable recent example is college basketball coach Billy Tubbs. During the 1997–98 season at Texas Christian University, as he had in the past, Tubbs took pride in crushing his opponents as badly as possible. In a 138–75 blowout of noted basketball power Delaware State, he not only kept his starters in until late in the game, he also was still using a press with four minutes to go. Tubbs is quoted in *Sports Illustrated* (January 1998) as saying: "Our job as coaches is to make our team look as good as it possibly can and the other team as bad . . . That's called winning."

To give Tubbs some credit, he does offer a reason for his view, although his reason isn't a very good one. To defend the traditional view of what might be called "blowout ethics," we will need to do more than simply respond to Tubb's seemingly thin view of what he's about as coach. His position, that there's nothing really wrong with "running up the score," is interestingly and powerfully defended by Nicholas Dixon. Dixon is no smirking curmudgeon, poking fun at the sentimentality of common views of sportsmanship. His case against what he calls the "anti-blowout thesis" is a strong challenge to one of the central assumptions associated with sportsmanship. His arguments show why the issue is important. It involves basic views about the nature of sport and our attitudes toward competition, the pursuit and display of excellence, and the importance of victory.

As I have said, my own intuitions are contrary to Dixon's position. He believes that no current model of sportsmanship, including my own, can show that pursuing a blowout is unsporting. If he is right, then, he says, my "intuition is no more than a prejudice" (OS, 11). I believe Dixon is wrong, and that there are good arguments to show why such behavior is unsporting. If this is the case, the traditional view is no mere prejudice. However, I do want to qualify what I am arguing. I am most familiar with the particularities of baseball, having played and coached this sport at virtually all levels for many years. Hence, my examples and my arguments will be directed in a sport-specific manner. I believe analogous arguments are effective for most other sports, but I'm convinced that good judgments about sportsmanship often require an insider's understanding and appreciation of the particularities of a sport and its relevant customs and traditions. I leave it to others to extend these arguments in obvious ways to other sports.

Nicholas Dixon argues against what he takes to be a widely held view of sportsmanship and blowouts. He calls this the anti-blowout thesis (AB):

AB: It is intrinsically unsporting for players or teams to maximize the margin of victory after they have secured victory in a one-sided contest (OS, 1).

Let's call a person who supports the traditional view of the relationship between sportsmanship and blowouts a "traditionalist," and let's call a person who rejects this view a "critic." Must the traditionalist support Dixon's formulation of the AB thesis?

First note that the AB thesis stresses the "intrinsic" nature of the actions at issue. This is an important aspect of Dixon's criticism of the traditional view. For example, he restates his thesis in this way: "there is absolutely nothing intrinsically wrong with pressing for a lopsided victory in a *competitive* game" (OS, 3); later he insists that lopsided defeats "are not intrinsically humiliating in the strong sense that they are prima facie morally wrong" (OS, 4). One can anticipate where the argument is heading. If pressing for a lopsided victory always expresses a morally bad intention, for example, wanting to humiliate an opponent, then such an action would be "intrinsically wrong." But it may not express such an intention, and the action's wrongness would then depend on the relevant intention. Hence, it wouldn't necessarily be intrinsically wrong to run up the score. Moreover, on consequentialist grounds, if such actions do not, in fact, humiliate opponents, then the actions would not be intrinsically wrong. Consider an instance of lying. A deontologist might hold that an act of lying is wrong just because it is an instance of a type of action: lying. A Kantian deontologist might further explain that an act of lying is absolutely intrinsically wrong because such an act could not be an expression of a good will, or the intention to act from duty, insofar as the moral rule (or maxim) describing the action could not be universalizable. A virtue theorist might hold that lying is intrinsically wrong because it is always an expression of dishonesty, a vice, rather than the virtue of honesty.

On the other hand, the act consequentialist evaluates an action in terms of the goodness or badness of the consequences that arise as a result of the action. For the act consequentialist, there are no intrinsically wrong actions, since the moral evaluation of the act depends on factors that are not intrinsic to the act.

Must the traditionalist hold that it is intrinsically wrong to attempt to maximize the margin of victory after victory has been secured? Not necessarily. It will depend on the moral theory held by the traditionalist. Such a theory would explain what makes actions right or wrong, or it would offer some account of the basis and nature of the virtues.

Consider again the example of lying. Kant's ethical theory was forced to confront one notorious problem: the possible conflict of two absolutely binding or exceptionless moral duties. In the standard textbook example, how could Kant's ethics give coherent guidance to a person hiding a Jewish family in Nazi-occupied Holland when the commandant comes to the house inquiring whether Jews are being harbored there? Kant holds that it is absolutely wrong to lie—no exceptions. In this situation, however, the duty to help persons fleeing Nazi oppression is stronger than the duty to tell the truth. But to say that it is not absolutely intrinsically wrong to lie, or that it could on occasion be morally permissible to lie, does not deny that it is prima facie morally wrong to lie. This is the language that W. D. Ross introduced to argue that lying is typically wrong.[2] We have a duty to tell the truth unless some more important duty overrides truth-telling in a particular situation. To say that we have a prima facie duty to tell the truth is to hold that in any situation there is a strong moral presumption against lying.

Likewise, a virtue theorist recognizes that honesty is a morally praise-worthy trait of character. But the Aristotelian emphasizes that honesty is not simply the strict adherence to an absolutely binding moral rule. It is a developed disposition to make wise choices in a whole range of situations that require not only resisting the temptation to tell outright lies. Good moral character may be expressed in situations in which it would not be virtuous to be *too* honest, as, for example, when Aunt Alice asks what you think about her beautiful new hat.

The view that lying is prima facie wrong, not absolutely wrong, or that the honest person may on occasion not tell the truth squares well with our common moral consciousness. To recognize the moral impor-tance of truth-telling or honesty, one need not be forced to defend the kind of absolutism characteristic of Kant's ethics. Nor does one need to agree with certain contemporary defenders of absolutism who believe that there are types of conduct that are "really right and wrong"; therefore, they must defend the view that it could *never* be right to engage in certain kinds of action.

Now we are in a better position to formulate the traditional view of the relationship between sportsmanship and blowouts. Dixon believes that the traditionalist must embrace the AB thesis as he formulates it. But the defender need not be saddled with this absolutist view. The tra-ditionalist may admit that there are occasions when maximizing the margin of victory might be called for. For example, there might be a sit-uation in a tournament where one of the tie-breakers for advancing to the championship is total runs scored. This might reasonably call for pursuing a lopsided victory. But such situations are relatively rare—or so the traditionalist maintains. Usually it's unsporting to attempt to run up the score, and that's the view that is widely and plausibly held in the sports community.[3] Finding a plausible counterexample to the AB the-sis need not defeat the traditional view. I will call this view the revised anti-blowout thesis (RAB):

RAB: It is prima facie unsporting for players or teams to maximize the margin of victory after they have secured victory in a one-sided contest.

One of the strengths of Dixon's argument is his attempt to force the traditionalist to think about the reasons for the traditional point of view of blowout ethics. I believe the critic is right that one can imagine situations in which maximizing the margin of victory is not unsporting. But the traditionalist maintains that these situations are relatively rare, and for a variety of reasons, pressing for blowouts will require quite strong overriding factors. In most cases, the traditionalist insists, these overriding factors are absent, and thus it is typically unsporting to run up the score.

What can be said in support of the RAB thesis? First, it seems natural to locate the unsportingness of running up the score in relationships to opponents. But it is important to describe in a psychologically appropriate manner the reactions of opponents to being blown out. It is sometimes said that the attempt to beat an opponent as badly as possible expresses the desire to humiliate him, since he will in fact be humiliated when he is badly beaten. However, that seems much too strong, for a number of reasons. It is more appropriate to say that suffering a lopsided loss is often embarrassing, for obvious and natural reasons. To lose is to fail, and to lose badly is to fail badly. Sport is an arena in which there are standards of excellence, and the desire to be good is at the heart of the competitive athlete's participation in sports. Being good as an athlete may not be as important, in some sense, as being good as a human being, or being good as a physician, teacher, or scientist, but it is a legitimate and strongly desired kind of goodness.[4] To lose is to fail to be as good as one wants to be in a certain situation, so losing badly normally carries with it the pain of recognizing the significant gap between one's desires and the reality of one's actual talents and abilities. "Pouring it on" or "rubbing it in," however one might describe the phenomenon, is rubbing the opponent's nose in his failure and at least momentary badness. To do so is typically an expression of a lack of graciousness and respect for others' feelings or emotions, just as it would be if Jill kept reminding Jack of how miserably he failed the scholarship exam. Hence, it is prima facie unsporting to attempt to crush the opponent as badly as possible because it fails, in a significant way, to respect one's opponent. It is analogous to situations in everyday life in which one person occasions in another, in an insensitive and sometimes callous manner, natural negative psychological reactions to loss and failure.

Of course, it's difficult to know what the reaction of opponents will be. But you can be certain of your own reactions, and because of this you are in a position to make use of one of the great principles of ethical life.

To be a good sport in particular, as well as being a good person in general, often requires that we consider the perspectives of other people and attempt to see things from an impartial perspective. Consider the Golden Rule, which encourages such impartiality as the key to morally appropriate conduct. For our purposes, the so-called "Silver Rule," "Do not do to others what you do not want them to do to you," is a particularly useful guide.[5] You may confront some opponent who both pursues blowouts and consistently accepts them without reproach, but in my experience such people are rare in sports. In most cases the Silver Rule would prohibit a competitor from wanting to crush an opponent as badly as possible, because of the competitor's own reactions to opponents who seek to do this to him and the moral appropriateness of impartiality.

A second important line of argument supports the RAB thesis. Sport is by its very nature competitive. But there are two different senses in which a game or a match might be said to be "competitive." In the weak sense, if I play against any opponent who literally *opposes* me and makes it possible to have a game or match, then the activity is competitive. In the strong sense, a game or match is competitive if it involves opponents whose skills or talents are relatively equal, where the game or match is a *good* one. It's good, because the outcome is a result of opponents whose talents are tested by the other, where dramatic tensions create uncertainty about the outcome (at least at some point after the game has begun), and where excellence is a result of being challenged to perform at one's highest level. In this sense a coach may thank his defeated, weaker team for being competitive against a stronger team, or he might offer consoling remarks that his weaker team made the stronger one work for victory. His remarks indicate another way to explain the distinction. The weak sense of "competition" simply makes a descriptive claim: as a matter of fact, a contest occurs in which there are opponents, rules, and the possibility of victory. The strong sense of "competition" carries some evaluative weight. To say that a game or match is competitive in the strong or evaluative sense indicates successful or good competition, hence the subject of possible praise.

What happens in a blowout? One of the following conditions obtain: the opponents are mismatched, in the sense that one is much stronger than the other, so the winner does not face a worthy, or "competitive," opponent; a usually worthy opponent plays unusually poorly; a player or team plays unusually well; one of the participants in the competition is either unusually fortunate or unusually unfortunate; or some combination of these factors occur. Since the issue of winning has already been resolved in a blowout, the outcome is not in doubt. The game is no longer—and perhaps was not from the start—competitive in the strong sense. In fact, competition in this sense has broken down. If players or teams attempt to maximize the margin of victory after they have secured victory in a one-sided contest, I believe they fail to respect true or real competition. True competition, good competition, requires being challenged or tested by worthy opponents. In a blowout this factor is at least momentarily absent.

Moreover, good competition often occasions excellence, the best performances that players and teams can achieve. These performances are expressions of the best things a sport has to offer, rare and wonderful moments amidst intense competition. In respecting good competition, players and teams show respect for the very sport in which they are engaged. This leads us to a more sport-specific understanding of the ethics of blowouts. Let's call this aspect of sportsmanship "respect for the game."[6] Consider a baseball game between a very good team and a very bad team (or a team having an unusually terrible game). Suppose the team being blown out makes numerous errors (both physical and mental). The pitcher is wild and has mediocre stuff, the catcher has bad hands and a weak arm, and so forth. Suppose the score is 18–0 by the third inning. The coach of the winning team is relentless in scoring more runs. He avoids substitutions and continues to steal bases, hit and run, bunt, and to take extra bases when possible, although the run-rule (the "mercy" rule) does not take effect until the fifth inning. One who loves baseball and respects its highest possibilities might say this isn't "real" baseball, by which he appropriately judges that the winning coach fails to "respect the game."

In fact, respect for the game of baseball requires respect for its traditions and customs, not just its central formal rules. Knowing and understanding these customs is an important part of sportsmanship in baseball. Knowing how to act in light of these customs is not always easy. It requires experience and good judgment. In addition, customs change. In baseball it's now more acceptable than in the past to steal bases when significantly ahead. Aluminum bats have made large leads more unsafe in high school and college baseball. So it's now more acceptable than it was in the past for a team to aggressively attempt to score more runs even when it has a large lead. But there is still some point at which it is judged to be unsporting in baseball to steal bases when ahead. It's permissible to throw inside, step out of the batter's box to disrupt the rhythm of a pitcher, quick-pitch, slide hard to break up a double play, and steal signs. On the other hand, blowout ethics is a central aspect of sportsmanship in baseball. When a team has a huge lead, players should not steal, bunt for a hit, squeeze, or do anything that they would normally do strategically in order to score more runs.

Does this mean that baseball players and coaches are required to "ease up" in blowouts, and wouldn't that be contrary to the duty to respect competition and opponents by playing as hard as one can at all times? Here I would make another important distinction. In one sense, to ease up might be to play less hard, to expend less effort. In another sense, to ease up involves strategy, not effort. In the second sense, to ease up is to avoid strategies that are usually taken to score runs. In a baseball blowout, it is appropriate to ease up in the strategic sense, not in the sense of effort. All players are required to play hard, even in a blowout. But one of the obvious things coaches can do to hold down the score is to put in backup players who will play hard but not be as effective in scoring runs. On the other hand, even backup players might be able to steal bases at will, but stealing bases in blowouts is strategically inappropriate.

The problems with such appeals to tradition in a moral argument is that they can always be undermined, in principle, by the normative question: "Well, I know it's a tradition (or custom), but why should I accept the tradition? Perhaps there are good reasons to reject the tradition." I recognize that there is a certain autonomy to such a normative query,[7] but the fact that some norm or kind of behavior is part of an established tradition grounds a presumption. The attempt to build a prima facie case against the pursuit of blowouts has moved from our relationship to opponents, to the nature of competition, and finally to the traditions specific to baseball. I suspect the tradition in baseball that judges as unsporting the pursuit of lopsided victories is grounded in the very concerns that we have been discussing. To respect baseball is to respect one's opponents and the specific competitive aspects of the game. When coaches or teams run up the score in baseball, they are judged to be in the business of embarrassment and shallow self-glorification; they are not in the business of what baseball is about. In the language of baseball, it's wrong to "show up" an opponent.

It's also important to note that athletic accomplishments in at least certain kinds of blowouts are tainted, or at least undervalued by the sports community. Players or coaches who attempt to "pad statistics" in blowouts show no respect for displaying excellence and no respect for the game. Significant athletic excellence requires worthy opponents who can challenge a team or player. Suppose the coach plays the Star for the entire game in the first round of a tournament against an extremely weak team. The coach, let's suppose, is a critic of the AB thesis and is committed to the "display of excellence" in a game, even a blowout. The Star goes five for five, hits two home runs, drives in eight runs, and gets the postgame interview as "star of the game." In the remaining games of the tournament he is hitless in ten at bats. In the championship game, he leaves eight runners on base and his team loses. He finishes the tournament hitting .333, leading all players in homeruns and runs batted in. Big deal. Did he have a good tournament? Should he be placed on the all-tournament team? Of course not.

We are now in a position to evaluate Dixon's case against the AB thesis. He believes that there are no good arguments for this thesis and that there are important considerations that positively count against it. First, let's consider what he takes to be two central lines of argument for the AB thesis. We'll call these the Gratuity Argument and the Humiliation Argument.

The Gratuity Argument goes like this:

1. In sport the only thing that matters is winning.
2. If the only thing that matters in sport is winning, then running up the score after victory is secured is gratuitous.
3. People ought to avoid gratuitous actions.
4. Therefore, people ought to avoid the attempt to maximize the margin of victory after they have secured victory in a one-sided contest. (OS, 3)

Dixon reasonably rejects the first premise because there are other important things that matter in sports. "Players who win blowouts can be justly proud of their display of athletic excellence, the personal and team records they have set, and the excitement provided for fans" (OS, 3).

The first odd thing about the Gratuity Argument involves what to make of the kind of prescription it offers. Perhaps from some point of view we ought to avoid unnecessary or groundless actions, but it's not clear what the moral force is of this "ought" in the argument. If winning is the only thing that matters in sport, then maximizing the margin of victory may be gratuitous, but why would such conduct be unsporting? Rather, it would seem to be unreasonable or irrational or unnecessary. I'm uncertain why Dixon thinks this is an argument for the intrinsically unsporting nature of pursuing blowouts.

Moreover, I agree with Dixon that there's more to sport than winning, or that winning is not the only thing that matters in sport. But given the arguments in the last section, appealing to the display of athletic excellence, records, or excitement for fans would not lead one to reject the AB thesis. As I have argued, crushing a weak opponent or beating up a normally worthy opponent who is having a bad day is not an adequate measure of athletic excellence, nor are such records achieved against weak opponents particularly noteworthy. In responding to this kind of argument, Dixon says this: "While the superior team's victory may never be in doubt, its manner of victory can be most revealing" (OS, 7). But beating a weak opponent by 20 runs in baseball reveals little more than beating the opponent by 10 runs. It often indicates more about the weakness of the opponent than the excellence of the winner. And the appeal to the excitement of the fans is irrelevant. The reaction of the fans is extrinsic to the essential elements involved in sports: competing with opponents, pursuing excellence and victory, and having fun. These are the key elements that ground our judgments about sportsmanship. There are other things besides winning that matter in sport, and it is reflecting on these things that leads one to *accept* the RAB thesis.

Dixon spends much more time examining what I will call the Humiliation Argument.

1. If players or teams maximize the margin of victory after they have secured victory in a one-sided contest, then the opponents who suffer such defeats are humiliated and diminished as human beings.
2. People ought not to humiliate other human beings.
3. Therefore, people ought not to maximize the margin of victory after they have secured victory in a one-sided contest. (OS, 3)

Unlike the Gratuity Argument, the Humiliation Argument clearly has moral force, since the actions in question supposedly harm or inflict a kind of cruelty on the defeated opponent. Dixon rejects the first premise of this argument, because he denies that losing badly in a sporting contest humiliates the defeated: "Neither victory nor defeat affects one's worth as a human being" (OS, 3). Nor is one humiliated as an *athlete*, rather than as a human being, because such a claim "indicates an inflated estimate of the importance of the outcomes of sporting contests" (OS, 4). Even if opponents *feel* humiliated, we need not be morally concerned about such reactions, since these negative perceptions would be based on a "misconception" (OS, 5) about the importance of the outcome of sporting contests.

I agree with much of what Dixon says here, but his objections to the Humiliation Argument leave untouched the strength of the considerations I have previously offered. Losing badly may not diminish one's worth as a human being, nor humiliate one in a strong sense, but it is the experience of loss and extreme failure, made public, and hence the actual occasion for quite negative perceptions. On the one hand, Dixon is right that sensitivity to negative perceptions need not always be respected. One need not respect the reactions of racists to interracial relationships nor the philistine's reactions to Michaelangelo's "David." On the other hand, embarrassment or psychological pain does morally count in our deliberations, especially when such reactions are not based on misconceptions or some kind of shallowness. The opponent who is crushed need not be suffering from any kind of intellectual or moral deficiency when he reacts negatively.

Dixon insists that he is not defending coaches and players who do want to humiliate their opponents, since the "wrongness of such actions consists in the *intention* to harm" (OS, 5). He simply denies that pursuing blowouts does harm, in the strong sense of "humiliate," and one may have morally permissible intentions in pursuing blowouts, insofar as players or teams may desire the display of excellence, setting records, and exciting fans. But if I am right, blowouts do typically embarrass. They also fail to respect both competition, and in the case of baseball, the game and its traditions.

Dixon also argues that "none of several currently favored theories of sportsmanship supports the AB thesis" (OS, 1). He discusses the view I have defended,[8] in which I primarily counter James Keating's well-known account of sportsmanship. My view, Dixon believes, does place moral demands on competitors. To see sportsmanship as a mean between the excessive seriousness of the ruthless competitor and the excessive playfulness of one who is frivolous and doesn't care about excellence and victory rules out cheating and "any form of disrespect for opponents" (OS, 9). I agree. Dixon denies that pursuing blowouts disrespects opponents. As I have argued, I believe such behavior typically does fail to respect opponents, but in a sense weaker than humiliation. So even my earlier account leads to the RAB thesis. I have offered elsewhere a much more extensive account of sportsmanship based on the foundation I had previously offered.[9] That book attempts to explain more fully the principles of respect, including respect for opponents and respect for the game, that are important expressions of sportsmanship so conceived. The arguments I have offered here and in *Coaching for Character* are based on my model of sportsmanship, so I would deny Dixon's claim about the relationship between at least one currently favored theory of sportsmanship and the traditional view of blowout ethics.

Dixon also seems to believe that my view wouldn't entail easing up in an uneven contest (assuming that the AB thesis does require players or teams to ease up), because a sense of playfulness seems more compatible with "continuing to entertain fans with exciting, innovative plays, taking advantage of the freedom that is provided by having already secured victory" (OS, 9). In response, I have two points. My view requires that players or teams ease up only in the strategic sense, not in the sense of effort. Playing hard shows respect for opponents, pursuing blowouts doesn't. Second, Dixon seems to misunderstand at least part of my emphasis on the playful character of sport. To stress that sport is competitive *play* is to emphasize the intrinsic value of the activity and the experiences and values associated with human play. Play has no essential connection to entertainment, and the competitive play of sports offers its primary values to participants, not spectators. Playfulness does not entail a commitment to entertain fans. The deep paradox of sport involves the conjoining of the seriousness of competition with a sense of playfulness that recognizes and affirms the ultimate triviality of these concerns. This paradox is the basis for attempting to judge what kind of behavior is appropriate for such activities. The spirit of play is important for sportsmanship because it infuses the pursuit of victory and relationships to opponents with a sense of realism or clear vision about the relative unimportance of sports and the inappropriateness of the "winning is the only thing" view of sports.[10] Such a view often leads to bad sportsmanship. However, sport is competitive, so the good sport must respect the conditions of competition: fair play and pursuit of excellence and victory.

There's much to admire in Nicholas Dixon's criticism of the AB thesis. Like Dixon, I believe that winning is not the only thing that matters in sport. I also agree that losing need not humiliate a person, since the outcome of relatively trivial activities like sporting contests is not as important as many persons seem to believe. He's right that overestimating the importance of victory often leads to cheating, drug abuse, and scandal (OS, 11). But such reflections need not lead to the rejection of the traditional view of blowouts. A deep concern for the value of sportsmanship supports the tradition in holding that it's usually unsporting to run up the score.

9 *Sport, Character,*
and Virtue

I think it's the commercials that did it. Most American sports
fans have seen them. You're watching a college athletic contest, time-
out is called, and the commercial advertisements begin to drone. Then
He appears. He's poised, articulate, and successful—I mean really successful! He's probably the CEO of a major corporation. He smiles and explains
that he was once a second-string guard at State University. The camera
pans to old footage of a State game where number 68, playing courageously with no face mask, is leading a sweep into the end zone—of course.
He tells us that playing sports taught him hard work, determination,
competitive drive, and teamwork, just those qualities of character that
he needed in order to be successful in megabusiness. Yes, intercollegiate
athletics is really important. Now back to the game . . . The announcers
then mention that State University is currently under investigation by
the NCAA for recruiting violations, tampering with transcripts, using
substitute test-takers for *scholar*-athletes, providing free cars for players,
and illegally providing bail money and support for drug rehabilitation.
Character, you say?

I confess at the outset that I find this issue vexing. Something like the
character building view of sport appears to be part of the prevailing orthodoxy of the sports world. It's not just the NCAA public relations people
who want to persuade others of the moral importance of participating in
athletic competition. Coaches, administrators, educators, and the ordinary

person on the street are often heard rejoicing in the lessons taught, the values conveyed, and the virtues developed by playing sports. Gerald Ford offers not a unique but surely a quintessential expression of this orthodoxy. "Broadly speaking, outside of a national character and an educated society, there are few things more important to a country's growth and well-being than competitive athletics. If it is a cliché to say athletics build character as well as muscle, then I subscribe to the cliché."[1]

On the other hand, it is difficult not to be skeptical of this cliché, not simply because it is trite or hackneyed or held by Jerry Ford and the majority of coaches we happen to have met. In *Sport: A Philosophic Inquiry,* Paul Weiss considers the character building view of athletics, only to dismiss it for what seem to be good reasons. In the context of ruminating on the attraction of athletics he describes the plausible view that good habits of character are developed by facing athletic challenges. However, to take the position seriously we would have to assume that most aspects of character are not formed much earlier than the age of sports participation. Moreover, it is not obvious that the character of children is developed by the sports experiences they often have, in which winning is overemphasized, injuries occur, and character is scarcely exemplified by screaming parents and coaches who lack self-control. "Sport does not, at least for some children, help them grow properly as bodies, and may hinder their growth in character."[2]

In addition, studies by social scientists have not been particularly kind to the orthodox view. One author concludes his review of ten years of research on the socialization effects of college athletic participation by saying that "the basic conclusion must remain that there is little valid evidence that participation in college athletics has any effect on the character of the athlete."[3] Another article's title sums up in a pithy manner the skeptical thesis: "Sport: If You Want to Build Character, Try Something Else."[4]

Also, we should not overlook the evidence of personal experience, however anecdotal and limited it might be. As I look back at my own experience, starting on ragged little baseball diamonds and cracker-box gymnasiums and ending with athletic competition for one of the major college athletic powerhouses in the country, I don't associate playing sports with building whatever character I happen to have. In fact it may have helped produce something akin to cynicism when I hear the pious declamations of Ford-like moralists. Institutions are poorly served by the charade of moral justification when they do nothing more than talk a good moral game. On the other hand—and it's just this interminable "on the other hand" that makes the issue so vexing—I think athletic participation has been important in the moral development of my oldest child, continues to be for the second, and I expect it to be for the youngest two. And then there's my philosophical colleague who told me that whatever character *he* happens to have was largely formed by participating in sports. What are we to make of so much conflicting evidence? What can a philosopher contribute to this issue?

There are a number of questions related to sport and character building that are philosophically interesting and relevant. Certainly the question whether sport does, in fact, cause the development of good character is in part an empirical one. But there are a host of other issues that can be addressed philosophically. What is it to have character? Good character seems to involve the question of virtue, for virtues are taken to be beneficial and praiseworthy traits of character. What is a virtue such that participation in sports might develop it? If sport did develop character or virtue, how would it do this? Are there moral dangers involved in sports participation? Are there natural threats to building character in sport? Which virtues might we expect to be developed by playing sports? Are there virtues specific to sports participation? Are there other important virtues that we wouldn't expect to be developed by sport? If there are, are they important for good character? Is there anything distinctive about sport, such that playing sports is especially important in developing character or virtue? (Gerald Ford appears to answer this question affirmatively.)

I would like tentatively to answer some of these questions by looking at some recent work in moral philosophy on the virtues.[5] In *After Virtue* Alasdair MacIntyre offers a conceptual account of the virtues that is particularly powerful as a way to get at some of the above questions. He argues that the natural home of the virtues resides in sustaining what he calls "practices," which, as we will see, include playing a given sport. He says of his theory that "this kind of conceptual account has strong empirical implications; it provides an explanatory scheme which can be tested in particular cases."[6] Hence, his theoretical account might help us make sense of the conflicting evidence found in various empirical studies concerned with sport and character. In the next section I pick out several of MacIntyre's main theses about the nature of virtue and relate these theses to sport. In the third section I examine MacIntyre's further arguments concerning virtue and the unity of a life. These arguments suggest that the character building thesis, if successful at all, is incomplete or offers a thin view of character. Finally, I look at other treatments of virtue and character to reinforce the view that sport only contingently and incompletely provides an arena for character formation.

In *After Virtue* MacIntyre attempts to write a philosophical history that will help us understand the problematic characteristics of our current moral discourse. For MacIntyre our current moral debates are characterized by disagreement because the rivals in these debates move validly from incommensurable moral premises. The problem is that "we possess no rational way of weighing the claims of one against another"[7] because we possess these premises as mere fragments, dislodged from the historical context in which they originally and specifically made sense. We experience moral language in an odd and paradoxical manner because we take moral reasons as impersonal criteria for action, yet the incommensurability of conflicting principles suggests that our ultimate moral principles are arbitrary, our moral positions nothing but expressions of private attitudes and feelings. MacIntyre's tour de force reconstructs the story of how we supposedly got ourselves into this mess, why we are unable to see this because of the prevailing ahistorical ways of doing moral philosophy, and how we might now confront this situation. The enlightenment project of justifying morality had to fail, and our emotivist, bureaucratic modern culture is the inevitable result. Only Nietzsche seemed to diagnose accurately the moral ills of modernism. We are left, in MacIntyre's view, with either an acceptance of Nietzsche's view that rational justification of morality fails and morality is "a set of rationalizations which conceal the fundamentally non-rational phenomena of will,"[8] or a return to some kind of premodern (or postmodern?) Aristotelian view of morality. To understand the dilemma of modernism and especially to appreciate the Aristotelian option, MacIntyre's narrative reconstructs the development of the notion of virtue in the ancient world and later. By the time the reader reaches the unifying chapter on the nature of the virtues he has encountered rich discussions of the virtues as lived and written about in Homeric society, in the Athens of Sophocles and Plato, and later, Aristotle, and in the world of New Testament writers and medieval thinkers.

The problem is the dazzling diversity of these accounts of virtues. "They offer us different and incompatible lists of virtues; and they have different and incompatible theories of the virtues."[9] Homer emphasizes physical excellence embodied in the warrior. Aristotle emphasizes *phronesis* (practical wisdom) and the virtues of an Athenian citizen. Faith, hope, and love are emphasized in the Christian tradition. Homer emphasizes qualities of character necessary for fulfilling specific social roles.

Aristotle stresses the role of virtue in relation to the telos of human nature. Christian virtues are also understood teleologically, but the good life for the Christian is in substantial ways quite different from the good life for the Athenian. MacIntyre discusses Jane Austen's notion that seems to combine the Homeric emphasis on social roles and Aristotelian teleology, and Benjamin Franklin's insistence on the virtues as useful.[10] What could these disparate accounts have in common? Is there a "core conception of a virtue" that can be derived from these different notions? MacIntyre's strategy is to understand virtue in relation to what he calls a "practice." Consider his central theses on the nature of the virtues:

> By a 'practice' I am going to mean any coherent and complex form of socially established cooperative human activity through which goods internal to that form of activity are realized in the course of trying to achieve those standards of excellence which are appropriate to, and partially definitive of, that form of activity, with the result that human powers to achieve excellence, and human conceptions of the ends and goods involved, are systematically extended.[11]

The first thing to note about MacIntyre's notion of a practice is how very broad it is. He mentions as examples such activities as farming, science, architecture, portrait painting, and chess. Even politics, in a sense, and helping to run a family could involve participation in a practice. For our purposes, however, one thing is quite clear. To play a sport is to engage in a practice. MacIntyre specifically mentions football and baseball in his discussion.[12] Crucial to his analysis is the distinction between internal and external goods. Suppose I teach my child to play baseball and he becomes an excellent young player. He might receive public recognition, a college scholarship, and even a professional contract. That is, he might achieve a variety of *external* goods—fame, education, money—from playing baseball. These are goods that can, logically, be achieved by engaging in other activities. For example, he might become well-known and respected in a community by starting a small business while still in high school. On the other hand, there are goods internal to the playing of baseball that cannot be explained, experienced, or understood apart from the specific context of the practice. For example, becoming an excellent line-drive hitter is an internal good in baseball. The list of possible internal goods associated with the practice of baseball appears to be quite long, including all of those skills necessary for becoming an excellent player or coach.

A practice involves standards of excellence and obedience to rules as well as achievement of goods.[13]

Internal goods arise because practices involve standards of excellence, ways of performing better or worse in achieving those goods. Practices develop as skills and abilities are advanced. Thus, practices have histories. They develop authoritative internal standards that provide objective criteria for performance. For example, in baseball it is understood that coaches know more than the players about how the game ought to be played. That is, they understand the tradition and try to show young players how to play better or well.

> External goods are . . . characteristically objects of competition in which there must be losers as well as winners. Internal goods are indeed the outcome of competition to excel, but . . . their achievement is a good for the whole community who participate in the practice.[14]

This point is also quite obvious in the context of sports. For example, Babe Ruth's power transformed the way in which higher levels of baseball are played. Dick Fosbury transformed high-jumping, and defensemen in hockey played differently after Bobby Orr's tremendous achievements. These are the most obvious examples, but successful innovations in playing and coaching specific sports appear often in less obtrusive ways. On the other hand, external goods like money, power, and fame are not typically communally shared. Little league all-star teams contain only a few players from the league; the headlines can only mention the hero; college athletic scholarships are limited; the Yankees need only so many catchers.

Now, how are we to connect these insights to the notion of virtue?

> A virtue is an acquired human quality the possession and exercise of which tends to enable us to achieve those goods which are internal to practices and the lack of which effectively prevents us from achieving any such goods.[15]

Whenever we engage in a practice we necessarily involve ourselves in a community of shared expectations, goals, and standards. As MacIntyre says, we subordinate ourselves to others with whom we share the experience of the practice. Certain things immediately follow from this. We must recognize both the authority of the tradition that has developed the standards informing a practice and authorities who are knowledgeable about the tradition and its standards. Some will be better than others in acquiring the abilities that enable a participant to achieve the goods internal to a practice. Those who are better *deserve* their lot. Participants must take *risks* since they may fail in achieving internal goods. To become better they must be *honest* about their shortcomings and respect authority. The conclusion about central virtues is easily purchased. "In other words we have to accept as necessary components of any practice with internal goods and standards of excellence the virtues of justice, courage and honesty."[16] MacIntyre insists, also, that such central virtues are required to sustain practices "whatever our private moral standpoint or our society's particular codes may be."[17] Hence, this scheme could satisfy the absolutist's desire for cross-cultural moral unity while retaining the relativist's sense of moral particularity.

We are now able to offer some initial tentative conclusions about sport and character in light of MacIntyre's account. Given the definitions of a practice and a virtue, it is easy to see why the character building view is so plausible. The young athlete needs to develop a keen sense of himself and his abilities in relation to the traditions of his sport. His development or simply his participation requires a certain honesty about himself, a respect for coaches who embody the tradition, a sense of who deserves or merits playing time, a feeling about the need for cooperation to achieve shared goals, courage in the face of failing to achieve standards, and persistence or determination in the attempt to achieve his goals. Since an athlete will participate in a variety of practices in life, if he really acquires or exercises justice, honesty, courage, and determination, because they enable him to achieve goods internal to his sport, he will benefit throughout life. At the same time, another interesting conclusion appears also to follow. It may be unsurprising that sports, as practices, might be occasions for the development of virtues. However, there is probably nothing distinctive, in this respect, about playing sports. The same could be said for participation in any practice. Contrary to what Jerry Ford might say, at this point the same arguments apply to arts, sciences, crafts, and so forth. If engaging in such practices might occasion the development of some central virtues, then the important thing is for young people to commit themselves substantially to *some* practice, not any specific one, like a sport. One might as well learn to play the violin rather than soccer.

Our conclusions are reinforced by considering Iris Murdoch's reflection on some related matters. For her, ethics ought to be concerned with the question, How can we make ourselves better?[18] (Notice Jerry Ford's answer to this question: Play sports!) She answers this question in the context of her view of human nature as essentially selfish, anxiety-ridden, and defensive.

> Our minds are continually active, fabricating an anxious, usually self-preoccupied, often falsifying *veil* which partially conceals the world. Our

states of consciousness differ in quality, our fantasies and reveries are not trivial and unimportant, they are profoundly connected with our energies and our ability to choose and act. And if quality of consciousness matters, then anything which alters consciousness in the direction of unselfishness, objectivity, and realism is to be connected with virtue.[19]

For Murdoch, the locus of moral development resides in experiences of "unselfing," in which the self pierces the veil of vanity and self-absorption and begins to see things as they are. While not claiming anything exclusive about the realm of the aesthetic, she emphasizes the moral power of experiences of natural beauty and art, in which the "brooding self" gives itself over to the reality of the world and forgets its obsessions. Good art confronts us with a more objective and less jaded sense of things. "Art transcends selfish and obsessive limitations of personality and can enlarge the sensibility of its consumer. It is a kind of goodness by proxy. Most of all it exhibits to us the connection in *human* beings, of clear realistic vision with compassion."[20]

As I suggested, Murdoch does not claim that art is preeminent in its role as educator of our moral vision. Recalling Plato's mistrust of the artist and his emphasis on mathematics as a *techne* (craft), she suggests that the virtues appear in many different kinds of human activities besides the arts. In sciences, crafts, and intellectual disciplines we see displayed "such concepts as justice, accuracy, truthfulness, realism, humility, courage as the ability to sustain clear vision, love as attachment or even passion without sentiment of self."[21] Murdoch's example is learning a language.

> If I am learning, for instance, Russian, I am confronted by an authoritative structure which commands my respect. The task is difficult and the goal is distant and perhaps never attainable. My work is a progressive revelation of something which exists independently of me. Attention is rewarded by a knowledge of reality. Love of Russian leads me away from myself towards something alien to me, something which my consciousness cannot take over, swallow up, deny or make unreal. The honesty and humility required of the student—not to pretend to know what one does not know—is the preparation for the honesty and humility of the scholar who does not even feel tempted to suppress the fact which damns the theory.[22]

Here we are not too far from MacIntyre's focus on the virtues required for the pursuit of goods internal to practices. Murdoch's stress on virtue as clear vision reinforces MacIntyre's sense of why the virtues are crucial to practices. For both, the self finds itself related to something over against which it must realistically come to be related. Murdoch says: "In intellectual disciplines and in the enjoyment of art and nature we discover value in our ability to forget self, to be realistic, to perceive justly."[23] I would add here that participating in sports *may* be able to educate us likewise, and that is why the character building view of sport should be taken seriously. Having said that, we might briefly pause to consider the downside of Murdoch's view before returning to MacIntyre's analysis.

If, as Murdoch suggests, the virtue-enhancing possibilities of an activity like a sport might reside in the way it occasions a sense of honesty, justice, and humility, (as selfless seeing of the way things are), then the extent to which young sports participants are not taught or helped to see things as they are will be morally inhibitive. Sport is a fecund area for dreams and fantasies, and wishful reveries are as much or more a part of the adult's experience as the child's. Think of the archetypical Little League parent, who pushes, goads, resents, blames, and punishes—all for the sake of a loving dream of athletic fame and wealth for a child whose talents might be limited and whose interests are sometimes even more meager. A child needs to be taught not only to have a keen sense of his strengths, in order to nurture ambition; he must also come to realize and have a keen sense of his own limitations, in order to make wise judgments about the plan of his life (more on this later). Murdoch mentions several difficult moral decisions, like situations involving care of the retarded or elderly, sustaining an unhappy marriage, or pursuing important goals that conflict with family relationships. For her, good moral judgments involve *seeing.* "The love which brings the right answer is an exercise of justice and realism and really *looking.* The difficulty is to keep the attention fixed upon the real situation and to prevent it from returning surreptitiously to the self with consolations of self-pity, resentment, fantasy and despair."[24] I believe Murdoch is right about this. One of the central barriers to building character in sport is the inability of people to perceive things truly.[25] Sometimes it's a matter of ignorance, as when a parent simply doesn't know enough about the traditions of a sport to realize a coach does understand who deserves to play or a child simply doesn't have enough natural ability to succeed in a given sport. Sometimes it's simply a function of illusion, as Murdoch says.[26] But the external pressures on the activity or practice are severe, as MacIntyre's further analysis shows.

As we have seen, when we engage in a practice we encounter others, both in an immediate and a historical sense. Hence the virtues mediate, in a positive sense, our human relationships internal to the practice. But something else happens in the historical life of practices:

> Practices must not be confused with institutions. Chess, physics and medicine are practices; chess clubs, laboratories, universities, and hos-

pitals are institutions. Institutions are characteristically and necessarily concerned with . . . external goods. They are involved in acquiring money and other material goods; they are structured in terms of power and status, and they distribute money, power, and status rewards.[27]

In the context of sports little needs to be said to interpret this point. We live in an age of massive commercialization of sports, beginning now even at the high school level and continuing through the college and professional levels. MacIntyre's distinction between practices and institutions, between internal and external goods, provides an enlightening way to view this much-talked about and much criticized phenomenon. Institutions are required to sustain practices, but the institutionalization of a practice carries clear moral dangers. When the primary focus of a practice is on competition for contingent external goods provided by institutional structures, a natural tension develops between the virtues required to attain internal goods, and qualities of character, vices, that may be helpful in the pursuit of fame, wealth, and power.

> The ideals and the creativity of the practice are always vulnerable to the acquisitiveness of the institution . . . the cooperative care for common goods of the practice is always vulnerable to the competitiveness of the institution . . . without justice, courage and truthfulness, practices could not resist the corrupting power of institutions.[28]

In large part, in our social context the goods of wealth, fame, and power are tied to the ethos of winning. The ethos of contemporary sport, related to the orthodoxy of character building, emphasizes winning—sometimes at all costs. "Show me a good loser and I'll show you a loser." "Winning isn't everything, it's the only thing." "If winning isn't important, why do they keep score?" Now, paradoxically, we are in a position to see why the emphasis on winning, in the context of the institutional pressures associated with practices, can undermine the moral message that is central to the orthodox view. For if winning is the key to achieving external goods, and the pursuit of external goods is overemphasized, then one may as well cheat to get the goods, that is, to win. But to cheat is to admit that the overruling reason to engage in a practice is to achieve *external* goods. It is to ignore the internal goods of the practice, the standards of excellence generated by the tradition, and the virtues required for pursuing and perhaps achieving such excellences. To cheat, as MacIntyre says, "so far bars us from achieving the standards of excellence or goods internal to the practice that it renders the practice pointless except as a device for achieving external goods."[29]

Such a view is very much what Christopher Lasch has in mind when he speaks of the "trivialization of athletics."[30] In the tradition of Huizinga, Callois, and other play theorists, he sees sport as a form of play precisely because it involves a game, an arbitrary construction of rules for no reason other than making the activity in question possible.[31] "The degradation of sport, then, consists not in its being taken too seriously but in its trivialization. Games derive their power from the investment of seemingly trivial activity with serious intent."[32] In MacIntyre's language, the point of sport as a practice is seriously to engage in the pursuit of relatively trivial internal goods. We don't take sport seriously when we allow the wholesale invasion of external goods as its primary raison d'etre. To do that is to ignore the internal goods of the practice. (Remember: internal goods are real *goods*.) Again, paradoxically it appears that the more appropriate way to defend sport's moral possibilities is to emphasize the "worthlessness" of sport; not to see it as a path to wealth and fame but as an occasion for momentary, enjoyable commitment and the achievement of a particular kind of excellence. We really appreciate and love the game of baseball when we appreciate great second base play or a beautiful swing, not just wins and losses. We love the tradition and enhance the moral possibilities of a given sport when we view such excellence as shared goods constituting the possibilities available for young players if they care to attend justly, honestly, and courageously to their sport.

Surely the most important sense of winning and competing courageously is to see winning as an internal good of significant yet trivial proportions. Perceiving sport as "splendid triviality" is perceiving it without illusion, in Murdoch's sense. We can still stress the value of winning as important because it is an essential part of the practice of a sport. But to overemphasize the value of winning is to diminish the numerous other internal goods of sports, and it is to point in a direction in which it becomes more difficult, not less, to be a good person. I suspect that the epithet associated with being a "winner" or being a "competitor" often has more to do with being ruthless than having a good character. Yet the moral discourse associated with sport muddles the issue. Since "winning" is so tied up with achieving external goods in our social context, and to "win" one must "compete," being competitive becomes the key virtue in sports. As MacIntyre says, "In any society which recognized only external goods competitiveness would be the dominant and even exclusive feature."[33] This is because external goods are much more the object of competition because of institutional and commercial pressures. So in our social and economic context the pressures are enormous. Perhaps it's not surprising that the mythical State University of the first paragraph of this chapter is faced with such a mess. MacIntyre's analysis puts the contemporary context of college athletics in proper perspective.

> Yet notoriously the cultivation of truthfulness, justice, and courage will often, the world being what it contingently is, bar us from being rich or famous or powerful . . . The virtues are always a potential stumbling block to this comfortable ambition. We should therefore expect that if, in a particular society the pursuit of external goods were to become dominant, the concept of the virtues might suffer first attrition and then perhaps something like near total effacement, although simulacra might abound.[34]

Still, although the psychological and economic forces that weigh against the moral possibilities of sport are great, other problems remain. MacIntyre stresses the importance of the virtues in sustaining practices. But some practices may be evil.[35] Or, for our purposes, some practices may be relatively trivial in relation to other important human activities, for example, having a good jump-shot versus being an excellent surgeon. Our commitments to a particular practice and the virtues sustaining our participation may conflict with other parts of our life.[36] An athlete might be universally admired for his courage and heroism on the athletic field, while he is miserable in sustaining his family, his friendships, and his other interests. After all, as Murdoch suggests, from the ethical point of view we are interested in how we can become better. That is why the character building thesis is of interest. How do the virtues associated with sport fit into life as a whole? Can the playing of sports contribute to making our life a unity, so we can order the goods of different practices?

MacIntyre attempts to place the virtues in a larger context by offering a rich and provocative discussion of human action and the self. Briefly, the major error committed by both analytic philosophers and the Sartrian brand of existentialism has been to interpret human action atomistically, ignoring the way in which action is embedded in a historical or narrative context that makes it intelligible. If we interpret some piece of human behavior we must appeal to the intentions of the agent; but these intentions can be made intelligible only by referring to a larger "setting," or a narrative history.[37] For example, driving west out of the city might be driving to the country to buy apples, momentarily escaping suburban boredom, leaving one's wife, going to see one's parents, testing a used car, and so forth. As MacIntyre says, "We place the agent's intentions . . . in causal and temporal order with reference to their role in his or her history; and we also place them with reference to their role in the history of the setting or settings to which they belong."[38] This means that "narrative history" is necessary to interpret human actions, and the self must be understood in terms of the way in which it is situated in the narratives it acts out. This applies also to others. "It is because we all live out narratives in our lives and because we understand our own lives in terms of the narratives that we live out that the form of narrative is appropriate for understanding the actions of others."[39]

This narrative conception of selfhood is fundamental for moral philosophy, because the question of what I ought to do can only be answered by placing my action in some larger narrative context. Human life is both unpredictable and teleological, since we're not quite sure what will happen to us, but we live as if our lives are moving toward certain ends, some of which are particular to individual lives, some of which we share with others.[40] MacIntyre sums up his main thesis:

> A central thesis then begins to emerge: man is in his actions and practice, as well as in his fictions, essentially a story-telling animal. He is not essentially, but becomes through his history, a teller of stories that aspire to truth. But the key question for men is not about their own authorship; I can only answer the question 'What am I to do?' if I can answer the prior question 'Of what story or stories do I find myself a part?'[41]

Now we are in a position to place the question of the virtues in a larger context. If my life is fragmented into a series of roles and a multiplicity of practices, how do I understand my life as a whole, as a unity, such that I can order the conflicting demands of the segments of my life? If the virtues sustain a variety of practices, how can I see my life as unified, such that the virtues still maintain their traditional Aristotelian role in relation to the teleological character of a human life? And for our purposes, how can we relate the answer to the character building view of sport?

MacIntyre's answer echoes Socrates' responses to these issues, although MacIntyre frames his answer in terms of the medieval conception of quest rather than the problem of the unexamined life. For MacIntyre, the "unity of a human life is the unity of a narrative quest."[42] But it is a quest that is typically Socratic. It is a seeking for answers to the ultimate moral questions of life without quite knowing what the answers would look like. It is understanding the problem of conflicting goods associated with the multiplicity of life's practices and seeking a notion of *the* good that would schematize these conflicts. In short, it is the attempt to answer the great Socratic question, How ought I to live?

> It is in looking for a conception of *the* good which will enable us to order other goods, for a conception of *the* good which will enable us to extend our understanding of the purpose and the content of the virtues, for a conception of *the* good which will enable us to understand the place of integrity and constancy in life, that we initially define the kind of life which is a quest for the good.[43]

The virtues sustain not only practices but our quest for the good. Courage, persistence, truthfulness, and justice are as much required in our quest for how best we ought to live as for our pursuit of goods internal to practices. However, for our purpose it is quite clear that something else is required. In this quest we seek understanding and good judgment concerning the relative merits of competing goods. We pursue philosophical knowledge, and for that we must develop the requisite intellectual virtues. To wonder about the good life we must develop a sense of reflectiveness, curiosity, questioning, skepticism, rationality, and wisdom. In short, we must become *philosophical*. The good life, the virtuous life, as Aristotle insisted, requires both intellectual and moral excellence. We need "the virtues necessary for philosophical inquiry about the character of the good," as MacIntyre says. He sums this up: "The good life for man is the life spent in seeking for the good life of man, and the virtues necessary for the seeking are those that will enable us to understand what more and what else the good life for man is."[44]

If it is intuitively clear why the character building view of sport is plausible when we consider the way in which the virtues sustain practices, I think it is just as clear that participation in sports has no intrinsic connection to the development of intellectual virtue. No doubt certain strategic skills are developed when someone learns to play and coach a sport. Understanding and quick judgment are called for. But what we are talking about here involves larger philosophical issues about the nature of the good life, and learning how to turn a double play or when to squeeze bunt appears to have nothing to do with answering Socrates' fundamental question. I suspect that the evidence for this claim must, necessarily, be anecdotal, but we know a number of things about contemporary sports that should make us skeptical about any connection between sports participation and becoming more reflective. We know that parents and coaches are often ready to sacrifice the long-term educational interests of their children and players for athletic success. From red-shirting junior high football players to the educational exploitation of college athletes, the stories are legion. One searches in vain for a coach to take the point of view described by MacIntyre. For example, John Wooden's "Pyramid of Success" mentions the following character traits: industriousness, friendship, loyalty, cooperation, enthusiasm, self-control, alertness, initiative, intentness, condition, skill, team spirit, poise, confidence, competitive greatness, ambition, adaptability, resourcefulness, fight, sincerity, honesty, integrity, reliability, patience, and faith.[45] Not mentioned in this laudable list are wonder, questioning, Socratic ignorance (uncertainty), skepticism, reflectiveness, and critical ability.

Let's close this section by performing a thought experiment. This thought experiment may only show that, given the current conditions in which sports exist, a certain kind of virtue is probably rather rare in the sports world, not that sports can never, in principle, be the vehicle of intellectual development. I suspect the outcome depends on education. First consider these quotes from famous football coaches.[46] "I will demand a commitment to excellence and to victory, and that is what life is all about" (Vince Lombardi). "Winning isn't everything, but it beats anything that comes in second" (Paul Bryant). "Winning is living" (George Allen). "Every time you win, you're reborn; when you lose, you die a little" (George Allen). "No one ever learns anything by losing" (Don Shula).[47] Now consider another kind of coach who believes that participating in sports can really be morally and intellectually profitable. Imagine his speech to his players, and consider whether this jars with our expectations. "Gentlemen, I know you've all had coaches who say things like 'Winning is living.' But I'm not one of them. I want you to look honestly at what you're doing. You're playing a rather silly game. Compared to other human endeavors it is relatively insignificant. Don't ever let your sport consume your life to the detriment of the other great goods in life. Sport is wonderful because it offers you an opportunity to commit yourself to a highly enjoyable physical endeavor. In doing this, sports can dramatize great moments of the human condition. You ought to see it as art, not war. In saying this, I don't want to sound as if I'm a final authority, for what I want you to do is really to think about the nature of your commitment to this game and how it stands in relation to the rest of your life. I want you to think about what really matters in life and what kind of person you are. Is life about winning and victory, solely? I'm not sure; I suspect it's not. Such a thesis sounds simplistic, even silly. What is success? Is it being famous and wealthy? What is happiness? Is it just becoming a great athlete? What will life look like after you quit playing sports? Is the value of competition as great as you find in our culture? What I want most from you is to play this game as well as you can, to enjoy it your utmost, and to think as well as you can about the kinds of questions it occasions. As for me, I'm not too sure about the answers to these questions, but I think reflecting on them is an important part of life and profoundly changes the nature of the person asking such questions. If you want to learn about life, read about Socrates, not famous coaches or athletes."

In the face of the cliché-ridden hype of commercialized sports and the contemporary stress on the external goods (money, prestige, fame) associated with sports participation, it is difficult to be very optimistic about the role of sports in occasioning the kind of reflectiveness and self-examination valued by the latter coach. But I am not wholly pessimistic, precisely because it *is* possible to approach sport in a way that provides reflective opportunities. While many players and coaches may unreflectively endorse the exclusive ethos of "Just win, baby!" there may be others who are more attracted by Phil Jackson's apparently reflective approach. Sport can, in fact, be a fertile ground for the growth of self-knowledge, whether the categories of self-examination are borrowed from contemporary psychology, Zen Buddhism, ancient Greek ethics, or the truisms of wise and experienced philosopher-coaches. Such opportunities can and should contribute to the growth of certain intellectual traits related to good character.[48]

Throughout this chapter I have assumed that our talk about "character" or having "good character" must have something essentially to do with virtue, since character must be described in terms of traits or dispositions we take to be constitutive of it. It is as if "character" means being virtuous, in a broad sense. Is there a way to look more specifically at character, to provide a more unified account of our talk about its development and presence? Let me say at the outset that I'm skeptical about pinning down such a notion in a very tight manner. I'm not sure that our talk about having character is governed by the sort of rules that would allow for a philosophical definition. I offer my own account because I think it helps us to understand something central about this area of our moral discourse, not that I have succeeded in defining what it means to have character or good character. (I'll use these interchangeably.)

I take my lead from some interesting remarks made by Anthony Quinton in his essay "Character and Culture."[49] He is interested in resuscitating the concept of character both in our cultural life and as an object of philosophical interest. After sketching a view of character he attempts to provide a historical account of its decline and describes its principal enemies in our everyday moral life. What is character? Quinton claims that "it is in essence resolution, determination, a matter of pursuing purposes without being distracted by passing impulse."[50] He believes this view is consistent with Plato's emphasis on prudence, courage, and moderation, since these virtues "are all dispositions to resist the immediate solicitations of impulse."[51] For example, as Aristotle also understood, courage is a response to our natural feelings of fear, while prudence is "settled resistance to whim."[52] Quinton sums up his notion of character or important qualities of character.

> They are, generally speaking, ways of deferring gratification, of protecting the achievement of some valued object in the future from being undermined by the pull of lesser objects near at hand.[53]
> It is the disposition or habit of controlling one's immediate, impulsive desires, so that we do not let them issue in action until we have considered the bearing of that action on the achievement of other, remoter objects of desire. Understood this way, character is much the same thing as self-control or strength of will.[54]

I find this a valuable general view of character, especially if it is conjoined with Murdoch's view of human nature as essentially selfish, self-preoccupied, and self-absorbed. For the desires that we must naturally battle are often those that insulate an inflated ego and prohibit the kind of objective seeing that is the foundation of virtue for Murdoch. In the context of sport and character we are interested in the possibilities for moral education provided for children, adolescents, and young adults by participation in sports. If the young are not always moral barbarians, they certainly do usually need the kind of training that responds to the immediate and often selfish impulses described by Quinton and Murdoch. It is possible now to construct a more specific account of character based on the moral psychology we have just outlined. Of what qualities does character consist? I offer this list in no particular order.

1. First of all, I associate character with a kind of strength that forces one properly to take responsibility for certain negative events that befall a person. Such events might make one look bad in the eyes of others and oneself. It is the courage to take responsibility for defeat and failure when appropriate, to be honest about one's self. I know of no neat virtue term that sums up this quality, but it is obviously a kind of responsibility. It is akin to a kind of self-reliance, and its opposite is the perpetual whiner, blamer, and excuse-monger. John McEnroe's lack of this quality is expressed in his constant paranoid complaints to officials, as if he has experienced more unfair and incompetent officiating than anyone in the

history of tennis. Lack of this quality is apparent throughout the sports world when officiating is blamed for defeat.

2. Character requires avoiding the impulse to succeed by cheating. A person of character is just or fair, in more than one sense. He is unwilling to take unfair advantage of another in order to gain his own advantage, and he is attuned to merit. He comes to see the way in which things are due, justly, to persons.

3. Character requires trustworthiness. In any social context reliable persons who resist the impulse to violate shared agreements are valued.

4. A person with character resists the impulse always to see things solely in terms of the way his own life is affected. Qualities like generosity, benevolence, and respect for others are important parts of character. Likewise, sensitivity to the social dimension of living produces a kind of civility in the person with character.

5. Surely character requires the resistance to impulses that might allow us to give up easily when life is difficult. Persistence and determination are important.

6. A person with character, in overcoming intense self-absorption, will appreciate the larger scheme of things and thus will have a diminished sense of his own importance. He will have a good sense of where his own abilities fit in various hierarchies of excellence. I agree with Murdoch when she stresses the centrality of this virtue. "Humility is not a peculiar habit of self-effacement, rather like having an inaudible voice, it is selfless respect for reality and one of the most difficult and central of all virtues."[55]

7. A person with character develops some sense of good judgment about what matters in life. In fact, it is this sense of good judgment that is the ground for resisting immediate impulses. As Quinton notes, "Strength of character, by holding in check impulses excited by what is immediately present, allows the cognitive harvest of our reasoning powers to have an effect on what we do."[56]

8. A person with character manifests a certain harmony, a balance among the parts of his character. There is a certain unity that provides a basis for what we might call the integration of the self. In short, all of the qualities of character seem to fit nicely and work harmoniously.

9. Finally, a person with character also is able to carve out a space for the particular goods of his own existence, and in making wise judgments about other competing matters, understands when it is important to remain committed to his own idiosyncratic plan of life. A person with character has integrity, in this sense.[57]

Quinton contrasts the characterless self of everyday morality with a self characterized by "cultivated and disciplined modes of choice, by which passive appetites are held in check and so brought into contention with longer term purposes."[58] This broadening of vision involves judgment about one's situation in the larger scheme of things and the requirements of living with others whose claims equal one's own. Character requires a self who is responsible, just, trustworthy, generous, respectful, civil, determined, humble and unpretentious, reasonable and wise, balanced, and has integrity. Whereas Quinton says that character is "comparatively unspecific, unlike abilities and skills,"[59] I think these relatively specific dispositions are a part of our concept of character. I agree with Quinton that character is a "fairly hard-won achievement,"[60] since developing these traits requires strength of will, practice, and sound judgment.

Now we are in a position to offer some tentative conclusions about the claim that sport builds character. Does sport build character? The best that can be said for this view is that sport can help build a part of character, especially if coaches and parents are good moral educators. But the notion of "character" is sufficiently rich and complex and the social, economic, and psychological pressures are so great that we should expect a very mixed moral result from sports participation. This is precisely what the empirical studies seem to show. As we have seen, the corrupting power of the institutionalization of sport and thus the emphasis on the pursuit of external goods produces an atmosphere in which internal goods are often underplayed or compromised. Winning, as the avenue to external goods, becomes the dominant ethos, and moral shortcuts naturally evolve. With the competition for external social goods comes the diminution of generosity or benevolence as key virtues specific to sports participation. Likewise, with fame, power, and money at stake, psychological variables like those described by Murdoch work against the virtuous seeing of the way things are. Thus the character building view is a fragment. It ignores these difficulties and seems to focus only on instrumental virtues that help us achieve the goals we might have in a competitive, business-oriented social world.[61] Also, it may have little or nothing to say about the importance of becoming reflective in working out the very questions that commitment to sports occasion. In short, my answer to the question as to whether sport builds character is the uninspiring "It depends." We are served best by attending to Wittgenstein's admonition to beware of our simplifying "craving for generality," respect particularities, attend to the phenomena, and see how various human experience is. If our task in life is to become better and help our children likewise, then participating in sports may help a person to become more responsible, fair, respectful, and determined. Unfortunately, it may have precisely the opposite effect. And, although it can, it need not have anything to do specifically with becoming wiser about how we ought to live. But thinking about the issues discussed here may produce a greater sensitivity concerning what we might do if we are really serious about the moral possibilities of sports.

10   *Respect for the Game*

In the previous discussion of the ethics of pursuing blowouts, one of the arguments against running up the score referred to the notion of "respect for the game."[1] The phrase at first seems too vague to be very helpful in understanding what it means to be a good sport or to function as a basis for making ethical judgments about conduct in sport. Yet this very language, or language close to this, is quite common in the everyday ethical discourse of the sports world. Consider a few examples. The retirement of Cal Ripken Jr. from major league baseball occasioned comments about the fundamental soundness of the way he played and his respect for the game. Sometimes older NBA players criticize the new generation of players for failing to respect the game. This sort of criticism has been given its quintessential expression in the fictional world of *the* baseball movie, *Bull Durham.* Crash Davis, journeyman catcher and tutor of the talented but erratic young pitcher, Ebby Calvin "Nuke" La-Loosh, is forced to explain why he dislikes his young, undisciplined pupil. Because, Crash explains, "You don't respect yourself, which is your problem, but you don't respect the game—and that's my problem." During a conversation with a college track coach, she condemned the behavior of certain athletes as an "insult to the sport," surely a lack of respect for the activities to which she was devoted. And there is obviously a connection between respect for the game and the familiar expression (and title of another sports film) "love of the game."

It is clear from a variety of usages that respect for the game often functions in the sports world as an important or even fundamental action-guiding, ethical principle: one ought to respect the game, or one ought to respect the type of activity characteristic of the sport in which one is involved. Sports participants ought to act in such a way that their activity expresses, embodies, or is consistent with an attitude appropriate for engaging in sport. The assumption is that action expresses attitudes, and a certain over-arching attitude, "respect," ought to be embodied in sports. The presence of such an attitude is the basis for praise. Its absence occasions ethical condemnation. I would like to consider the suggestion that respect for the game, far from being merely a vague, sentimental, and nostalgic aspect of sportstalk, is actually the description of a significant attitude that may describe the unity of the good sport's perspective. As the reader recalls, sportsmanship can be viewed as conduct arising from our attitudes, and these attitudes must be appropriate for one who engages in sport. Earlier, I argued that the virtue of sportsmanship should be viewed in Aristotelian terms, as a mean between excessive seriousness and excessive playfulness and the disposition to act consistently in light of this mean. It's not difficult to work out some of the practical implications of this notion, as I did then. But respect for the game is more suggestive and fecund. It is possible to analyze this notion, to say something about the constituent aspects that are suggested by its uses in the sports world and that arise because of a perceptive understanding of the nature of sport. This is appropriate after the examination in the last chapter of the implications of viewing sport as a practice, in MacIntyre's sense. Respect for the game also calls attention to the attitude or perspective of the good sport in a more explicit manner than the concept of sportsmanship. Even in its everyday usage in the sports world, "respect" suggests an attitude of esteeming or valuing some phenomenon, in the sense that one must attend to something outside one's self, larger than the self, a reality that demands that one takes account of its nature, value, or interests. It is common to perceive the ethical viewpoint as a perspective from which some larger set of interests or demands must be considered beyond the selfish or narrow interests of an individual. This understanding of the ethical is also suggested by the use of "respect for the game" in the sports world.

What does it mean to speak of respect for the game? What could it mean? As usual, I'll have one eye fixed on the more general issue, while occasionally glancing at particular cases from the sport upon which I've had my attention fixed for many years—and whose authority has generated my respect. My general conclusions, however, do not seem to be idiosyncratic; other games make similar demands.

Let's begin to unpack the notion of "respect for the game" in a manner that will mirror the view of sport, play, and ethical reflection developed in this book. Central to an understanding of sport are the notions of play, game, and practice, in MacIntyre's sense. Each of these notions leads to a narrowing of one's reflective focus, toward the relevant sport-related phenomena that are set apart from other worldly phenomena in important ways. This narrowing of one's reflective focus leads to a description and conceptualizing of sport in terms of various interpretive responses to the notions of the internal and external. To think of sport in terms of play turns one's attention inward, toward a world of play with its intrinsic rewards and internal attractions. Of course, there's something metaphorical or figurative about such language, because playful activity often exuberantly engages the actor in the world. However, as Huizinga and others insist, play is separate, set apart from the concerns of the everyday world. The freedom of play suggests that we are liberated as we identify with the activity and we value it for its own sake. But the play of sport is not mere frolic. It is constituted by rules, and in most cases it is neither incorrect nor misleading to speak of such activities as games. When we esteem or value a sport, our attention is fixed on the activities internal to the game, where space, time, and distinctive meanings are defined in terms of a play world. New goals, intrinsic to such a world, become significant. We appreciate sport as the playing of a certain kind of game, whose very existence arises because of the rules that define it and whose rules are constructed merely to bring such an activity into being. Furthermore, the games associated with sports are by their very nature competitive. Sport is competitive play. A game is a contest with another, an opponent, without whom the contest would not occur. In sport, I am opposed; I enter a world in which others act against me or my goals in quite explicit ways. This opposition, however, takes place in the context of a practice.

Participation in a sport is involvement in a practice, a "socially established cooperative human activity."[2] Recall the essential components of a practice. Participation in a practice involves the attempt to realize internal goods. Such goods are defined in terms of standards of excellence characteristic of the practice. The attempt to achieve goods internal to a practice involves the desire to realize a certain kind of excellence, which is possible only if one understands and submits to the authority of such standards and is obedient to the rules or guidelines that define the practice. The internal goods of a practice are available only to practitioners;

such goods represent the possibility of extending human powers with regard to the means and ends that constitute the practice. Unlike the external goods available to those outside of the practice (goods subject to worldly competition), the internal goods of a practice, while occasioned by the competition to achieve excellence, are good for the entire practice community. They represent goods for the practice itself, not simply for the individual who improves, transforms, or revolutionizes the practice. In this sense, internal goods are shared goods.

Thinking of sport in terms of the concept of a practice (as well as the concept of play) changes the ethical tone and atmosphere of sports participation. Because sport is essentially competitive, it is natural for some to think that the desire to win trumps all other sport-related goals, and the opponent must be treated as the enemy in a zero-sum game. Alienation, estrangement, separation, conflict—no wonder that some find competition to be necessarily problematic and even harmful for human relationships and psychological well-being.[3] However, the exclusive focus on competition and winning leaves out practice-related concerns that shift our ethical focus in a significant way. A practice is a cooperative human activity, in which a community of practitioners have shared concerns, expectations, and goals. In sport it is the game that binds the community together, and the game is a larger reality that generates the standards of excellence over against which the individual defines his own achievements and his sport-related identity. It is the game that demands the attention of the players attempting to achieve a particular kind of goodness, and it is the game that benefits when achievements are understood as shared goods.

Thus it appears that there is a structure of involvement in sports, with various moments that arise as a participant becomes increasingly devoted to her sport. It is within this structure that respect for the game can be understood, and such an attitude seems naturally to arise among members of the practice community who become serious about the possibilities related to becoming a good player. Consider these moments, offered not necessarily in temporal order, but as structural aspects of involvement: being set apart, giving oneself over to the object, submission to authority, obedience to constitutive rules, and desire to become good or to achieve excellence. Perhaps "being set apart" is especially significant in reflecting on the roots of sport in play, but the other moments of involvement are reflected in other practices. Consider again Iris Murdoch's account of learning a language as a lesson in the development of virtue.

If I am learning, for instance, Russian, I am confronted by an authoritative structure which commands my respect. The task is difficult and the goal is distant and perhaps never attainable. My work is a progressive revelation of something which exists independently of me. Attention is rewarded by a knowledge of reality. Love of Russian leads me away from myself towards something alien to me, something which my consciousness cannot take over, swallow up, deny or make unreal. The honesty and humility required of the student—not to pretend to know what one does not know—is the preparation for the honesty and humility of the scholar who does not even feel tempted to suppress the fact which damns the theory.[4]

The language in this passage is striking if we think in terms of learning to play a sport and attempting to become a good player. The novice is thrust into a new world, set apart, with an authoritative structure over against which the player must begin to understand his own abilities and potentialities. If the young player wants to become better, he must submit to those who understand the practice and its standards of excellence. Apprenticeship is demanding. Coaches pursue an education in attentiveness to the object, to the sport understood as a practice, with rules, standards, techniques, and traditions and customs that must be respected if there is to be a realistic possibility of achieving the goals that naturally arise when the desire to play the game arises. Possibilities are projected into an ideal made possible by the practice, a standard of achievement toward which members of the practice community are directed, a notion of perfection against which achievements, both individual and team, are measured. To put the issue more abstractly, "respect for the game" expresses one's attraction to the good made possible by the practice, by the sport in question.

Although the preceding analysis may seem abstract and hopelessly out-of-touch with the way sport is actually practiced, I don't think this is the case. Undoubtedly, in contemporary sports we see the win-at-all-costs ethos and we understand the pressures related to the desire for external goods. The motivations associated with sports participation are mixed. Excellence leads to victory, and victory often occasions external goods—notoriety, praise, recognition, honor, fame, prestige, scholarships, and money. Respect for the game, however, is typically related to a perspective that is far from unusual. The point of playing is to play well—that's the ultimate goal demanded by participation in the practice. Cooking, teaching, building, leading—if the practice attracts, so does the good. The point is to become good. In sport, to play well is the ideal, the good at which the participants ought to be striving. Anything less fails to esteem or value the possibilities, the real internal goods, made possible by participating in the practice. It may be disingenuous for a purist coach or player to deny that winning is *a* goal of playing, but it need not be, and shouldn't be the *only* goal.

For many people, a surprising example of the emphasis on focusing one's attention on the game and the internal goods made possible by participating in a sport comes from comments made by Bob Knight, one of the greatest college basketball coaches of all time, and apparently one of the most competitive. Consider these comments about his approach to basketball.

> You can't make every game out like it's the national championship game. But over the course of a season you've got to develop a sense of pride in performance. Winning just isn't enough. You win on Wednesday playing sloppily against a mediocre team and you go out on Saturday and play the same way against a good team and you get your ass beat.
>
> Winning is the last of all criteria that I think you should use to determine how well you're playing. When the way you've won a game just isn't good enough, you show your players why: you talk about turnovers, missed block-outs, fast-break points allowed, fouls committed—to show your team, "We just didn't play well."
>
> . . . You're trying to get players to understand that how they play is a hell of a lot more important than whether or not they win.[5]

For Knight, the goal of playing, that is, the goal of competing, is to play well, and winning is, of course, not wholly irrelevant. It's a natural by-product of the more basic goal and sometimes, though not always, a criterion by virtue of which we make judgments about excellent play or the achievement of internal goods. However, its importance is subsumed and put in its place by the larger ideal—playing the game well. Perhaps Knight's famous volatility and impatience has more to do with his overwhelming love and respect for *basketball*, not his ruthless desire for victory. It is also noteworthy that Knight's focus on the game leads him to remarks that have an explicit ethical tone reminiscent of McIntyre's emphasis on the way in which internal goods are shared within the practice community. Knight says: "My third coaching cornerstone was an appreciation of basketball as something to be mastered but always, every day of every year, to be studied with an unflagging zeal for answers—and a duty to pass them on."[6]

Murdoch describes what happens when we attempt to learn a language. Bob Knight reflects on the necessity of *studying* basketball, helping players think about the game and attempt to understand it.[7] Their reflections mirror my own experience as a philosophy teacher. Apprenticeship in the practice of philosophy is unsettling for many students for a variety of reasons. The usual explanation involves the natural reaction to having one's fundamental beliefs questioned. However, the questioning takes place in the context of learning the relevant ground rules of philosophy: that beliefs must be defended by arguments and acquired only after a rigorous and prolonged process of critical reflection. Many beginning philosophy students are unwilling to submit to the tradition, the rigorous ground rules, and the noetic austerity that it supposedly entails. Others, however, develop what seems to be an apt attitude toward the study of philosophy. Some students want to know what they will get from the study of philosophy, but the only goods they initially recognize are external to the practice, and philosophy becomes the trivialized pursuit of such goods: a mark on a transcript, a requirement satisfied, an awkward hurdle to be overcome in the pursuit of a degree, a job, or a career. Others, however, develop an attitude that esteems or values the activity itself and the goods made possible by engaging in it—a certain kind of critical facility and insight that arises in reading texts, reconstructing and formulating arguments, appreciating objections, and pursuing the truth in philosophical matters. In this case, a student becomes acquainted with a different world—the world of philosophy, where a practice community participates in a shared activity with common goals, expectations, and standards of excellence. The teacher, that is, the good teacher, conveys her respect, even love, for the practice, and if she is successful such an attitude may arise even in those students who will choose not to pursue the activity further in any serious manner. Even educational institutions within which the practice of philosophy is taught often endorse this end by putting the goal on the course evaluation form: Did the teacher help the student "gain respect" for the discipline?

In any case, the respect at issue has practical effects. While the student's attention is narrowed and the focus is on the nature of the activity, the student's vision is simultaneously broadened toward the possibilities available within the historical development of the practice. "The honesty and humility required of the student—not to pretend to know what one does not know—is the preparation for the honesty and humility of the scholar who does not even feel tempted to suppress the fact which damns the theory." Murdoch insists that moral consequences arise when the student's attention is seriously fixed on the reality of the practice and the self is given over to the structures of authority inherent in the activity. Bob Knight wants his players to focus on the game and be motivated primarily by the goal of playing well. To become good in philosophy you must think for yourself—naïve, unreflective hubris or dishonest borrowing is ruled out at the start. These comparisons are appropriate because the structures of commitment, of respect, are similar across different practices. Now let us consider sport more exclusively and describe the consequences of the sports participant gaining respect for the activity in which she is engaged. I'll attempt to provide both descriptive comments concerning how references to respect for the game actually function, and some suggestions about how the principle ought to function in certain kinds of ethical reflections in sport.[8]

In general, respect for the game, as an ethical principle, often functions as the basis for a judgment about the relative importance of the sport in question and the relative unimportance of one individual player or participant. The principle often calls attention to selfish conduct or various forms of self-aggrandizement. Given a certain understanding of the sport, with its history and traditions, a natural continuation of such an interpretation is humility and appreciation for one's place in the tradition.[9] A great player in professional sports is sometimes praised because "he never thought he was bigger than the game." Ripken and Gretzky carry themselves with grace and humility; Ricky Henderson and Dennis Rodman are found lacking. Achieving the good or a high degree of excellence in a sport need not lead to an inflated ego; it may instead lead to "unselfing," in Murdoch's sense, if it is connected with the appreciative largeness of vision characteristic of those who respect the game. What are more specific aspects of respect for the game and what are the practical effects of such attitudes? Given the background discussion in the book, we can now proceed more briefly than we might have without such a background.

1. Respect for Rules

Since games are defined by the rules without which these activities wouldn't exist, to respect the game is to respect the rules that define the activity and make possible the attempt to become good—and win. Respect for the game requires a stringent respect for fair play, or the intention to play according to the implicit agreements embodied in the rules. By violating the agreements that make the sport possible and by attempting to gain an unfair advantage over an opponent, the cheater trivializes the sport in question by reducing it simply to a means by which other goods are achieved. The sportstalk cliché, "Jones is only interested in winning," if taken literally, is not necessarily grounds for praise, since the player or coach may attempt to win by cheating. The cheater reduces sport to an instrument for achieving external goods, rather than the locus for the possibility of achieving an intrinsically satisfying set of internal goods occasioned by agreements with others. The cheater thumbs his nose at the relevant standards of excellence and thus fails to value or esteem the practice itself. In an important sense, the cheater has expelled himself from the play world since he is no longer playing the game at all. (Recall the incompatibility thesis.) Instead of being praised for his competitiveness—"Everyone cheats; he's only doing what he is forced to do to win"—the cheater should be shunned and judged accordingly by the practice community. The cheater loves the practice and the play world too little—and worldly goods too much.

2. *Respect for the Spirit of Competition*

Respect for the game entails respect for an essentially competitive activity. Sport is a contest, not mere frolic, with winners and losers, successes and failures, exhilaration and even despair. In sport, something is at issue and opponents come together to seek resolution within the play world or the practice community constituted by the rules. Players assume that their opponents are motivated by the same goals and are equally serious about the pursuit of excellence and the desire for victory. Sport involves struggle, tension, and uncertainty because of its internal seriousness. Hence, respect for competition means esteeming or valuing the seriousness characteristic of those who participate in the sport. Such respect leads to the grateful recognition that the values internal to the sport are not possible unless worthy opponents are available. When Cal Ripken Jr. is praised for his respect for the game, part of what might be meant involves the sense that a player is obliged to attempt to play as hard as he can, with intensity and devotion, to not give up under difficult circumstances, to be the best opponent he can be in terms of standards of good play. In this sense, an appreciation of the competitive nature of sport may lead the player to consider the perspective of his opponent, who is also seriously engaged and equally susceptible to disappointment and discouragement. The respectful player would never allow the contest to degenerate into disrespectful festivity because of a lopsided score, nor would he "show up" his opponent in various ways. Mickey Mantle used to run around the bases with his head down after he hit a home run in order to avoid embarrassing the pitcher. Respect for competition involves respecting an opponent who is the condition for the possibility of achieving the goods made possible by participation in a sport.

3. Respect for the Spirit of Play

Given the emphasis on play in this book, it is hardly surprising to insist that respect for the game means respect for a playful activity, a reminder that a game is first of all an activity whose value is internal to the activity and relatively trivial in relation to other human activities and values. Sport is competitive play, serious nonseriousness, splendid triviality, joyful uselessness. To respect the game of baseball, qua playful activity, is to insist that the game never be reduced to a mere instrument for the production of some other value that others insist must be available in order to salvage the value of the sport: character, entertainment, social identity, money. Coaches and players (and fans) usually do not need to be reminded that sport is competitive, but it is important to remind them that sport isn't war, that opponents aren't enemies, that winning isn't all that matters, that external goods aren't the only justification for playing a sport, and that the product shouldn't overshadow the process. Respect for the playful character of sport should involve generosity, an attitude that rules out taunting, trash talking, fighting, and excessive violence—a perspective that attempts to relate to an opponent gracefully and generously both during competition and after a victory or a difficult defeat.

4. Respect for the Game's Traditions and Customs

As we have seen in the examination of cheating in an earlier chapter, one of the most interesting but difficult aspects of respecting the agreements that are relevant for fair play arises because a sport is more than simply a collection of explicit rules. The actual playing of a sport also involves a prescriptive atmosphere in which rules are interpreted in various ways and expectations arise concerning what is appropriate conduct in relation to both written and unwritten rules. For example, in basketball committing a strategic foul late in a game is not bad sportsmanship; it's good and expected strategy. An explicit rule is violated, but the customs of the sport not only allow such conduct; fouling is strategically required.

The game of baseball provides clear examples of this aspect of respect for the game. Respect for baseball requires knowledge, experience, and good judgment in relation to conduct embedded in the historical reality of the game. Intent, often crucial for ethical evaluation, is interpreted against a background of the relevant customs, and players and coaches are held responsible for knowing such prescriptive ideals. Ignorance may not be excused. Stealing signs, breaking up the double play hard at second, throwing inside, quick-pitching, stepping out of the batter's box to break up the pitcher's rhythm, bunting, stealing bases—all are "part of the game." Yet it's contrary to the customs of baseball to bunt, steal, or hit and run when far ahead, just as the customs disallow attempting to injure an infielder by sliding with high spikes, or yelling "swing" as the ball crosses the plate during the game. Various verbal tricks are also considered to be "bush league," the negative ethical concept that contrasts with respect for the game of baseball. The notion is that the game ought not to be cheapened by conduct that seems alien to the internal demands of the practice, as interpreted by the tradition. Appropriate strategy is filtered through the tradition, which interprets what is to count as internal goods, real game-specific excellence, and what is to count as cheap trickery, cheating, culpable ignorance, disrespectful conduct toward opponents, and self-aggrandizement.

I should add I'm not unaware of the problems associated with apologists who refer to what is "part of the game" to excuse behavior that has in *fact* become customary but is problematic and ought to be condemned. Reference to the customs and traditions of a sport must sometimes be related to other principles, or to other aspects of respect for the game or sportsmanship to evaluate the appropriateness of the behavior in question. Cal Ripken Jr. is a part of a larger tradition to which he submits, yet he is also responsible for the formation of new customs in his decisions about what to preserve and respect and what may require some transformation. It's not clear why regular fist-fights should be a part of hockey. Nor is it clear why uncivil displays toward umpires should be expected in baseball, nor why bench-clearing brawls after every inside pitch represent an expression of a perceptive understanding of the game. There is no algorithm to help us distinguish those customs that ought to be preserved from those that should be rejected, but there is also no mystery concerning the kinds of reasons to which one might appeal in ethical reflection. Taunting and trash-talking may have become a part of the game in many sports but that doesn't mean such behavior is justified. These actions fail to respect opponents, the very nature of athletic competition, as well as basic norms of civility and decency. Surely that's not what sport is about, so these actions fail to appreciate or value the very activity in which they arise. Respect for the game is the basis for making good judgments about such matters.

5. Respect for Achievement and Excellence

Since practices have standards of excellence, the achievement of internal goods is possible, and the young player of a sport must recognize the relevant standards in order to become good. To respect the game is to recognize and appreciate the possibilities for achievement made possible by participating in the practice. Recognizing and appreciating excellence in a sport is crucial for a player. Such recognition is the basis for accurate judgments about her own abilities and may fuel the desire for improvement, as well as a humility that is joined with realistic expectations for achieving the internal goods of the practice. Respect for excellence is also crucial for relations with opponents, because reactions to winning and losing are related to judgments about what constitutes being good in the sport. Respect for achievement and excellence requires that competitors give credit where credit is due, to acknowledge when they are beaten by a superior opponent instead of whining, making excuses, and rationalizing—the opponent was lucky, the officials were terrible, game conditions were awful. Respect for the game requires accepting responsibility for defeat because the opponent played better and graciously acknowledging that the *game* determined the outcome, not external factors generated by excuse-mongering.

Respect for the game also involves an admiration for those who have played well in the historical development of the sport, and an appreciation for being part of something that is historically larger than an individual self. Our sports heroes are those who have played the game the way it ought to be played, in terms of the ideals of excellence that have developed and the moral qualities that are required for such achievements. George Will has a useful comment:

> It requires a certain largeness of spirit to give generous appreciation to large achievements. A society with a crabbed spirit and a cynical urge to discount and devalue will find that one day, when it needs to draw upon the reservoirs of excellence, the reservoirs have run dry. A society in which the capacity for warm appreciation of excellence atrophies will find that its capacity for excellence diminishes.[10]

Respect for the game "requires a certain largeness of spirit" in the way in which Will argues, as well as the way in which Murdoch (and even Bob Knight) traces the self's movement from preoccupation with itself to submission to an "authoritative structure that commands respect." Respect for "reservoirs of excellence" expands the self, undermines cynical smallness, and generates the honesty and humility that Murdoch associates with being a good student and a committed scholar. The task is to see clearly what we're doing.

———————

Throughout this book I have emphasized the importance and the practical implications of gaining a proper perspective on sport. Will's comment about "largeness of spirit" is analogous to the emphasis on the larger perspective on sport I have described. If being a good sport involves the attainment of a more reflective and detached attitude about participation in sport, this will also naturally give rise to acts of benevolence or altruism that seem to be more rare in sports today. If you love or respect the game, the act of playing fairly and enthusiastically with a good opponent will be the foremost goal for you, so acts of generosity are the natural consequence of such an attitude.

As I did in the first chapter of the book, I'd like to close with comments from someone outside the academic world. Perhaps the view of sport found here will seem unrealistic and naïve to some. I admit that the language of play, freedom, the aesthetic, detachment, absurdity, sportsmanship, and good character scarcely resonates for many at the higher levels of sport, as if such talk is best left back at the YMCA in the context of T-ball, youth soccer fields, and lowered baskets. Even high school sports, not to mention college and professional athletics, seem to be more about dog-eat-dog competition, winning, and anticipation of external rewards than the kinds of notions I have stressed. Yet even at the highest levels of money-mad professional sports, it's still possible to see the thing for what it is. Arguably the most successful coach in professional sports in the last few years has been Phil Jackson, whose teams have won numerous NBA championships. His book, *Sacred Hoops,* is a must read for any aspiring philosopher-coach. Many things that Jackson says will resonate with readers of this book.

> It was Super Bowl Sunday. When we arrived at the hotel I told the players to get some pizzas and beers after practice and watch the Super Bowl in their hotel rooms. 'You guys need to get together and remember what you're doing this for,' I said. 'You're *not* doing it for the money. It may seem that way, but that's just an external reward. You're doing it for the internal rewards. You're doing it for each other and the love of the game.'[11]

Jackson says that at one point in his coaching career, "I realized I needed to become more detached emotionally and put the game in the proper perspective."[12] He speaks of "opponents as partners in the dance"[13] and of his attempt to teach players "to embrace a non-belligerent way of thinking about competition"[14] He says he attempted "to talk regularly about ethics" to his players.[15] Finally, he mentions the importance of play.

> When I was a player, I used to have a slogan scotch-taped to the mirror in my apartment: 'Make your work play and your play work.' Basketball is a form of play, of course, but it's easy for players to lose sight of this because of the pressures of the job. As a result, my primary goal during practice is to get the players to reconnect with the intrinsic joy of the game. Some of our most exhilarating moments as a team came at these times. That's certainly true for Jordan, who loves practice, especially the scrimmages, because it's pure basketball, nothing extra.[16]

As Jackson says, we should not lose sight of the intrinsic joy of the game, for that's the locus of the powerful but paradoxical attraction of sport as well as the ground for wise attitudes and good conduct. Perhaps we need intermittently to be reminded of this, as I have tried to do here.

NOTES

Chapter 1: Sport, Bodily Excellence, and Play

1. Paul Weiss, *Sport: A Philosophic Inquiry* (Carbondale: Southern Illinois University Press, 1969), 217.

2. See, for example, the following useful collections: Ellen Gerber and William Morgan, eds., *Sport and the Body: A Philosophic Symposium*, 2d ed. (Philadelphia: Lea and Febiger, 1979); Robert G. Osterhoudt, ed., *The Philosophy of Sport: A Collection of Original Essays* (Springfield, Ill.: Charles C. Thomas, 1973); William Morgan and Klaus Meier, eds., *Philosophic Inquiry in Sport* (Champaign, Ill.: Human Kinetics, 1988, 1995); David Vanderwerken and Spencer Wertz, eds., *Sport Inside Out: Readings in Literature and Philosophy* (Fort Worth: Texas Christian University Press, 1985); William Morgan, Klaus Meier, and Angela Schneider, eds., *Ethics in Sport* (Champaign, Ill.: Human Kinetics, 2001); and M. Andrew Holowchak, ed., *Philosophy of Sport: Critical Readings, Crucial Issues* (Upper Saddle River, N.J.: Prentice Hall, 2002).

3. Paul Weiss, *Philosophy in Process*, vol. 5 (Carbondale: Southern Illinois University Press, 1971). For an excellent essay that attempts to relate the entire development of Weiss's thinking on sport in *Philosophy in Process* to his finished product, *Sport: A Philosophic Inquiry*, see Paul Kuntz, "Paul Weiss: What is a Philosophy of Sport?" *Philosophy Today* 20 no. 3 (fall 1976): 170–89. The major problem with Kuntz's essay is that he strongly emphasizes Weiss's developmental and often tentative formulations found in *Philosophy in Process*. Kuntz leaves me with the impression that Weiss doesn't really have a finalized theory of sport; rather, Weiss supposedly endorses a theory that dialectically subsumes the best of *four* different theories. But this interpretation is belied by a close attention to what Weiss considers his finished theory found in *Sport: A Philosophic Inquiry*.

4. Weiss, *Sport*, chapters 3, 4, 5.

5. *Ibid.*, chapters 7, 8.

6. *Ibid.*, chapters 9, 10.

7. *Ibid.*, 17.

8. *Ibid.*, viii.

9. Michael Novak, *The Joy of Sports* (New York: Basic Books, 1976), xiv.

10. Weiss, *Sport*, 4.

11. *Ibid.*

12. *Ibid.*, 10.

13. *Ibid.*, 3.

14. *Ibid.*, 10.

15. *Ibid.*, 143.

16. *Ibid.*, 10–11.

17. *Ibid.*, 12.

18. *Ibid.*, 13.

19. *Ibid.*, 14.

20. *Ibid.*, 18–36.

21. *Ibid.*, 36.

22. *Ibid.*

23. Keith Algozin, "Man and Sport," *Philosophy Today* 20 no. 3 (fall 1976): 190.

24. Weiss, *Sport*, 4.

25. Frank McBride, "Toward a Non-Definition of *Sport*," in *Sport and the Body*, ed. Gerber and Morgan, 50. For an interesting response to the criticisms of the attempts to define sport see William Morgan, "Some Aristotelian Notes on the Attempt to Define Sport," in *Sport and the Body*, ed. Gerber and Morgan, 53–65.

26. Paul Kuntz calls this theory of sport "pleasure in play" in "Paul Weiss," 173.

27. Weiss, *Philosophy in Process*, vol. 5, 518.

28. Weiss, *Sport*, 24.

29. *Ibid.*, "Play, Sport, and Game," chapter 9.

30. Kuntz, "Paul Weiss," 173.

31. Johan Huizinga, *Homo Ludens: A Study of the Play-Element in Culture* (Boston: Beacon Press, 1955); Roger Caillois, *Man, Play, and Games*, trans. Meyer Barash (New York: The Free Press of Glencoe, 1961).

32. Huizinga, *Homo Ludens*, 3.

33. *Ibid.*, 13.

34. *Ibid.*, 28.

35. Caillois, *Man, Play, and Games*, 3.

36. Weiss, *Sport*, 134.

37. See Kenneth Schmitz, "Sport and Play: Suspension of the Ordinary," in *Sport and The Body*, ed. Gerber and Morgan, 22–29. The essay also appears in *Philosophic Inquiry in Sport*, ed. Morgan and Meier, 29–38.

38. Weiss, *Sport*, 133.

39. *Ibid.*

40. Kuntz, "Paul Weiss," 173.

41. Richard L. Schacht, "On Weiss on Records, Athletic Activity and the Athlete," in *The Philosophy of Sport*, ed. Osterhoudt, 26. See in that volume the article by Scott Kretchmer, "Ontological Possibilities: Sport as Play," 64–78.

42. Weiss, *Sport*, 139, 140, 141.

43. *Ibid.*, 18.

44. George Sheehan, *Running and Being: The Total Experience* (New York: Warner Books, 1978), 78.

Chapter 2: The Freedom of Play

1. Weiss, *Sport*, chapter 1.

2. Novak, *Joy of Sports*, xi.

3. *Ibid.*, xiii.

4. Huizinga, *Homo Ludens*, 2.

5. *Ibid.*

6. *Ibid.*, 4.

7. See Huizinga, *Homo Ludens*, 7, 8, 13; Caillois, *Man, Play, and Games*, 9; Novak, *Joy of Sports*, 43; and Weiss, *Sport*, 134.

8. Weiss, *Sport*, 134.

9. Huizinga, *Homo Ludens*, 3.

10. *Ibid.*

11. Frithjof Bergmann, *On Being Free* (Notre Dame, Ind.: University of Notre Dame Press, 1977).

12. *Ibid.*, 18.

13. *Ibid.*, 17.

14. *Ibid.*, 19.

15. *Ibid.*

16. *Ibid.*, 37.

17. *Ibid.*, 55–78.

18. *Ibid.*, 60.

19. *Ibid.*, 78.

20. *Ibid.*, 91.

21. *Ibid.*, 92.

22. Novak, *Joy of Sports*, 41.

23. See George Sheehan, *On Running* (New York: Bantam Books, 1978), 185–96; and *Running and Being*, 71–83.

24. Schmitz, "Sport and Play," 31.

25. *Ibid.*

26. Huizinga, *Homo Ludens*, 13.

27. *Ibid.*, 28.

28. I realize that dance might be rule-governed, but it certainly need not be. Consider a young child who spontaneously dances, with great joy and enthusiasm, to some rhythmic piece of music. If there is any doubt about this point, you might turn on the television and watch some dance show. Even Huizinga says of dance that "it is always at all periods and with all people pure play, the purest and most perfect form of play that exists."

29. Caillois, *Man, Play, and Games*, 9.

30. *Ibid.*

31. *Ibid.*, 10.

32. Allen Guttman calls this "organized play," as opposed to "spontaneous play." See *From Ritual to Record: The Nature of Modern Sports* (New York: Columbia University Press, 1978), chapter 1.

33. See Melvin Rader, ed., *A Modern Book of Esthetics*, 5th ed. (New York: Holt, Rinehart and Winston, 1979), 14–17.

34. Quoted by Anthony Skillen in "Sport: A Historical Phenomenology," *Philosophy* 68 (1993): 343.

Chapter 3: Sport, the Aesthetic, and Narrative

1. Drew Hyland, *Philosophy of Sport* (New York: Paragon House, 1990), 125.

2. Jean-Paul Sartre, *Nausea*, trans. Lloyd Alexander (New York: New Directions, 1964). I will abbreviate the title and refer to it as *N*. Also, I will cite all specific references to the novel in the body of the chapter.

3. John Dewey, *Art as Experience* (New York: Capricorn Books, 1958). I will abbreviate the title and refer to it as *AE*. Also, I will cite all specific references to Dewey's text in the body of the chapter. All quotations will come from chapter 3, "Having an Experience."

4. As a matter of fact, a book has been written describing and analyzing only two games. See Keith Hernandez and Mike Mryan, *Pure Baseball: Pitch by Pitch for the Advanced Fan* (New York: Harper Collins, 1994).

5. Monroe Beardsley, *Aesthetics: Problems in the Philosophy of Criticism*, 2d ed. (Indianapolis: Hackett, 1981), 524–56.

6. *Ibid.*, 530.

7. Also see Joseph Kupfer, *Experience as Art: Aesthetics in Everyday Life* (Albany: State University of New York Press, 1983) for a more lengthy treatment of the aesthetic possibilities in ordinary life. Kupfer has also been influenced by Dewey. Chapter 5, "Sport—The Body Electric," is especially interesting.

8. Alasdair MacIntyre, *After Virtue*, 2d ed. (Notre Dame, Ind.: University of Notre Dame Press, 1984).

9. *Ibid.*, 208.

10. *Ibid.*, 211.

11. *Ibid.*

12. *Ibid.*

13. *Ibid.*, 212.

14. Richard Lischer, "The Limits of Story," *Interpretation* 38 (Jan. 1984): 26–38.

15. *Ibid.*, 30.

16. *Ibid.*

17. *Ibid.*, 31.

18. See A. Bartlett Giamatti, *Take Time for Paradise: Americans and Their Games* (New York: Summit Books, 1989), especially chapter 3, "Baseball as Narrative," for a loving reflection related to these comments.

19. Huizinga, *Homo Ludens*, especially chapter 1.

20. Schmitz, "Sport and Play," 29–38.

Chapter 4: Play and the Absurd

1. See Huizinga, *Homo Ludens*; Caillois, *Man, Play and Games*; and Eugen Fink, "The Ontology of Play," *Philosophy Today* 18 no. 2 (summer 1974), 147–61, or his "The Oasis of Happiness: Toward an Ontology of Play," in *Game, Play, Literature*, ed. Jacques Ehrmann (Boston: Beacon Press, 1968).

2. Schmitz, "Sport and Play," 29–38.

3. Drew Hyland, "Athletics and Angst: Reflections on the Philosophical Relevance of Play," in *Sport and the Body*, ed. Gerber and Morgan, 22–29.

4. Joseph Esposito, "Play and Possibility," in *Philosophic Inquiry in Sport*, ed. Morgan and Meier, 175–81.

5. Keith Algozin, "Man and Sport," in *Philosophic Inquiry in Sport*, ed. Morgan and Meier, 183–87.

6. Albert Camus, *The Myth of Sisyphus*, trans. Justin O'Brien (New York: Vintage Books, 1955), 89.

7. Richard Taylor, *Good and Evil* (New York: Macmillan, 1970), 257–58.

8. Caillois, *Man, Play, and Games*, 5–6.

9. Robert Osterhoudt, "The Term 'Sport': Some Thoughts on a Proper Name," in *Sport and the Body*, ed. Gerber and Morgan, 5.

10. Taylor, *Good and Evil*, 260.

11. Taylor also discusses this possibility in *Good and Evil*, 259–60.

12. Camus, *Myth of Sisyphus*, 21.

13. Thomas Nagel, "The Absurd," in *Mortal Questions* (New York: Cambridge University Press, 1979), 13.

14. *Ibid.*

15. *Ibid.*, 14.

16. *Ibid.*, 15.

17. *Ibid.*, 19–20.

18. Huizinga, *Homo Ludens,* 8.

19. Schmitz, "Sport and Play," 24–25.

20. Huizinga, *Homo Ludens,* 8.

21. *Ibid.*

22. Fink, "The Ontology of Play," 156.

23. Novak, *Joy of Sports,* 40.

24. Nagel, "The Absurd," 20.

Chapter 5: Sport and the View from Nowhere

1. Thomas Nagel, *Mortal Questions* (Cambridge, UK: Cambridge University Press, 1979). I will refer to this book as *MQ* and cite all specific references to it in the body of the text.

2. Thomas Nagel, *The View From Nowhere* (New York: Oxford University Press, 1986). I will refer to this book as *VN* and cite all specific references to it in the body of the text.

3. See this essay in *Mortal Questions,* 196–213.

4. The standard arguments against such conventionalism (also called "normative relativism," "prescriptive relativism," or "conventional ethical relativism") can be found in most introductory ethics textbooks. For example, see James Rachels, *The Elements of Moral Philosophy,* 4th ed. (Boston: McGraw-Hill College, 2003), or Luis Pojman, *Ethics: Discovering Right and Wrong,* 4th ed. (Belmont, Calif.: Wadsworth Publishing Company, 2002).

5. See chapter 7, "Freedom," in Nagel, *The View From Nowhere,* and "Moral Luck," in *Mortal Questions.*

6. See Nagel's widely discussed "What is it Like to be a Bat?" in *Mortal Questions.*

7. The phrase is J. L. Mackie's in *Ethics: Inventing Right and Wrong* (Hammondsworth, UK: Penguin, 1977). The contemporary literature on moral realism is extensive. For an excellent collection of articles, see Geoffrey Sayre-McCord, ed. *Essays on Moral Realism* (Ithaca: Cornell University Press, 1988).

8. For a clear defense of the notion of the "moral point of view," see the introductory chapter in Peter Singer, *Practical Ethics,* 2d ed. (Cambridge, UK: Cambridge University Press, 1993).

9. See, for example, the following discussions: Bernard William's criticism of utilitarianism in *Utilitarianism: For and Against* (Cambridge, UK: Cambridge University Press, 1973); Susan Wolf, "Moral Saints," *Journal of Philosophy* 79 (1982): 419–39; and Nagel's "Living Right and Living Well," in *The View From Nowhere.*

10. See Nagel's discussion "The Fragmentation of Value," in *Mortal Questions.*

11. For example, see Peter Unger, *Ignorance: A Case for Skepticism* (Oxford: Clarendon Press, 1975), for a defense of global skepticism. A more local skepticism might deny that we can have, for example, moral or metaphysical knowledge, while holding that scientific claims remain warranted.

12. See Nagel, "The Absurd."

13. The judgments about sports that we might make from a relatively "objective" perspective—remember that the distinction is a matter of degree—are not unitary. I do not believe that sports are reduced to absurdity based on all objective views of it. Later I argue that the development of moral character in sport represents a form of "objective reengagement" after reflective detachment has seemed to undermine the objective

significance of sports participation. Some kind of objective viewpoint can obviously recognize valuable aspects of sports participation, including psychological, physical, and social benefits, as well as the intrinsic value of noninstrumental activities. Nevertheless, at some point objectivity generates a perspective from which judgments about the relative triviality of sports participation are occasioned, especially when certain aspects are emphasized to the exclusion of others. Likewise, subjectivity in sports is a complex phenomenon. It includes intersubjective elements insofar as sports are social practices that involve shared goods, as well as more subjective elements like the joys of playful exuberance, personal well-being, and a sense of achievement.

14. Bernard Suits, "The Elements of Sport," in *Philosophic Inquiry in Sport*, ed. Morgan and Meier, 8.

15. *Ibid.*, 19.

16. Klaus Meier, "Triad Trickery: Playing with Sports and Games," in *Philosophic Inquiry in Sport*, ed. Morgan and Meier, 28.

17. Suits, "Elements of Sports," 11.

18. *Ibid.*, 10.

19. *Ibid.*

20. *Ibid.*, 11.

21. Huizinga, *Homo Ludens*. Also see Schmitz, "Sport and Play."

22. I am following Nagel's structure here. See *VN*, 218–21.

23. See Michael Novak's insightful discussion of the "New Sportswriters" in *Joy of Sports*, chapter 14, "Jocks, Hacks, Flacks, and Pricks."

24. Both Nagel and Joel Feinberg offer useful comments on irony. Nagel recommends an ironic view of life in "The Absurd," while Feinberg comments favorably on this suggestion in "Absurd Self-Fulfillment," in *Freedom and Fulfillment: Philosophical Essays* (Princeton: Princeton University Press, 1994). The quote comes from Feinberg's essay.

25. The reference is to the appearance of the article in *Philosophy and the Human Condition*, ed. Tom Beauchamp and Joel Feinberg (Englewood Cliffs, N.J.: Prentice-Hall, 1984), 601–2.

26. The distinction between the internal and external goods of a practice is made by Alasdair MacIntyre in *After Virtue*, chapter 10.

27. See Clifford and Feezell, *Coaching for Character*, chapter 3.

28. See George Will's discussion in the conclusion to *Men at Work: The Craft of Baseball* (New York: Macmillan, 1990).

29. I discuss this more extensively in chapter 9 of this book.

30. See Clifford and Feezell, *Coaching for Character*.

31. See Kierkegaard's discussion in *Concluding Unscientific Postscript*, trans. Walter Lowrie (Princeton: Princeton University Press, 1971), 177–88.

32. See Robert McKim's analysis of the appropriateness of "tentative" religious belief because of "widespread and deep disagreement" about religious matters among those with "intellectual integrity and some relevant expertise," in "Religious Belief and Religious Diversity," *Irish Philosophical Journal* 6 (1989): 275–302.

33. Martin Heidegger uses quite different language to make the point that persons are ontologically unique because they can reflect upon their life and choose what to be and to do. Da-Sein, or human being, is "being about which this being is concerned." "And because Da-Sein is always its possibility, it *can* 'choose' itself in its being, it can win itself, it can lose itself, or it can never and only 'apparently' win itself." See Joan Stambaugh's translation of *Being and Time* (Albany: State University of New York Press, 1996), 39, 40.

34. Joel Feinberg makes this important point in "Absurd Self-Fulfillment."

35. I have argued that Nagel is not right about his global claims of life's absurdity. See "Of Mice and Men: Nagel and the Absurd," *Modern Schoolman* 61 no. 4 (1984): 259–65.

Chapter 6: Sportsmanship

1. There is some dispute whether we should say that the cheating coach's team won. Bernard Suits, in "What is a Game?" in *Sport and the Body*, ed. Gerber and Morgan, 12–13, argues that in a strict or logical sense one cannot win by cheating. The game is defined by its rules, so one cannot win the game by breaking the rules, since, in that case, one would not be playing the game at all. On the other hand, Craig K. Lehman, in "Can Cheaters Play the Game?" *Journal of Philosophy of Sport* 7 (1981): 41–46, argues that the conventions of sport may allow some breaking of the rules (e.g., Gaylord Perry throwing a spitball or an offensive lineman holding) without thinking that the violator has ceased to play the game because of such nonobedience. I am sympathetic to Lehman's arguments, but the so-called "incompatibility thesis" is not crucial to my arguments in this chapter. I simply start with a paradigm example of unsportsman-like behavior, and the cheating coach is a good place to start since such behavior violates the rules of basketball and the unwritten conventions of proper conduct in the sport.

2. Here I am using the term "bad sport" to describe the cheater as someone who displays poor sportsmanship. In *The Grasshopper: Games, Life and Utopia* (Toronto: University of Toronto Press, 1978), chapter 4, Bernard Suits distinguishes the trifler, the cheater, and the spoilsport. What I mean by "bad sport" is not what Suits means by "spoilsport." In the broad sense in which I am using the notion, the trifler, cheater, and spoilsport are all bad sports.

3. James Keating, "Sportsmanship as a Moral Category," *Ethics* 75 (Oct. 1964): 25–35. Keating's views are extensively discussed in *The Philosophy of Sport*, ed. Oster-houdt. His views are noted by Carolyn Thomas in *Sport in a Philosophic Context* (Philadelphia: Lea and Febiger, 1983), and by Warren Fraleigh in *Right Actions in Sport: Ethics for Contestants* (Champaign, Ill.: Human Kinetics Publishers, 1984). The paper is anthologized in *Sport and The Body*, ed. Gerber and Morgan; in *Philosophic Inquiry in Sport*, ed. Morgan and Meier; and in *Ethics in Sport*, ed. Morgan, Meier, and Schneider.

4. James Keating, *Competition and Playful Activities* (Washington, D.C.: University Press of America, 1978).

5. *Ibid.*, 39–42.

6. *Ibid.*, 43.

7. *Ibid.*, 47.

8. *Ibid.*, 43–44.

9. See *The Object of Morality* (London: Methuen, 1971), chapter 2. Warnock's comments attempt to describe generally "the human predicament" and the way in which morality serves to better the human predicament by countervailing "limited sympathies."

10. Keating, "Sportsmanship as a Moral Category," 52.

11. *Ibid.*, 43.

12. See Suits, "What is a Game?"

13. Keating, "Sportsmanship as a Moral Category," 44.

14. Richard Taylor, *Metaphysics*, 3rd ed. (Englewood Cliffs, N.J.: Prentice-Hall, 1983), 106.

15. *Ibid.*, 107.
16. Keating, Sportsmanship as a Moral Category," 50.
17. Schmitz, "Sport and Play," 22.
18. Huizinga, *Homo Ludens*, 13.
19. Schmitz, "Sport and Play," 23.
20. *Ibid.*, 24–25.
21. *Ibid.*, 26.
22. *Ibid.*
23. Suits, "What is a Game?" 14.
24. *Ibid.*, 15.
25. *Ibid.*, 17.
26. The conclusion concerning intrinsic satisfaction is mine, not necessarily Suits's. I leave open the question whether his account of "lusory attitude" would agree or disagree with this conclusion. See his discussion in *The Grasshopper*, 38–40 and 144–46. His comments on page 40 seem close to the conclusion I offer, but his later comments on professional game-playing lead elsewhere.
27. Schmitz, "Sport and Play," 27.
28. Aristotle, *Nicomachean Ethics*, trans. Terence Irwin (Indianapolis: Hackett, 1985), 1106b.
29. *Ibid.*, 1107.
30. Schmitz, "Sport and Play," 27–28.
31. Drew Hyland's "Competition and Friendship," in *Sport and the Body*, ed. Gerber and Morgan, 133–39, offers an excellent analysis of how competition always involves the risk of degenerating into an alienating experience, but it need not. Competitive play can be a mode of friendship. This essay also appears in *Philosophic Inquiry in Sport*, ed. Morgan and Meier, 231–39.
32. Aristole, *Nicomachean Ethics*, 1094b.
33. These comments are from Irwin's translator's notes, 313.

Chapter 7: On Cheating in Sports

1. See Oliver Leaman, "Cheating and Fair Play in Sport," in *Philosophic Inquiry in Sport*, ed. Morgan and Meier, 277–82; and Craig Lehman, "Can Cheaters Play the Game?" *ibid.*, 282–87. Oliver Leaman's article also appears in Morgan, Meier, and Schneider, eds. *Ethics in Sport*, 91–99. Craig Lehman's article has recently been anthologized in *Philosophy of Sport*, ed. Holowchak, 172–77. Later in this chapter I critically discuss the central arguments in both articles.
2. See Peter Singer, *Animal Liberation* (New York: Avon, 1975).
3. Nagel, *Mortal Questions*, x.
4. For a clear discussion of the tax-cheat see Fred Feldman, *Introductory Ethics* (Englewood Cliffs, N.J.: Prentice-Hall, 1973), 97–98. Also see Colin Strang, "What If Everyone Did That?" in *Right and Wrong: Basic Readings in Ethics*, ed. Christina Hoff Summers (New York: Harcourt Brace Jovanovich, 1986), 51–62, for an insightful discussion of the kind of reasoning that is involved when we think about the ethics of cheating.
5. Suits, "Elements of Sport,"43.
6. William Frankena, *Ethics*, 2d ed. (Englewood Cliffs, N.J.: Prentice-Hall, 1973), 49.
7. See Fred D'Agostino, "The Ethos of Games," in *Philosophic Inquiry in Sport*, ed. Morgan and Meier, 42–49, for an important analysis that stresses what I will call the

prescriptive atmosphere of games. D'Agostino says that "any particular game has an ethos as well as a set of formal rules. By the ethos of a game I mean those conventions determining how the formal rules of that game are applied in concrete circumstances" (42). D'Agostino seems most interested in how the ethos of a game would sometimes permit conduct that is impermissible in terms of the formal rules of the game. I am also interested in the way in which the prescriptive atmosphere of a game may proscribe conduct that is permissible in terms of rules. What is at issue is the conflict between formalist and conventionalist approaches to cheating and sportsmanship. There are two types of examples of conduct to be kept in mind: impermissible in terms of rules but permissible in terms of an ethos or prescriptive atmosphere; permissible in terms of rules but impermissible in terms of an ethos.

8. Leaman, "Cheating and Fair Play," 279–80.

9. *Ibid.,* 280.

10. *Ibid.*

11. See Beardsley, *Aesthetics,* for a discussion of aesthetic complexity, especially 462–69.

12. Leaman, "Cheating and Fair Play," 281.

13. Lehman, "Can Cheaters Play The Game?" 286.

14. *Ibid.,* 283.

15. *Ibid.,* 284–85.

16. *Ibid.,* 285.

17. *Ibid.*

18. *Ibid.,* 283.

19. *Ibid.,* 279.

20. I think Aristotle makes a similar point in talking about certain vices. In the *Nicomachean Ethics,* 1107a, he says:

> But not every action or feeling admits of the mean, for the names of some automatically include baseness, e.g. spite, shamelessness, envy (among feelings), and adultery, theft, murder, among actions. All of these and similar things are called these names because they themselves, not their excesses or deficiencies, are base.
>
> Hence in doing these things we can never be correct, but must invariably be in error. We cannot do them well or not well—e.g. by committing adultery with the right woman at the right time in the right way; on the contrary, it is true unconditionally that to do any of them is to be in error.

21. I wish to thank Jim Hendry, former head baseball coach, Creighton University, for suggesting some of the interesting examples found in this chapter.

Chapter 8: Sportsmanship and Blowouts

1. Nicholas Dixon, "On Sportsmanship and 'Running Up the Score,'" *Journal of the Philosophy of Sport* 19 (1992): 1–13. I will refer to this article as OS and cite page references to Dixon's article in the body of the text.

2. W. D. Ross, *The Right and the Good* (Oxford: Clarendon Press, 1930).

3. I would not deny that there are other situations in which pursuing blowouts might be justified. For example, blowouts might have some strategic significance for future games played in a series. In professional basketball or baseball, a blowout in the first game of a playoff series might shake the opponent's confidence. On the other hand,

soundly thrashing an opponent and then easing up, in a strategic sense, usually would seem to have the same effect on the opponent's confidence. It's interesting that a friend of mine, a former major league baseball player, used precisely the same example—pursuing a blowout against an opponent you would play in the future—to argue that "running up the score" is a bad idea because it causes your opponent to be more highly motivated in the rematch. Since my view is that such behavior is prima facie wrong, the factors involved in each particular situation are relevant. Still, my arguments show why the overriding factors must be quite strong in order to pursue blowouts.

4. In *After Virtue*, chapter 14, Alasdair MacIntyre distinguishes between the internal goods associated with human practices, including sports, and external goods. For example, becoming an excellent hitter is an internal good in baseball. If a player becomes excellent enough, he may have the opportunity to acquire external goods like money and fame when he becomes a professional player.

5. See Clifford and Feezell, *Coaching for Character*, 36–37, for a brief discussion of applying the Silver Rule as a practical guide to "respect for opponents."

6. In chapter 10 I say more about this important principle of sportsmanship.

7. See Thomas Nagel, *The Last Word* (New York: Oxford University Press, 1997), chapter 6, for a penetrating discussion of what I have called the autonomy of normative query. Nagel speaks of "the more general truth that the normative can't be transcended by the descriptive."

8. See chapter 6.

9. See Clifford and Feezell, *Coaching for Character*.

10. Iris Murdoch connects virtue with "seeing the way things are" in "The Sovereignty of Good over Other Concepts," in *The Sovereignty of Good* (New York: Schocken Books, 1971).

Chapter 9: Sport, Character, and Virtue

1. Gerald R. Ford, "In Defense of the Competitive Urge," in *Sport Inside Out*, ed. Vanderwerken and Wertz, 247. The essay originally appeared in *Sports Illustrated* (1974).

2. Weiss, *Sport*, 29.

3. Christopher Stevenson, "College Athletics and 'Character': The Decline and Fall of Socialization Research," in *Sport and Higher Education*, ed. Donald Chu, Jeffrey Segrave, and Beverley Becker (Champaign, Ill.: Human Kinetics Publishers, Inc., 1985), 264.

4. This essay, by Bruce Ogilvie and Thomas Tutko, also appears in *Sport and Higher Education*, ed. Chu, Segrave, and Becker, 267–73. See also Dorcas Susan Butt, *Psychology of Sport*, 2d ed. (New York: Van Nostrand Reinhold, 1987), especially chapters 9, 10.

5. See Gregory E. Pence, "Recent Work on Virtues," *American Philosophical Quarterly* 21 no. 4 (Oct. 1984): 281–97 for an informative overview. A more recent collection, *Virtue Ethics*, ed. Roger Crisp and Michael Slote (New York: Oxford University Press, 1997), contains a helpful introduction and many of the influential pieces on virtue ethics.

6. MacIntyre, *After Virtue*, 196.

7. *Ibid.*, 8. See chapter 2.

8. *Ibid.*, 117.

9. *Ibid.*, 181.

10. *Ibid.*, 180–85.

11. *Ibid.*, 187.

12. *Ibid.*, 187, 190. It is interesting to note that MacIntyre's notion of a practice is helpful in distinguishing a game from a sport. In his sense, sports are practices, whereas a game isn't necessarily a practice. See also Suits, "Elements of Sport," 39–48.

13. MacIntyre, *After Virtue*, 190.

14. *Ibid.* The point is wonderfully exemplified in an anecdote described by David Halbertstam in *Summer of '49* (New York: William Morrow, 1989), 175. Ted Williams' passionate devotion to the art of hitting caused him to give tips to opposing players. The Boston owner, Tom Yawkey, asked him to stop helping the competition. Williams is quoted as having responded to his owner, "Come on . . . The more hitters we have in this game, the better it is for the game. Listen, when you're coming towards the park and you hear a tremendous cheer, that isn't because someone has thrown a strike. That's because someone has hit the ball." Williams was interested in a shared internal good; Yawkey's interest was in external goods.

15. *Ibid.*, 191.

16. *Ibid.*

17. *Ibid.*, 192.

18. Iris Murdoch, "The Sovereignty of Good," 78.

19. *Ibid.*, 84.

20. *Ibid.*, 87.

21. *Ibid.*, 89.

22. *Ibid.*

23. *Ibid.*, 90.

24. *Ibid.*, 91.

25. Think of John McEnroe's behavior in this respect. The problem concerns his incivility and lack of respect for an opponent. But the incivility and disruptive behavior seem to be a function of his seeming paranoia, as if referees were always out to get him, or he was at the mercy of their incompetence. In fact, a more realistic judgment would be that referees sometimes err but are for the most part accurate in their judgments.

26. Murdoch, *The Sovereignty of Good*, 93.

27. MacIntyre, *After Virtue*, 194.

28. *Ibid.*, 194.

29. *Ibid.*, 191.

30. Christopher Lasch, *The Culture of Narcissism* (New York: Warner Books, 1979), 194–97. See all of chapter 5, "The Degradation of Sport."

31. *Ibid.*, 191.

32. *Ibid.*, 195. Lasch describes sport as "splendid futility."

33. MacIntyre, *After Virtue*, 196.

34. *Ibid.*

35. *Ibid.*

36. *Ibid.*, 201–2.

37. *Ibid.*, 204–8.

38. *Ibid.*, 208.

39. *Ibid.*, 212.

40. *Ibid.*, 215.

41. *Ibid.*, 216.

42. *Ibid.*, 219.

43. *Ibid.*

44. *Ibid.* I do not discuss the third stage of MacIntyre's account of the virtues, since it adds little to my discussion. The virtues also sustain the particular traditions of which

I find myself a part. These traditions serve as the particular background out of which I understand myself as embedded in a past and within which I come to understand my future possibilities.

45. Quoted in *Sociology of North American Sport,* 3rd ed., ed. D. Stanley Eitzen and George Sage (Dubuque, Iowa: Wm. C. Brown, 1986), 55.

46. *Ibid.,* 60.

47. This last quote by Don Shula is particularly interesting, since it appears to be so patently false. One wonders why he would say something like this.

48. See Drew Hyland's discussion, "Sport and Self-knowledge," in *Philosophy of Sport,* 70–87. Phil Jackson's approach to sport and coaching is nicely expressed in *Sacred Hoops: Spiritual Lessons of a Hardwood Warrior* (New York: Hyperion, 1995). For an interesting discussion of the "philosopher coach," see Gary Walton, *Beyond Winning: The Timeless Wisdom of Great Philosopher Coaches,* (Champaign: Ill.: Leisure Press, 1992).

49. Anthony Quinton, "Character and Culture." The essay originally appeared in *The New Republic* (1983). I will refer to the pagination of the essay as it appears in Christina Hoff Sommers and Fred Sommers, eds., *Vice and Virtue in Everyday Life,* 2d ed. (New York: Harcourt Brace Jovanovich, 1989).

50. *Ibid.,* 614.

51. *Ibid.*

52. *Ibid.*

53. *Ibid.,* 615.

54. *Ibid.*

55. Murdoch, *The Sovereignty of Good,* 95.

56. Quinton, "Character and Culture," 615.

57. See MacIntyre's comments on integrity, 203, and constancy, 241–43, in *After Virtue.*

58. Quinton, "Character and Culture," 620.

59. *Ibid.,* 614.

60. *Ibid.*

61. In *Quandaries and Virtues* (Lawrence: University of Kansas Press, 1986), Edmund Pincoffs distinguishes between instrumental virtues and noninstrumental virtues. Noninstrumental virtues include aesthetic virtues (both noble, e.g., dignity, and charming, e.g., wittiness), meliorating virtues (including mediating virtues, e.g., tolerance, temperamental virtues, e.g., cheerfulness, and formal virtues, e.g., politeness), and moral virtue. See chapter 5. In relation to the question of having character, see his interesting discussion "On Becoming the Right Sort," chapter 9.

Chapter 10: Respect for the Game

1. The discussion in this chapter is related to the analysis of "respect for the game" found in chapter 6 of *Coaching for Character,* a book I co-authored with Craig Clifford. In that chapter we suggest that "respect for the game includes the full range of respect that makes up the virtue of sportsmanship. Someone who shows disrespect for an opponent, a teammate, a coach, or an official is at the same time showing disrespect for the game; conversely, a genuine respect for the game necessarily includes an understanding of the need for respecting all of its participants as essential to the game"(62). The view that "respect for the game" summarizes many important aspects of sportsmanship was crystallized for me when I later read the fine article by Robert Butcher and Angela Schneider, "Fair Play as Respect for the Game," in *Ethics in Sport,* ed. Morgan,

Meier, and Schneider, 21–48. The article first appeared in the *Journal of the Philosophy of Sport* 25 (1998): 1–22. Unlike Butcher and Schneider, I prefer to speak of "sportsmanship" rather than "fair play," precisely because the former suggests just the sort of broader concerns I discuss. I associate fair play primarily with a commitment to abide by the explicit and implicit agreements involved in sports participation. Being a good sport also involves the spirit of play, respect for good competition, appreciation of impersonal internal goods, and perhaps even benevolent action. It's not clear to me why they speak of fair play rather than sportsmanship. At one point they say: "When we talk of fair play, the standard we tend to adopt is one that refers to the spirit of the game, rather than the letter of its rules" (30). I quite agree. That's why I prefer to speak of sportsmanship or the virtue of being a good sport. They also offer the following useful claim: "On the sport-is-play approach, the central feature of sport is its nature of being set apart" (26). I use this helpful language, derived from Huizinga, when I emphasize the nature of sport as play.

2. See the discussion of MacIntyre's concept of a "practice" in chapter 9.

3. See Alfie Kohn's critique of competition in *No Contest: The Case Against Competition* (Boston: Houghton Mifflin, 1986).

4. Murdoch, "The Sovereignty of Good," 89.

5. Bob Knight with Bob Hammond, *Knight: My Story* (New York: Thomas Dunne Books, St. Martin's Press, 2002), 29.

6. *Ibid.*, 18.

7. *Ibid.*, 22, 23.

8. See Clifford and Feezell, *Coaching for Character,* for a somewhat more extensive account of each aspect of respect for the game, as well as for additional practical implications.

9. See Joel Kupperman's discussion of the relation between descriptive claims about the human condition and appropriate or apt attitudes in *Classical Asian Philosophy* (New York: Oxford University Press, 2001), 149–59. He argues that the logical relation between facts and ethical conclusions is neither deductive nor inductive, yet there *is* some sort of logical relation involved. On page 158 he says that "certain kinds of guidance in life seem a natural continuation of the picture of the world that is provided. Should this be viewed as logic or as coherent storytelling? Any reader can explore her or his own view on this." Likewise, this issue has been a recurrent theme in this book. Given certain descriptive claims about the nature of sport, some attitudes toward sport are more apt or appropriate. Certain attitudes appear to be a natural continuation of the picture of sport I have offered here.

10. Will, *Men at Work,* 329.

11. Jackson, *Sacred Hoops,* 162.

12. *Ibid.*, 121.

13. *Ibid.*, 136.

14. *Ibid.*, 137.

15. *Ibid.*, 124.

16. *Ibid.*, 123.

INDEX

absurd, 48–53, 54–55, 69, 70, 78–79
adventure, 34–35
aesthetic experience, 38–39, 41–42
Algozin, Keith, 9, 46–47
Allen, George, 137
Aristotle, 7, 94–96, 103, 126, 127, 136, 139, 165n20
athlete, 7, 10–11, 14, 15–16, 86–87, 88–89, 90
Austen, Jane, 127

Beardsley, Monroe, 41, 165n11
Beauchamp, Tom, 162n25
Bell, Clive, 30
Bergmann, Frithjof, 23–25
bracketing ordinary life, 13, 15, 27, 31, 45, 46, 91
Bryant, Paul, 137
Bullough, Edward, 30
Butcher, Robert, 168n1
Butt, Dorcas Susan, 166n4

Caillois, Roger, 5, 12–13, 22–23, 28–29, 46, 48–49
Camus, Albert, 48, 51–53
character, 124, 125, 138–42
Chu, Donald, 166n3
Clifford, Craig, 162n27, 162n30, 166n5, 168n1, 169n8
competition, 85–87, 116–17, 122, 133, 145–46, 151–52, 169n3
consequentialism, 65, 113
Crisp, Roger, 166n5
custom, 107–109, 117–18, 152–54

D'Agostino, Fred, 164n7
dance, 28, 159n28

definition, 10, 11, 103, 158n25
deontologist, 113, 114
Dewey, John, xii, 30, 37–42, 47
Dixon, Nicholas, 111–15 passim, 119–22
Dostoyevsky, 23

easing up in sports, 118, 121–22
Esposito, Joseph L., 46
ethos of games, 164–65n7
excellence, 6–8, 11, 16, 18, 118, 127–28, 132, 147, 154
experience, an, 38–39, 41–42

family resemblances, 10
Feinberg, Joel, 74, 162n24, 162n34
Feldman, Fred, 164n4
Fink, Eugen, 46, 48, 54
Ford, Gerald, 124
Fraleigh, Warren, 163n3
Frankena, William, 100
freedom, 13, 21–22, 23–25, 29, 49, 53, 55, 145
frolic, 27–28, 29, 91, 95, 145
fun, 11, 12, 14, 22, 69, 79

games, 68–69, 91, 92, 100, 101, 145
Gerber, Ellen, 157n2, 163n3
Giamatti, A. Bartlett, 32, 160n18
Guttman, Allen, 159n32

Halberstam, David, 167n14
Heidegger, Martin, 162n33
Hendry, Jim, 165n21
Hernandex, Keith, 159n4
Holowchak, M. Andrew, 157n2
Homer, 126, 127

Huizinga, Johan, xi, 5, 12–13, 21–23, 28–29, 46, 54, 91, 145
humiliation in athletics, 115, 120–21, 122
humility, 74–76, 77, 130–32, 155
Hyland, Drew, 32, 164n31, 168n48

identification, 24–25, 29
incompatibility thesis, 97, 107, 163n1
injustice, 100
institutions, 131–32
internal and external goods, 127–29, 131–34, 138, 141, 145–46, 148, 162n25, 167n14
intrinsic value, 14, 38, 45, 49–50, 69, 87, 93, 122, 155–56
irony, 53, 55, 57, 74, 77, 78, 162n24
Irwin, Terrence, 95–96
isolationism and contextualism, 30–31

Jackson, Phil, 138, 155–56, 168n48

Kant, Immanuel, 113–14
Keating, James, 85–91, 94, 121
Kierkegaard, Soren, 77, 162n31
Knight, Bob, 148, 154
Kohn, Alfie, 169n3
Kretchmer, Scott, 158n41
Kuntz, Paul, 12, 15, 157n3
Kupfer, Joseph, 160n7
Kupperman, Joel, 169n9

Langer, Suzanne, 9
Lasch, Christopher, xiii, 133, 167n30
Leaman, Oliver, 104–107, 109, 110
Lehman, Craig, 107–109, 110, 163n1
Lischer, Richard, 43–44
Lombardi, Vince, 137

MacIntyre, Alasdair, xiii, 42–43, 125–37, 145, 162n26, 166n4
Mackie, J. L., 161n7
Mantle, Mickey, 151
McBride, Frank, 10
McEnroe, John, 105, 139, 167n25
McKim, Robert, 162n32
Meier, Klaus, 68, 157n2

mean between extremes, 94–96, 121, 144
meaninglessness, 48, 51
Moore, G. E., xv
morality, 76–77
Morgan, William, 157n2, 158n25, 163n3
Murdoch, Iris, 129–31, 133, 134, 139, 141, 145–46, 148, 150, 154, 155, 166n10

Nagel, Thomas, 52–57, 59–66, 67, 70–79 passim, 97, 161n9–10, 162n24, 166n7
narrative, 42–45, 134–36
Nausea (Sartre), 34–37
Nietzsche, 126
Novak, Michael, xi, 5, 19–20, 26, 56, 162n23

objectivity, 58, 59, 60–66, 67, 161–62n13
Oglivie, Bruce, 166n4
Osterhoudt, Robert, 49–50, 157n2

Parcells, Bill, 58
Pence, Gregory, 166n5
Perry, Gaylord, 107, 108
Pincoffs, Edmund, 168n61
Plato, 126, 130
player versus athlete, 14–15, 88–89, 93
play world, 14, 31, 54–56, 87–88, 95
Pojman, Louis, 161n4
polarized thinking, 89–90
practices, 127–29, 131–32, 134, 144, 145–46
prescriptive atmosphere, 100–103, 109

Quinton, Anthony, 138–39, 140–41

Rachels, James, 161n4
Rader, Melvin, 159n33
respect, 144, 150–55, 168–69n1
Ripken, Jr., Cal, 143, 153
Roquentin, Antoine (in Nausea), 34–37, 40–42, 45
Ross, W. D., 114

rules, 13, 14, 28, 50, 68, 76, 84, 87, 99–100, 104–109, 145, 146, 150–51, 164–65n7

Sartre, Jean-Paul, 34–37
Sayre-McCord, Geoffrey, 161n7
Schacht, Richard, 15
Schmitz, Kenneth, 27, 45, 46, 53, 91–92, 93, 95
Schneider, Angela, 157n2, 163n3, 168n1
self, 23–26, 27, 28, 29, 70, 73, 140–41
seriousness and nonseriousness, 13, 25, 28, 31, 52–59, 66, 69, 92–93, 95
Sheehan, George, 17, 159n23
Shula, Don, 137
Silver Rule, 116, 166n5
Singer, Peter, 161n8, 164n2
Sisyphus, 48–51
skepticism, 53, 56, 65–66, 70
Skillen, Anthony, 159n34
Slote, Michael, 166n5
Socrates, 135–36, 138
spirit of play, 95, 122, 152
Stevenson, Christopher, 166n3
Strang, Colin, 164n4
subjectivity versus objectivity, 60–66, 67, 70, 71–73
Suits, Bernard, 68–69, 92–93, 100, 163nn1–2, 164n26, 167n12

Taylor, Richard, 48, 51, 89–90

teaching philosophy, 24, 26, 148–49
Thomas, Carolyn, 163n3
Tolstoy, Leo, 30
tradition. *See* custom
trivialization of athletics, 133
Tubbs, Billy, 111–12
Tutko, Thomas, 166n4

Undergroundman, 23
unfair advantage, 84, 98–99, 102–110 passim
Unger, Peter, 161n11
universalizability, 98, 113

Vanderwerken, David, 157n2
virtue, 83–86 passim, 94–96, 114, 125–30, 134, 136, 166n10, 167–68n44, 168n61

Wallace, Mike, 58
Walton, Gary, 168n48
Warnock, G. J., 86, 163n9
Weiss, Paul, x, xi, xii, 3–12, 14–18, 19–21, 124, 157n3
Wertz, Spencer, 157n2
Will, George, 32, 154, 162n28
Williams, Bernard, 161n9
Williams, Ted, 167n14
winning at all costs, 95
Wittgenstein, Ludwig, 10, 103, 141
Wolf, Susan, 161n9
Wooden, John, 137

RANDOLPH FEEZELL is a professor
of philosophy at Creighton University.
He is the author of *Faith, Freedom and
Value: Introductory Philosophical
Dialogues* and coauthor of *How Should
I Live?: Philosophical Conversations
about Moral Life* and *Coaching for
Character: Reclaiming the Principles
of Sportsmanship.*

*The University of Illinois Press
is a founding member of the
Association of American University Presses.*

*Composed in 9.5/12.5 Trump Mediaeval
by Celia Shapland
for the University of Illinois Press
Manufactured by Maple-Vail
Book Manufacturing Group*

*University of Illinois Press
1325 South Oak Street
Champaign, IL 61820-6903
www.press.uillinois.edu*